Seal of Approval

Studies in Popular Culture
M. Thomas Inge, General Editor

Seal of Approval

The History of the Comics Code

Amy Kiste Nyberg

University Press of Mississippi   *Jackson*

Manufactured in the United States of America

01 00 99 98   4 3 2 1

The paper in this book meets the guidelines for permanence and durability of the Committee on Production Guidelines for Book Longevity of the Council on Library Resources.

Library of Congress Cataloging-in-Publication Data

Nyberg, Amy Kiste.
  Seal of approval : the history of the comics code / Amy Kiste Nyberg.
      p.   cm. — (Studies in popular culture)
    Includes bibliographical references and index.
    ISBN 0-87805-974-1 (alk. paper). — ISBN 0-87805-975-X (pbk. : alk. paper)
    1. Comic books, strips, etc.—United States—History and criticism.   2. Wertham, Fredric 1895–1981.   3. Comic books and children—United States.   4. Censorship—United States.   5. Popular culture—United States.   I. Title.   II. Series: Studies in popular culture (Jackson, Miss.)
  PN6725.N953   1998
  741.5'973—dc21   97-21789
                                                                           CIP

British Library Cataloging-in-Publication data available

Contents

Introduction

The comics code seal of approval bears the message "Approved by the comics code authority" and first appeared on the covers of comic books in the mid-1950s. The comics code is a set of regulatory guidelines primarily concerned with sex, violence, and language drawn up by publishers and enforced by the "code authority," a euphemism for the censor employed by the publishers. Comic books passing the prepublication review process are entitled to carry the seal of approval. This study of the origins and history of the comics code examines how and why such a code came into being and the code's significance both historically and to comic book publishing today.

The code was originally implemented in response to a public outcry over comic books in postwar America when comic book content was linked to a rise in juvenile delinquency, and this book begins with a chronology of the controversy that provided the impetus for industry self-regulation. The chronology is followed by a detailed account of how the code was implemented, enforced, and modified. Along the way, this examination of the comics code also explores the evolution of a medium and the public's attitude toward comic books since the introduction of the modern comic in the mid-1930s. The perception of comic books and their audience is central to understanding the comics code both in postwar America and today. What this book does not do, quite intentionally, is provide a detailed analysis of the comics themselves. While some examples of crime and horror comics are discussed in relation to the criticism they generated, the histories of the characters, their creators, and their stories have been told elsewhere. Rather, I approach the history of the comic book code from the perspective of the industry, identifying the events that led to the creation of the code, examining ways in which it was formulated and implemented, and analyzing the impact it had on comic book publishing.

To begin, it is important to recognize that the postwar comic book controversy has its roots in earlier attitudes toward comic books and toward popular culture more generally. Most of the investigations of the comics code to date have focused on criticisms of comic books in the postwar period, specifically 1948 to 1954, but by limiting their study to this time frame, researchers have failed to recognize important links between the campaign against comic books and previous efforts to control children's culture. Far from being an isolated instance of Cold War hysteria, the debate over comic books fits into a broad pattern of efforts to control children's culture. As film, radio, and comic books each were introduced and became part of children's leisure activities, guardians of children's morality renewed their attacks on the mass media.

From the outset, symbols of social authority over childhood and children's reading, particularly teachers and librarians, defined comic book reading as a problem. They expressed fears that the comic book was leading children away from better literature and creating a generation of semiliterates. When academic researchers began to test some of the assumptions educators were making about comic books, however, their findings demonstrated that comic book reading made little difference in the acquisition of reading skills, in academic achievement, or in social adjustment. Despite these research findings, the criticism of comic books persisted because the fears about comic books, rather than being based on empirical evidence, were rooted in adult beliefs and attitudes about children's leisure time activities. Adults' concern stemmed in large part from fears that children's culture, especially the control of leisure reading, had escaped traditional authority. Adults believed that children's free time should be spent in constructive activities that would improve their mental and physical well being, failing to understand the appeal of comic books, which they perceived as simplistic, crude, and lacking artistic or literary merit. Reading comic books was, plain and simple, a waste of time and money. The struggle between children's taste and adult authority was presented as a "challenge" to be faced and a "battle" to be won; adults sought to substitute their own choices for the comic books favored by children.

Alarm over this contamination of children's culture failed to produce a sustained public reaction. Evidence suggests that the "problem" of comic books entered public discourse only after those seeking to control children's culture, allied with church and civic groups that traditionally enforced standards of public morality, were able to gain the attention of the popular press. The major factor in the success of the campaign against comics was the linkage of comic book reading to juvenile delinquency, a problem representing the ultimate loss of social control over children. When the antecedents of the postwar campaign against comics are understood, it becomes clear that while the debate shifted from an emphasis on education and morality to one of law and order, the fundamental concern—social control of children—remained the same. The impetus for the shift in the debate was the emergence of experts such as psychiatrist Fredric Wertham, whose crusade against comics was a significant factor in focusing public attention on the medium and in legitimating the views of those who saw comic books as a threat to children.

In this book, I investigate the ways in which the attack on comics was carried out. At the local level, civic and religious groups acted to impose standards on comic books and brought pressure to bear on the retailers in their communities. These groups, which had no legal power, used the economic threat of boycotts to force retailers to remove from their shelves comic books deemed unsuitable. Such decency crusades were aided by ratings lists published by the Catholic Church's National Office of Decent Literature and by the Cincinnati Committee for the Evaluation of Comics, whose lists were published in *Parents' Magazine*. These efforts attracted the attention of lawmakers at the state and national level. In the years following World War II, several states appointed legislative committees to study the problem and recommend laws aimed at curbing undesirable comic books. At the national level, the investigation of comic books was carried out by the Senate Subcommittee to Investigate Juvenile Delinquency, which undertook a study of the relationship of the mass media to the problem of delinquency.

The key witness at the Senate hearings and the leader of the crusade against comics was Wertham. He took the position that comic books were harmful, and he pressed for legislation restricting the sale of comic books to children under age sixteen. But Wertham's argument was much more complex than the idea he was often accused of perpetrating: that there was a direct causal link between comic book reading and juvenile delinquency. The problem of juvenile delinquency, he believed, stemmed from the fact that society was trapped in a "cult of violence" of which comic books were simply a manifestation. While he acknowledged that eliminating harmful comic books would not solve the problem of juvenile delinquency, he was convinced that such action would be a step in the right direction.

Many media scholars have dismissed Wertham's work as an example of early, unsophisticated social science research into media effects, and contemporary social scientists criticized Wertham for his lack of scientific methodology and his failure to present quantitative evidence to support his findings. I argue, however, that the image of Wertham as a misguided pioneer in media effects research is erroneous. In fact, Wertham attacked the emerging social science approach to media effects research, calling instead for a multidisciplinary study of mass media. He believed his approach, which he called the clinical method, with its detailed case histories, observation, and follow-up, was the only valid way to study long-term media effects.

Despite Wertham's efforts, the Senate subcommittee failed to recommend any legislative remedy for the problem of comic books, instead calling on the industry to police itself. The passage of the comics code in October 1954 pacified many of the groups calling for censorship and put to rest any fears that the industry would be regulated by the government. The models for self-regulation of the comic book industry were the codes adopted by other mass media. Since many of the criticisms of film were repeated almost verbatim about comic books, the film industry provided a compatible model for comics publishers, and the comics code is nothing more than a rewrite of the Film Production Code of the 1930s. The bulk of the comics code dealt with crime and horror, the two topics that had brought public ire down on the heads of publishers. The code continued to allow publication of crime comics within new, strict guidelines but banned publication of horror comics. But publishers went beyond the criticisms voiced against comics to address the complaints of groups more concerned with morality than delinquency, adding provisions dealing with language, costume, and the portrayal of family values, following the lead of the Film Production Code in these areas.

There is a persistent belief among the fan-historians that the comic book industry was nearly destroyed by the comics code, a view accepted by academic researchers. Such a view ignores other, more important influences. While the years following the adoption of the code were a period of upheaval in the industry, the implementation of the comics code was only part of the explanation for the industry's difficulties. First, the distribution problems the industry experienced in the mid-1950s were due not to retailers' resistance to carrying the "controversial" comics but rather to the decision by American News Company, which distributed more than half of all comic books published at the time, to pull out of magazine distribution following federal antitrust action. The demise of American News Company left many publishers without a way to distribute their titles. Second, many of the companies that went out of business were simply victims of a more general economic hardship brought about by the drop in sales of comic books. This decrease was attributable to two factors. One was negative publicity about comic books, but a second factor was the increasing competition from television for children's leisure time. James Baughman, in his analysis of the impact of television on mass media industries in postwar America, has suggested that the introduction of television marginalized other mass media, forcing them increasingly to compete for a share of the audience's time that was not being spent watching television. Although Baughman does not address comic books specifically, it is clear from his analysis that the failure of comic books to regain their status as a mass medium can be linked to much broader trends in all media industries. The scramble by comic book publishers to reestablish themselves in the marketplace was mirrored by similar efforts among newspaper publishers, magazine publishers, film companies, and radio networks.

It is true that some companies, such as William Gaines's E.C. Comics, were casualties of the new standards; in fact, most fan-historians focus on the demise of E.C. Comics as an example of the impact of the code. But what happened to Gaines was the exception rather than the rule. Many publishers continued to add new titles, and by the end of the decade, with the reintroduction of the superheroes who would launch the "Silver Age" of comics, the comic book industry regained some of the ground it had lost a few years earlier. Gaines's comic books from that period have been reprinted for new generations of fans, and today E.C. Comics are recognized as a significant contribution both for their artwork and their storytelling. If there is a "canon" of comic books, E.C. Comics may be found at the head of the list. This reverence for E.C. Comics of the 1950s helps to explain why the demise of Gaines's company is equated to the destruction of an entire industry in that period. It is important to separate the impact of the code on the creative output of the industry from its impact on comic book publishing. While one may argue that the comics code harmed the creative development of comic books, it is much more difficult to support the argument that the comics code almost destroyed the comic book publishing industry.

Gaines was not the only publisher unhappy with the code. Those who sat on the executive board of the Comics Magazine Association of America, the trade organization formed and supported by the publishers to administer the code, would debate the provisions and the very need for a code at almost every meeting. Changes were made to the code in 1971 and again in 1989. In 1971, changing social values, the emergence of underground "comix," and a depressed market combined to force the publishers into relaxing some of the restrictions on comic book content to allow publishers to bring their comics more in line with contemporary standards. Regulations on both the depiction of sex and violence were rewritten, and a section on how to show drug use and abuse was added. But the four publishers who remained active in the Comics Magazine Association of America during the late 1970s and the 1980s—Archie, Marvel, Harvey, and DC—continued to challenge the need for a code. The next change to the code, enacted in 1989, was due in large part to changes in comic book distribution and audience demographics and to competition from a new group of "independent" comic book publishers. Instead of selling comics only through the magazine distribution system, publishers began, in the 1970s, to market comic books through a new network of distributors and retailers developed exclusively for comic books. In addition, the audience for comic books, rather than being the preteens of the 1940s and 1950s, was more likely to be older teens or young adults. And finally, a number of upstart companies began to publish comics that were more experimental and adult in their themes. The 1989 code eliminated the detailed lists of what was forbidden, instead offering a more general set of "principles" in various categories. A second portion of the code, not intended for public distribution, gave more specific editorial guidelines to publishers, editors, and artists. Despite the seeming flexibility built into the 1989 version of the code, it is still clearly the intention of the comic book publishing industry that comic books carrying the code seal of approval be appropriate for children of all ages.

Much of the narrative history of the comics code that follows will be familiar to students of the medium, although the discussion of the implementation and enforcement of the comics code is the first such discussion to draw on the archives of the Comics Magazine Association of America. But in two important ways, this study of the comics code challenges the way in which this period of comic book history has been understood. First, I argue that Wertham's role in the crusade against comics has been largely misinterpreted by fans and scholars alike, who dismiss his findings as naive social science, failing to understand how his work on comic books fits into the larger context of his beliefs about violence, psychiatry, and social reform. Second, I reject the view that the comics code nearly destroyed the comic book industry, suggesting that this is far too simplistic a conclusion to draw about the impact and significance of the code.

Few books are a solo effort. I would like to thank those who helped along the way: Robert McChesney, who made it possible for me to write the dissertation that became this book; Julie Ratliff, who provided valuable advice on cutting a six-hundred-page manuscript down to size; M. Thomas Inge, whose critical reading was enormously helpful; my colleagues in the Comic Art and Comics Area of the Popular Culture Association, who heard many of the chapters in the form of conference papers and offered much-appreciated feedback; my grandmother, Macy Snyder, who instilled in me a love of reading; my parents, Bruce and Eleanor "Petey" Kiste, for all their support; and finally my husband, John, whose love makes all things possible, including this book.

Chapter 1

Comics, Critics, and Children's Culture

The audience for comic books in postwar America was much different from what it is today. Readers today are more likely to be older teens and young adults, mostly male. Comic book reading has become associated with the phenomenon of collecting comic books, and a specialized market catering to the collector has given rise to comic book specialty shops. But in the 1940s and 1950s, comic books were widely available at grocery stores, news stands, and corner drug stores, and children were the primary audience. In the days before television, comic book reading was a major leisure activity for children. Partly because of the ubiquitous nature of the medium, children's fascination with comic books became a topic of concern for parents, teachers, and librarians and an area of investigation for researchers. The analysis that follows of the early criticism of comic books shows that almost from the beginning, comic book reading was defined as a problem.

Studies of readership made by comic book publishers and academic researchers showed that nearly all children read comic books.[1] Comic books were most popular with children in the upper elementary grades; more than 90 percent of the children in the fourth, fifth, and sixth grades reported they read comic books regularly, averaging at least ten comics a month. For this age group, comic book reading appeared to be an activity enjoyed by both boys and girls. Readership was lower among adolescents and adults; still, 30 percent of young adults reported reading comic books. Their popularity alarmed parents and educators. While the comic book was a new phenomenon, the problems it posed had been faced earlier with the introduction of the dime novel, the comic strip, and the film.

Many of the complaints about comics were resurrected from earlier debates surrounding the introduction of these other media.

Dime novels, which were inexpensive pamphlets featuring simple stories recounting the adventures of explorers, cowboys, or soldiers, were first published during the Civil War. Historian Merle Curti notes that although dime novels were intended for an audience of working-class adults, the stories held great appeal for children as well, so publishers began to produce dime novels specifically for the juvenile reader (172). As audiences became more jaded, the clean-cut heroes gave way to "bad" heroes like Jesse James and Billy the Kid. Next, publishers began offering sophisticated crime and detective stories (Hart 154–56). The decline in the literary quality of the stories, along with the addition of more lurid cover illustrations, led to an attack on dime novels by vice societies, formed in many major cities in the years following the Civil War. These groups originally targeted pornography, but after their vice campaigns eliminated or drove much of that material underground, the societies broadened the scope of their work (Broun and Leech 187). The leader in these efforts was Anthony Comstock, the head of the New York Society for the Suppression of Vice. Comstock's attack on the dime novel, the topic of his book *Traps for the Young*, published in 1884, marks the first major controversy in the history of American children's culture.

The criticism of comic books also has its roots, not surprisingly, in the criticism of the comic strips that inspired the creation of the "funny books." Newspapers began printing Sunday supplements devoted exclusively to comics as early as 1894. Early comics were populated by characters drawn from the working class, usually immigrants, and their humor was very physical. The emphasis on vulgar humor (often featuring the misbehavior of urban slum children) combined with the crude production values of the time offended the literary and artistic sensibilities of the middle class. The disrespect for authority and the cruelty of the pranks depicted in the strips also concerned parents and educators, who worried about the impact that such depictions would have on children, and groups in several cities organized a highly focused protest against the comics. In her analysis of early comic strips, Elsa Nystrom notes that while such protests produced a flurry of activity between 1906 and 1911, the growing concern about the involvement of the United States in world affairs and the country's entry into World War I put an end to the crusade. In addition, the profitability and popularity of the comic strip ensured it would survive despite its critics (201–2).

The introduction of movies created a new target for censors. Film scholars Edward deGrazia and Roger Newman note that almost immediately after the introduction of the silent "photoplays," concerns were raised about the social effects of films, and various groups began to denounce the irresponsibility of movie makers. Immigrants and children were of special concern, since they were considered particularly vulnerable to film's effects (7). Legislation was introduced as early as 1915 to create a federal film censorship body. The threat of federal censorship led the industry in 1916 to launch its first attempt to police itself. Throughout the 1920s and early 1930s, the film industry struggled with self-regulation, adopting guidelines but failing to devise a way to enforce its standards.

The next push for film censorship came from the Catholic Church. In November 1933, at the annual meeting of Catholic bishops, the organization appointed a committee on motion pictures (Martin 32). The committee created the Legion of Decency, a campaign designed to persuade Catholics to boycott films that the church felt offended decency and Christian morality. The film industry reacted by creating the Production Code Administration in June 1934 and appointing Joseph Breen as its head. Under the new code, studios were forced to submit scripts to Breen for approval and fines were established for violation of the code.

Also in the 1930s, concern about comic strips surfaced again as strips shifted their focus from humor to the action and adventure. During this decade, strips such as Flash Gordon, Jungle Jim, Tarzan, and others debuted. Many lamented the passing of the "funny" strips, and the popularity of the nonhumorous strip with young readers alarmed some educators and critics. One study published in 1937, an analysis of comic strips appearing in the Boston papers, concluded that many of the adventure strips were not suitable for juvenile consumption. In addition, the researcher argued, children and adults alike who read comic strips regularly ran the risk of lowering their artistic appreciation (Gay 206).

By the end of the decade, though, the popularity of comic books shifted attention to this newest mass medium. The first national attack on comic books came from Sterling North, literary critic for the *Chicago Daily News*. In an editorial on May 8, 1940, headlined "A National Disgrace," North noted that almost every child in America was reading comic books. Nearly ten million copies were sold every month, taking a million dollars out of the pockets of children. He examined 108 comics available on the newsstands, concluding that at least 70 percent of them contained material that no respectable newspaper would think of accepting. He argued that the old dime novel could be considered classic literature compared to the comic book, which he described as "badly drawn, badly written and badly printed—a strain on young eyes and young nervous systems ... [that] spoil a child's natural sense of color, their hypodermic injection of sex and murder make the child impatient with better, though quieter stories."

North concluded his editorial by calling for parents to become aware of what their children were reading and to furnish a good substitute. He wrote: "The antidote to the 'comic' magazine poison can be found in any library or good bookstore. The parent who does not acquire that antidote for his child is guilty of criminal negligence." More than forty newspapers and magazines reprinted the editorial. The *Daily News* reportedly received twenty-five million requests for reprints of the editorial for distribution in churches and schools across the country, and letters supporting North's crusade against the comic book poured into the newspaper office. Nearly a year later, the newspaper was still receiving an average of one thousand requests a day for reprints of the editorial (Frakes 1350; North 16).

North's objection to comic books has its basis in the reaction of cultural elites to popular culture. High culture is valued for its individuality and aesthetic complexity, whereas popular culture is dismissed because of its mass distribution and its perceived lack of literary or artistic merit. North believed there could be little value in a comic book produced quickly and cheaply for mass consumption and profit. This elitist criticism was influential in shaping public attitudes toward comics, since it was the opinions of the elite, quoted by newspaper and magazine journalists as experts, that appeared in print. Another significant aspect of North's criticism was his identification of the comic book specifically as a form of *juvenile* literature, despite the fact there is nothing inherent in the form itself that limits its appeal to children. Comic strips, which share many of the same characteristics of comic books, are considered appropriate reading for all ages. By first identifying and then denigrating the comic book as a form of juvenile literature, North and other critics were instrumental in helping to shape public perception that comics books were exclusively for children.

This marginalization of comic books, then, goes beyond the issue of high versus popular culture and beyond consideration of form. Two factors are at work. First, reading context played a part in North's rejection of the comic book. Comic strips appeared in newspapers, which gave the comic strip a legitimacy not enjoyed by comic books. On the other hand, children became the primary purchasers of comic books, which attached a certain stigma to adult comic book reading. The second factor had to do with the comic book industry's emphasis on the superhero genre during the early years of comic book publishing. The dominance of the superhero characters was largely responsible for creating the strictly juvenile audience for comic books. When Superman proved to be enormously popular with children and therefore extremely profitable, publishers rushed to flood the market with their own version of the superhero. Before long, other genres that might have attracted an older readership were crowded out or abandoned. While the superhero has occasionally attracted a wider audience, evidenced by the success of the campy Batman television show in the 1960s and the more recent revivals of Superman and Batman in film and on television, the traditional superhero comic of the Golden Age seemed to have little appeal for adults.

One other aspect of North's editorial merits discussion: his failure to recognize an essential difference between traditional children's literature and the comic book. To North and other critics, comic books were just a new kind juvenile literature with too many illustrations and not enough text. But these critics were mistaken. The comic book was a new medium altogether, a medium that relied on the interaction of words and pictures to tell stories in a unique way, with its own highly developed conventions of interpretation that bore more resemblance to film than to literature or drawing. Reading comic books was teaching young readers a whole new vocabulary, one that was largely foreign to adults, because adult readers did not immerse themselves deeply enough in this new cultural form to learn its language. The conflict over comic books became generational, not unlike the battle that raged later over rock 'n' roll.

While the public attention to comics generated by North died down, the arguments in North's editorial resonated with opinions and attitudes held by teachers and librarians and inspired a lively dialogue about the problem of comic books in their professional journals. Some educators rejected comics outright and sought to ban them from classroom and home, but the majority, perhaps more realistically, looked upon comics as a challenge to teachers, librarians, and parents, who needed to understand children's attraction to comics and then find substitutes for the undesirable leisure reading material. The journal articles reiterated North's assertion that children could be weaned from comic books if teachers and parents presented them with attractive and appropriate juvenile literature. Dozens of articles in the professional journals proposed various strategies for how to win the battle against comic books.

For example, the *Wilson Library Bulletin* reported that a St. Louis librarian was waging a simple, but successful, campaign against "the highly colored enemy." To entice young readers away from comic books, the librarian selected various juvenile titles and displayed them on shelves labeled "Funny Books" and "Heroes and Supermen." Instead of finding the adventures of Clark Kent, alias Superman, children were handed books about Robin Hood, Baron Munchausen, and Paul Bunyan ("Comic Menace" 846–47). In another article, librarians were encouraged to place new emphasis on book presentation and storytelling hours. In addition, teachers and parents were advised to pay more attention to the "non-literary, non-aesthetic child" in order to encourage the reluctant reader (Bechtel 300–303).

Teachers, too, were drawn into the war against comic books. One high school English teacher compiled a list of books that might be offered as alternatives to comics, characterizing his task as "missionary work among my comic-book heathens" (Dias 143–45). An Arizona teacher had her freshman English class analyze the comic books they read and generate a list of reading material that had the same appeal as the comics but that, at the same time, was more acceptable. She concluded that since these suggestions came directly from the students themselves, teachers would be able to provide substitutes that were as attractive as comic books. This "gradual substitution," rather than an outright prohibition, would be the most effective strategy against comic book reading (Kinneman 333–35).

One solution to the comic book "problem" came from the publishers themselves, in the form of educational comics. The publishers of *Parents' Magazine* announced in its March 1941 issue that they were entering the comic book publishing business. The magazine reproduced the North editorial, and editor Clara Savage Littledale added: "It was widely reprinted. But nothing really happened. Now, however, the publishers of *Parents' Magazine* are doing something about it. They have launched, as a substitute, a really good well-drawn comic magazine entitled *True Comics*" (26).

The publishers of *True Comics* argued that children liked comic books because they were colorful and their format was quick and easy to read. In addition, the stories offered adventure, tales of daring and courage, and a chance for hero worship. The publishers pointed out that trying to substitute good books did not work; children read the books but keep right on reading comics, too. Banning comics did not work because children could read them at a friend's house. The answer was to substitute reading material that offered all of the same features of the comic book but substituted desirable content (Littledale 26). The first issue of *True Comics* featured "real life heroes" such as Winston Churchill and Simon Bolivar.

Littledale believed that parents and teachers would approve of the comics because of their educational value, while children would be delighted with the pictures and stories about "real" people. To add respectability, the publishers of *True Comics* appointed a junior advisory board of youthful movie stars, among them Shirley Temple and Mickey Rooney, to make sure the magazines would appeal to children, and a senior advisory board featuring such luminaries as George H. Gallup, director of the Institute of Public Opinion; David Muzzey, emeritus professor of history at Columbia University; and Littledale.

The first issue was a success. *Publishers Weekly* reported the comic sold 300,000 copies ten days after its publication in early March, and the Canadian edition of 40,000, titled *True Picture Magazine,* was also a sellout. An extra 10,000 copies were printed for American distribution and an extra 25,000 for Canadian distribution. Although the comic was scheduled to come out every two months, sales convinced the publishers to issue the comic book monthly. Publisher George Hecht actively promoted his new company by releasing circulation figures showing the impact an educational comic could have. At a luncheon hosted by *Parents' Magazine* during Children's Book Week in October 1941, Hecht told his audience that children between the ages of nine and fourteen spent 75 percent of their leisure time reading comic books. The industry offered 125 different titles on more than 100,000 newsstands. Fifteen million comic books were sold a month, adding' up to 180 million a year. Hecht compared those figures to the sales figures for children's books, where sales of 5,000 copies of a title was considered good.

A competitor entered the field of educational comics in fall 1941 with *Classic Comics;* the title of the series would be changed in 1947 to *Classics Illustrated.* In these comics, publisher Albert Kanter adapted literary classics into comic-book format. By 1946, the company had produced 28 titles and sold about 100 million copies. More than 20,000 schools reported using the comic books. They were also sold on the newsstands, in department stores, and in bookshops ("Classic Comics" 1736). In 1942, Max Gaines, who edited the All-American Comics line for National Comics, brought out *Picture Stories from the Bible,* which won Catholic sanction and approval from an advisory board of Protestants and Jews. Each story was prefaced with appropriate citations for finding it in the Old Testament ("Biblical Comic" 55). Also in 1942, a comic book designed for distribution in Catholic schools, *Topix Comics,* was published and featured stories about the pope and about Catholic saints and also included biblical stories (Doyle 556).

The addition of the "educational comic" brought a new dimension to the debate. While there had been nearly universal agreement that better literature should be substituted for comic books, educators were divided over whether introducing a comic book with educational content was a satisfactory compromise. Some educators objected to the form as well as the content of the medium. For example, a *Wilson Library Bulletin* editorial reminded teachers and librarians that their job was to train children how to read and make them want to read good literature. The practice of "fighting comics with comics," while an improvement, did nothing to eliminate the crudeness of the medium with its bad taste in color and design and its sensationalism. The *Bulletin* editorial argued that the comics reader was "a damaged child, incapacitated for enjoyment of the more serene pleasures of the imagination." It concluded by expressing skepticism that the children would be taken in by the attempt to convert their favorite leisure activity to an educational one, noting, "The reaction of children of my own acquaintance to *True Comics* is that it is a pale imitation of 'the real thing'" ("Libraries, to Arms!" 670). Louise Seaman Bechtel, writing for *The Horn Book,* called the *Parents' Magazine* publication a remarkable experiment, but hoped that that magazine would keep its cheap price and informational content while gradually dropping its "imitation-comics approach" (298). Others, however, approved of the new venture. An editorial in *The Educational Forum* titled "Our Comic Culture" suggested that in a society that has been conditioned by motion pictures to acquire information visually, the comic book could serve an educational function. The author suggested that educators were "cultural isolationists" who needed to make an impartial evaluation of mass culture. The editorial concluded, "The comic on the newsstand can show us not a little about how to teach" (84).'

The popularity of comic books with youthful readers and the ongoing debate among educators brought the comic book to the attention of the academic community. Since the introduction of comic books, teachers and librarians had been making assumptions about the impact of comics on children's reading. These assumptions can be summarized as follows: comics tend to crowd out reading of a more desirable type; they are too easy to read and spoil the taste for better reading; the adventures are so fantastic that children do not acquire an understanding of the world that comes from better literature; there is little progression of reading experience in comics; the artwork is of inferior quality; and the books are poorly printed on cheap paper and hard on the eyes.

Early academic studies focused on establishing reliable readership figures for various age groups and on investigations of the relationship between comics and the development of reading skills such as vocabulary. Some of these studies were of comic strips rather than comic books, with researchers arguing that comic books were basically collections of the strips and conclusions about one could be applied to the other.

One of the first studies, done by Florence Brumbaugh, examined the effects of comic strips upon the written English of children. She asked eight hundred New York City school children between the ages of eight and thirteen to draw a cartoon and then analyzed the content of the word balloons. She concluded that the English found in comic strips carried over into the language of children "too often to be attributed to chance." This influence was reflected in their use of "faulty English" and the inclusion of stars, exclamation points, and dashes to express profanity and strong language (63–64). However, a study done by Robert Thorndike, an education researcher at Columbia University, of vocabulary used in the most popular comic books revealed that the bulk of language in comics was standard English rather than slang. Comics averaged about ten thousand words of reading matter, refuting the assumption that comics were all pictures and very little text. The reading difficulty was a fifth- or sixth-grade reading level, consistent with the age group with whom the comics were most popular. Thorndike concluded that comics provided a substantial amount of reading material at a level appropriate for a child in the upper elementary grades or junior high school (113).

A survey of fourth, fifth, and sixth grade students in Philadelphia in 1938 completed by George E. Hill and M. Estelle Trent showed that the average child read about twenty-three comic strips all the time and reported reading ten more sometimes. Although white children read more comics than black children, the researchers concluded that this was because black children were from homes that did not take the newspaper or subscribed to fewer newspapers. They also found girls read fewer comic strips than boys. When questioned about why they liked comics, the children said they were exciting and full of action. The element of humor played a minor role in their enjoyment. In comparing the reasons given for reading comics to the reasons given (in other research) for selecting movies and radio, the researchers found that reasons given were similar. Noting that theirs was an exploratory study, Hill and Trent called for a more thorough analysis of the field and suggested that studies be done to determine what effect comics had on children's conduct (36).

In 1941 researcher Paul Witty, whose research efforts would dominate the academic inquiry into comic books over the next two decades, published the first of several readership studies. Witty's interest in comics went back to the 1920s, when he and H. C. Lehman published *The Psychology of Play Activities,* which devoted a portion of one chapter to a readership study of the Sunday funnies. In that research, Witty and Lehman found that reading the funnies was the most popular play activity for children ages eight to fifteen (Witty, "Children's Interest" 100). He began his research into comic book readership with a study of the same age group on which Hill and Trent focused: upper elementary students. His findings, based on surveys and interviews with students in the Chicago suburb of Evanston, suggested that the conclusions Hill and Trent reached about comic strip readership could also be applied to comic books. Witty discovered that reading comic books was the most popular of all reading pursuits, and children chose comics that provided excitement and adventure over humorous ones. In addition, the appeal of comic books was seen to be similar to that of cinema and radio.

In the same issue of *Journal of Experimental Education,* Witty published a study that compared heavy and light readers of comic books to test the validity of the assumption that comic book reading was harmful and should be discouraged. What he found was that in terms of intelligence, academic achievement, and social adjustment, there was no difference between the two groups. Witty studied their reading patterns and discovered that the amount of comic book reading did not significantly affect the other types of reading done by the children. In fact, some of the heavier readers were following reading programs that were "varied, rich and generally commendable," while other children who read few comics had inadequate reading patterns ("Reading the Comics" 105–9).

One concern about comic books supported by research was the accusation that they were bad for children's eyes. Matthew Luckiesh and Frank K. Moss conducted studies on twenty-four comic books and found they failed visibility tests. Comic book lettering was poor and of small size, the printing and paper were of poor quality, the lettering was often placed on a colored background, and the word balloons lacked adequate spacing between lines of dialogue. Luckiesh and Moss's conclusion: "Comic books represent a great step backward in safeguarding the eyesight of children" (24).

This review of early research suggests that most of the critics exaggerated the effects of comics. Reading comic books, even to the exclusion of other activities, seemed to make little difference in reading skills, academic achievement, or social adjustment. The attacks against comic books persisted, however. Critics, ignoring the research findings, continued to insist that comic book reading was harmful and that parents and educators should do whatever they could to redirect their children's interest in the medium. Even Witty, in summarizing his research in *National Parent-Teacher,* downplayed the results of his research, suggesting that it would be a mistake to assume that comic books were harmless. Although his research revealed no immediate effects on academic achievement or behavior, he believed that children were developing reading tastes that were "far from desirable" and that comic book reading contributed to "a decline in artistic appreciation and a tolerance of shoddy experience and language." Witty recommended to parents that the rehabilitation of children who have "this problem" (reading comics) could be accomplished by providing a good selection of children's books at home and making an effort to encourage reading that is "accurate, dependable and sound" (30).

Why did adults find children's preoccupation with comic books disturbing, despite evidence that suggests that it was an apparently harmless leisure activity? An analysis of the criticism suggests two reasons why many adults continued to attack the comics: first, adults believed that children's leisure time should be spent in constructive activities that would improve either their mental or physical well-being; and second, adults were genuinely puzzled over why children were attracted to something adults perceived as crude, simplistic, and lacking in any literary or artistic merit.

For example, an article in *Catholic World,* arguing that a desire to read comic books was neither normal nor necessary, asserted that parents who allowed their children to read comic books demonstrated that they have "lost control" of the child. Comic book reading was characterized as a waste of time and money. The article added: "But such waste is inevitable in children who have not been taught to use their leisure for work as well as play." Parents must realize that "every time their children sit down to peruse a comic book their own failure as parents is being exposed" (Doyle 556–57). In a *New Republic* article by former *Vogue* editor Marya Mannes, spurred by her eight-year-old son's "addiction" to comic books, Mannes wrote that she rationed him to two a week. Her objections to comics echoed the criticism leveled against them in the professional press. She disapproved of her son's reading because comic books required no effort, no concentration, no imagination, and no thought: "They are, in fact the greatest intellectual narcotic on the market." She also asserted that comic book reading was a waste of time that could be spent "learning, playing, or dreaming." Instead, Mannes wrote, "Every hour spent in reading comics is an hour in which all inner growth is stopped" (20–22). Calling comic book reading "a perversion of American tradition" because of comics' emphasis on wish fulfillment, James Landsdowne condemned comic books for creating children who were daydreamers and loafers. He concluded that getting rid of comic books would bring children back in touch with reality, a necessary step in preventing "a country of doers from becoming a country of leaners" in order to keep democracy strong (14–15).

In addition to condemning comics as a waste of leisure time, much of the space in articles about comic books was devoted to offering explanations for why children found comic books attractive. Once those reasons were discovered, parents and educators could then substitute good juvenile literature. For example, *Scholastic* magazine wrote that comic books were "crude, absurd, over-stimulating, and take time which could well be spent on something else. Why do children read them?" The author suggested that comic books fill a void in children's lives for adventure and heroic tales, and that comic books were easy to get used to since they followed naturally from the comic strips that children and their parents had read. Finally, comics were popular because parents have failed to purchase good books for their children. Two solutions were proposed: first, adults should supply other picture books that would give the child what he finds in the 'comics' without its "harmful effects;" second, publishers should develop a wide range of books available at a low price (Aldrich T-1).

Nine reasons were listed for why children liked comics in an article appearing in the September 1942 issue of *The School Executive*. The author, an elementary teacher, noted that while the adult's viewpoint on the comic magazine had been widely publicized, educators should focus instead on what children believe about comics. He interviewed students in the fourth through seventh grades to produce his list. Among the reasons children gave for reading comics were that they were cheap, exciting, amusing, and easy to read; that children enjoyed collecting them; that children were unaware of other books available; and that children read them because all the other children were reading them. The author concluded that he did not condone comic magazines because they were terrible literature, influencing children's reading tastes and making children "bloodthirsty" (Reynolds 17).

One freshman English teacher, Harriet E. Lee, asked her students to keep track of all unassigned reading and wrote that the results were "disturbing" because comic books topped the list. Lee incorporated units on comic books into her class work, drawing several conclusions from the students' work and her own observations: comic books are escape literature, discouraging the realistic facing of problems and encouraging wishful thinking; students who read comics exclusively were immature; and comic books fail to provide the "spiritual uplift" and "fine thinking" present in fine writing. Other teachers were encouraged to teach students to be discriminating in their selection of magazines and to steer students away from the comics (678).

In an experiment in the Toledo Public Library, librarians selected twenty-five comic books that could only be read in the library and displayed them next to popular books featuring adventure and humor that could be checked out. The children invariably selected books to check out and then took comic books off the rack to read. Librarian Ethel Wright noted the children "were entirely unaware of the literary difference between the two types of reading material which had been made available to them." When librarians questioned children about why they liked comics, they reported the children were "almost inarticulate" and answered in an offhanded manner that they thought the comic books were funny or exciting or interesting (833).

While they were in the minority, some educators took a more optimistic attitude toward the new medium. They felt that comic books presented a unique opportunity for educators to adapt the techniques to classroom use, using comics as a "stepping stone" or "bridge" to better reading. Ruth Strang, who interviewed and surveyed children ranging from first graders to high school seniors, reported that children believed parents took comics too seriously. The children themselves offered a variety of reasons for liking comics. Among them were the desire for adventure and suspense, the desire for relaxation and escape, the comics' use of art and color, and their low price. Strang concluded that educators, rather than seeking to eliminate comics, should instead work for their improvement and utilize them as an educational tool, advocating moderation rather than abstinence, recognizing that comics meet the needs of children at certain stages of development (342).

Josette Frank, a staff advisor on children's books for the Child Study Association of America, took a moderate stance, suggesting in an article in *Progressive Education* that comic books had potential in teaching reading in schools. She noted that the language, in terms of difficulty as measured by school standards, was quite respectable. In addition, children could be taught to evaluate their own comics on the basis of story content and good taste ("People" 30). In the spring 1942 issue of *Child Study,* the official publication of the Association, Frank expanded this idea, pointing out that children should not be made to feel self-conscious and apologetic about their reading tastes. Exposure to a wide range of reading materials was the way in which children learned to differentiate and discriminate among them. She added, "If we use their comics wisely and tolerantly we will find that their young readers will progress to other books and other heroes which will serve these same interests" (76, 90). In the same publication a year later, Frank (writing with Mrs. Hugh Grant Straus) addressed the issue of use of leisure time: "These are a waste of time only if we believe that children's hours must all be spent in ways which will be educationally and culturally profitable." Frank and Straus pointed out that adults do not know what the children get from comics "that seems to them so rewarding." Until educators and parents understand the attraction of comics, they argued, it would be useless to try to substitute other reading or even to select children's comic books for them (117).

W. W. D. Sones, a professor of education at the University of Pittsburgh, advocated incorporating comics into classroom instruction. Comics could be especially helpful in working with slow readers and those students who were disinterested and sometimes rebellious toward school subjects presented in a more formal way, Sones argued. He provided a list of activities that incorporated comics in instruction of language, social studies, science, math, and art. He noted, "There are better books to read than comics, but this current out-of-school activity may be exploited to improve reading skills, broaden informational backgrounds, and by comparison and contrast, lead to other and more acceptable tastes in reading" (14).

Some educators offered a more spirited defense of comics. Two children's librarians, in an article published in *Library Journal* in March 1942, suggested that adults were being "Victorian" and should abandon the idea that children are "wistful-eyed little darlings who are instinctively and innately delicate, untouched by the world." The reasons children gave for reading comic books amounted to "nothing but a normal love of excitement, adventure and hero worship"; their reactions to comics were natural, since "it is entirely human to be excited about the unusual or the sensational." Most children's books, on the other hand, are written down to childish levels, and strive to be correct, innocuous, and entertaining all at the same time, the authors argued. While they agreed that comic books represented a mass literature that was "not particularly distinctive," they did not believe it was harmful (Williams and Wilson 204–6).

One of the staunchest defenders of comic books was Harvey Zorbaugh, a professor of education at New York University and editor of the *Journal of Educational Sociology.* The December 1944 issue of the journal was devoted to the topic of comic books, and Zorbaugh put together a collection of articles that took a generally moderate position on comic book reading. Authors included Sidonie Matsner Gruenberg, director of the Child Study Association of America; her colleague, Josette Frank; child psychiatrist Lauretta Bender; and W. W. D. Sones of the University of Pittsburgh. Zorbaugh opened the issue with an editorial that reprinted Sterling North's attack on comic books and added: "It is time the amazing cultural phenomenon of the growth of the comics is subjected to dispassionate scrutiny. Somewhere between vituperation and complacency must be found a road to the understanding and use of this great new medium of communication and social influence. For the comics are here to stay" ("Editorial" 194).

The comic book publishers capitalized on this moderate attitude on the part of some educators, appointing them to advisory boards in an effort to counteract criticism. For example, the Superman-DC Comics Board included child psychiatrist Lauretta Bender, and education professors W. W. D. Sones, Robert Thorndike, and C. Bowie Millican. Pearl S. Buck and Gene Tunney also served as board members. The Fawcett Editorial Advisory Board included Sidonie M. Gruenberg of the Child Study Association, education professors Harvey Zorbaugh and Ernest G. Osborne, and Maj. Al Williams, a famous aviator and author (Abelson "Comics Part II"

82). This strategy would later backfire; the experts who defended comics were denounced by critics as "paid apologists" for the industry (see chap. 3).

Lauretta Bender and her colleague Reginald Lourie, child psychiatrists at Bellevue Hospital, were the first psychiatrists to go on record about comic books. At a psychiatric association meeting they presented a paper on comic books that was published in the *American Journal of Orthopsychiatry* in July 1941. Their study was undertaken partly because of the growing concern of parents and educators about comic books and partly to test clinical observations made about disturbed children who also were comic book readers. Bender and Lourie described comic books as modern folklore, noting that the omnipotent superheroes had their parallels in fairy tales; replacing magic with science was simply expressing basic ideas in contemporary terms. Comic books, with their excitement and adventure, offered a type of mental catharsis to young readers that served a healthy purpose. Bender and Lourie concluded: "The chief conflict over comic books is in the adult's mind" (547–48). These findings were given wider circulation when a summary of Bender and Lourie's research was published in *Science News Letter* August 23, 1941, with the headline: "Let Children Read Comics; Science Gives Its Approval" (124). The Bender and Lourie study also would be widely cited in subsequent articles about comics.

These psychiatrists and others who tried to analyze the appeal of comic books by looking for parallels between comic book superheroes and other heroic figures failed to realize that the superhero represented a new heroic archetype. Although those who created the costumed heroes drew on the popular culture of the day, the superhero was a new concept; so new, in fact, that the term *superhero* was not coined until several years after the appearance of Superman, the first comic book superhero. Superhero characters set comic books apart from the other media and contributed to the comic book's growth from a newsstand novelty item to a mass medium. In hindsight, it is easy to see the impact these superheroes had on American popular culture as the superhero is updated and reinvented for each new generation. Except for a brief time in postwar America, the superhero genre has dominated comic book publishing. Rather than trying to determine how comic book superheroes were like other heroic figures in American culture, educators and researchers should have studied the ways in which superheroes are different. Answering those questions would have helped explain the appeal of the superhero and would have gone a long way toward demonstrating why attempts by critics to substitute other reading material were doomed to failure.

One generalization about the criticism of comic books that can be made from this analysis of both professional and academic journal articles is that academic researchers were generally more tolerant and supportive of comic book reading than teachers and librarians. This might have been due in part to the familiarity the academics had with research that suggested many of the assumptions held about comic books were not valid. Also, they were more removed from the "problem" of the presence of comic books in children's everyday lives, while teachers and parents were faced with making decisions about comics in the classroom or home.

Criticism by educators and some academics attracted only intermittent public attention in the 1930s and early 1940s. Not until the end of the war would attacks on comics lead to a public demand for action. The most frequently advanced explanation for this delay is that the content of comic books shifted as the industry searched for new ways to entice readers who had lost interest in the colorful costumed superheroes who peopled the pages of the comic books prior to and during the war. The publishers turned to the familiar genres of pulp fiction for their ideas and produced, among others, comic books that featured themes of crime and horror. Although superhero comic book violence took place in fantastic, fictional worlds, the crime and horror comic book stories were acted out in very realistic settings. When this violence was rendered quite graphically and sold to children by an industry that had fewer restrictions than film, radio, or television, these "new" comic books brought down the wrath of the public on an industry that many felt had gone too far in its search for profits.

While shifts in public taste and the resulting publishing trends certainly played a part in feeding the controversy that sprung up around this new medium, there are several other possible explanations for why comic books did not attract sustained public attention until after the war. First, comic books were not the product of a new technology in the same way that film, radio, and television were. Early comic books were reprints of comic strips, which had been part of American culture throughout the twentieth century. The "old" technology posed fewer threats than the new electronic media. In addition, public concern about mass media often has roots in the research done by academics, and most scholars engaged in mass media research during this period focused more intensely on the electronic media. Such investigations dominated the academic discourse about media effects and children throughout the 1900s. Of the 242 articles and books that researchers Ellen Wartella and Byron Reeves catalogued, only five studies were done of newspapers, comics, magazines, and reading in general (124). Wartella and Reeves's overview of research on children and mass media between 1900 and 1960 reveals that there were three distinct "epochs" of research clustered around film, radio, and television, and the three "obviously correspond to the introduction and dissemination of the three technologies" (125). Delayed public reaction might also be attributed to the initially slow growth of the comic book medium. Although the comic book debuted in 1934, it was not an immediate success. It was not until the boom in 1939–1940 that the comic book became a strong presence in American culture. The fact that World War II broke out just at the time comic books became popular in America probably forestalled most criticism. The American public had more pressing concerns.

But perhaps the biggest reason why comic book reading failed to capture public attention and generate public outrage until after the war was that it was not until the postwar period that comic book reading became linked to the rising concerns about juvenile delinquency. This linkage introduced an entirely new element into the debate and shifted the discourse from being one about the impact of comic book reading on children's culture to broader fears about media effects on behavior. Although earlier critics had mentioned concerns about comic books relating to children's behavior and the fears that children would imitate what they read, their main complaint was that comic books were not good literature. The explicit accusation that comic book reading was a factor in juvenile delinquency was not made until the publication of the work of a noted psychiatrist, Fredric Wertham, who would emerge as a national spokesman in the debate over comic books.

Concern over comic books and children's culture and worries about comic books and juvenile delinquency, however, both have their roots in the way comic books represented a threat to adult authority over children. Children's literature did not emerge as a distinct field of publishing until the 1920s, and it wasn't until then that library schools began to offer specialized courses in children's literature (Meigs 395–400). But by the time the comic book made its debut, the supervision of children's reading had been largely given over to teachers and professional librarians in public and school libraries, so it is not surprising that these professionals would be the first to raise the alarm about comic books.

The "child consumer" was a relatively minor element in the juvenile fiction market; children did not purchase their own books, and usually the adult making the purchase also selected the books. The major market for children's books was not individual parents but school and public libraries. In addition, most magazines aimed at children relied primarily on subscription sales rather the newsstand purchases and targeted adult purchasers (Duke 13, 19). The comic book, however, was an alternative to reading sanctioned by adult authority, and children's leisure reading escaped the control of parents and professionals. The comic book was inexpensive and easily accessible, and children had a wide range of titles from which to select. The fact that adults frowned on such reading no doubt made comics even more appealing to children.

The addition of comic book reading to the ways in which children spent their leisure hours also reflected a broader trend toward the commercialization of children's culture. As historian Stephanie Coontz notes, marketing strategists in the 1950s would target children with advertising, bypassing parental authority to appeal directly to American youth as consumers (171). Historians Ellen Wartella and Sharon Mazzarella studied the emergence of "youth culture" in the United States, noting that beginning in the 1920s, public concern and media attention was given to the emergence of "an autonomous peer-oriented leisure-time culture, a culture independent of adults, outside the home, unsupervised, and increasingly commercialized" (178). In the 1930s and 1940s, high school students increased the amount of time spent outside the home, often with mass media that were beginning to be specifically marketed to them (182).

As documented by historian James Gilbert, the concern over juvenile delinquency stemmed in large part from this increasing visibility of teenagers and teen culture in postwar America. Gilbert writes that teens' speech, fashions, music, and mores puzzled and distressed Americans, who searched for ways to interpret this behavior. In the early 1950s, one theory caught hold of the public imagination: mass culture, including comic books, film, and other consumer entertainment aimed at youth, had "misshaped a generation of American boys and girls" (Gilbert 12–14). In addition, juvenile delinquency became an issue during the war years, Gilbert suggests, because evidence suggested crimes committed by children had increased significantly. Juvenile experts had anticipated just such an increase due to the social stresses caused by the war as men entered the service and women entered the work force, disrupting family life (25–28).

Gilbert attributed the rising concern about juvenile delinquency in the postwar period to three factors. First, the increased interest in juvenile delinquency meant that more attention was given to the topic in the popular press, making the problem more noticeable. Second, law enforcement agencies, prodded by public opinion, stepped up their monitoring of teenage behavior, resulting in more arrests and generating statistics that supported the notion that there was an increase in delinquency. Third, changes in youthful behavior meant that delinquency was redefined to encompass a broad range of activities not previously considered delinquent (71). Gilbert writes, "The point is a large portion of the public thought there was a delinquency crime wave, and they clamored to understand how and why this was happening" (77).

While most professional social workers, psychologists, sociologists, and criminologists denied any direct link between mass media and delinquency, focusing instead on the family environment as the cause, this conclusion did not produce a solution to the problem. The public chose to embrace a more satisfying explanation: the idea that modern mass culture, particularly radio, the movies, and comic books, was turning children into delinquents. Gilbert writes:

> For many Americans, mass culture in this equation solved the mystery of delinquency. It was an outside force guided from media centers in New York and Hollywood. It affected all classes of children. It penetrated the home. And it appeared to promote values contrary to those of many parents. It seemed, in other words, to be the catalyst that provoked generational conflict. Thus as the movement to control delinquency grew in the early 1950s, one of the most important corollary developments was the impulse to investigate, control, and censor mass culture. (77–78)

As a result, the mass media were targeted as causes of delinquency and there was broad public support for regulation of the mass media industries. Elimination, or at least regulation, of mass media was a simple, direct solution to the threat facing American children. Comic books were especially vulnerable because of public perceptions that they targeted child readers and because they were the least regulated of any of the mass media.

The early critics, who focused on the form and quality of comic books, were influential in the way that they first defined comic book reading as an activity strictly for children and then attacked comics for being unsuitable juvenile literature. Once comic books were perceived as primarily a medium aimed at children, the stage was set for later critics to shift the attention from the form to the specific content of comic books, raising questions about their impact on children's behavior. They represented comics as threat to law and order, rather than simply a bad influence on children's education, and sparked a reaction where earlier critics had failed.

This reaction took two forms. First, usually at the local level, civic and religious groups sought to impose informal controls on comic books by pressuring retailers to remove comics judged to be unsuitable or offensive; second, at the state and national level, many critics sought to impose formal governmental controls on the industry in the form of laws prohibiting publication of certain types of comic books. The next chapter will examine these efforts in detail.

Chapter 2

Censorship Strategies

Comic book crusaders fought their battle on two fronts. Critics undertook community decency crusades, often ignited by a Sunday sermon against the evils of comics, suggested by a local librarian who was the guest speaker at a women's club luncheon, or triggered by an article appearing in a popular national magazine or local newspaper. Then, as community crusades gained attention, legislators responded by launching investigations of comic books and proposing legislation to control or stop their distribution. The decency crusaders, although they occasionally invoked city ordinances dealing with obscene material, did not have the force of the law behind their demands. Instead, they relied on negative publicity and its resulting economic consequences as the primary tools in achieving their objectives. Legislators, on the other hand, sought legal remedies by drafting ordinances and statutes that outlawed the sale of certain types of comic books to minors. Such laws could be enforced by police and the courts and violators punished with fines, time in jail, or both.

The decency crusade has a long history, and one of the earliest crusaders was Anthony Comstock. As a result of his lobbying, Congress passed the first comprehensive obscenity law in 1873, known as the Comstock Act. That fall, Comstock formed the New York Society for the Suppression of Vice, an outgrowth of his work for the YMCA begun in 1872. While Comstock was empowered by the state to make arrests under the charter granted to the society, he found the threat of legal action was sufficient in most cases (Boyer 10). His crusade against the dime novels popular in that period can be compared to the campaign against comics some 60 years later (Mark West 43). Like comics, the dime novels really could not be prosecuted under existing statutes, since they were not obscene, so Comstock resorted to economic pressure, urging parents: "Let your newsdealer feel that, in just proportion as he prunes his stock of that which is vicious, your interest in his welfare increases and your patronage becomes more constant" (Comstock 42). These tactics would prove just as effective against comics as they had been against dime novels.

The efforts in the postwar period against comics, however, were much more organized. Crusaders took to the streets in teams, armed with lists of objectionable comic books, visiting local newsstand dealers and urging them to remove the "bad" comics from their stands. These community decency campaigns occurred nationwide and were organized by church groups, women's clubs, parent-teacher associations and others who heeded the alarm raised about comic books and juvenile delinquency. In most cases, the campaigns were highly successful; retailers visited by such teams agreed to remove whatever titles the crusaders identified as objectionable. The decency campaigns operated in relative isolation, and there was no national effort to organize or coordinate a campaign against comics. But decency campaigns were able to draw upon the work of two groups that reviewed comic books and provided the lists used to purge local newsstands of bad comics. One was the National Office of Decent Literature (later known as the National Organization for Decent Literature), a Catholic Church organization. The other was the Committee on the Evaluation of Comic Books in Cincinnati, whose work was publicized by *Parents' Magazine.*

The Catholic Church's success with the Legion of Decency, which pressured the film industry into enforcing a self-regulatory code and also established a rating system that provided Catholic filmgoers with a list of approved films, led to the establishment of the National Office of Decent Literature in December 1938. NODL was the only pressure group formed to direct attention against literature at the national level (Blanchard 186). In the beginning, NODL was concerned only with magazines and published a list of those it found objectionable, titled "Publications Disapproved for Youth." The organization was concerned with materials available to youth, and it did not pass judgment on adult reading material. The introduction of paperback books and comic books broadened the range of publications available to children and youth at newsstands, and NODL responded by expanding its activities in 1947 to evaluate these publications. The stated goals of the NODL program were to remove objectionable comic books and other publications from the places of distribution accessible to youth, to encourage publishing and distribution of good literature, and to promote plans to develop worthwhile reading habits during formative years (Gardiner 110).

It is interesting to note that the NODL goals incorporated both the "elite" criticism against comics, discussed in the previous chapter, with the criticism of the content of comics. The idea that comics were bad literature and encouraged children to develop undesirable reading habits was still an underlying force in such campaigns. It demonstrates that earlier criticism of comics, instead of being abandoned when the content of comics came under scrutiny, was incorporated into the later campaigns against comics. This helped to forge links between the various groups who objected to comics on different grounds. Although teachers and librarians had an agenda different from that of the morality crusaders from various religious organizations, each saw the campaign as a means to an end. In much the same way, psychiatrist Fredric Wertham would strike an alliance with conservative religious groups, whose objections to comics extended far beyond the concern with violence to their "moral" content, in order to try to get legislation passed to ban the sale of comics to minors.

The concern with "morality" as well as violent content is reflected in the criteria used by NODL in its reviews of comics. Publications rated as objectionable by NODL exhibited one or more of the following characteristics:

1. glorified crime or the criminal
2. described in detail ways to commit criminal acts
3. held lawful authority in disrespect
4. exploited horror, cruelty, or violence
5. portrayed sex facts offensively
6. featured indecent, lewd or suggestive photographs or illustrations
7. carried advertising which was offensive in content or advertised products which may lead to physical or moral harm
8. used blasphemous, profane or obscene speech indiscriminately and repeatedly
9. held up to ridicule any national, religious or racial group. (Gardiner 110)

Under the NODL procedure, magazine titles were reviewed twice a year. One individual read the magazine, wrote an opinion, and returned it to the national office. Five others reviewed the initial opinion, and if all rated the magazine objectionable, it was placed on the "objectionable" list. The procedure for reviewing books was somewhat more elaborate, and NODL selected reviewers who appreciated "literary values" (Gardiner 111). The organization confined its activity to material available at newsstands and did not investigate libraries or book stores (117). Comic book titles also were evaluated every six months. A committee of 150 mothers, divided into groups of five, received a specified number of comics. Each group member read and rated the comics as either acceptable, borderline, or objectionable. If all five found the comic book acceptable, it was set aside for six months. If, after six months, another group of reviewers also rated the title acceptable, it was placed on the list distributed by NODL of "acceptable" comics (111). NODL published a separate "White List" of acceptable comics, listing unacceptable comics with other "condemned" publications. One typical NODL monthly list contained thirty-five condemned comic books, along with the titles of 440 unacceptable paperbacks and magazines (Blanchard 187).

The NODL lists were made available to the general public; individual parishes were urged not to post the list, however, since the office did not want the list in the hands of adolescents who might be enticed to search out material that the church had condemned. Catholics were urged to use the lists in local decency campaigns. The NODL literature outlined specific procedures for conducting such campaigns. Every two weeks, members of the local committee were to visit each establishment selling magazines, comics, and paperback books. Members were urged to work in teams of two or three, with each team assigned to visit three dealers.

On the first contact, teams were encouraged to explain the purpose of the decency crusade, emphasizing that the goal was to protect "the ideals and morality" of youth. The team gave the dealer a NODL list and got permission to examine his racks at two-week intervals. This inspection, the literature advised, was to be offered as a voluntary "service" to the dealer, with members explaining that they understood that many proprietors simply did not have the time to check their racks. When the team found something objectionable, they were to report it to the manager. If the manager refused to take action, the decency crusade team was to leave the establishment silently, rather than confront the manager, and report the refusal to their pastor. Lists of stores that cooperated with the local decency crusades were announced in church and printed in parish publications (Gardiner 112). In some cases, cooperative store owners were issued certificates of compliance, but the national office discouraged that practice, pointing out that the dealer could continue to display the certificate while restocking his shelves with objectionable material (117).

NODL promoted the lists as tools for the busy retailer, noting that ideally, sellers should exercise their own moral responsibility rather than abdicate to any group or list, but that it was unrealistic to expect the retailer to read everything on his racks (122). The decency crusades targeted retailers rather that publishers because, according to NODL literature, "most of the filthy books and magazines are put out deliberately by publishers who know that they will sell. They are not interested in their effect on youth, and cannot be reasoned with" (115).

To get widespread support for conducting decency crusades, NODL urged Catholics to form citizens' committees made up of members of educational, social/fraternal, and religious organizations. At the initial meeting of the committee, examples of the types of literature of concern to the community were shown. The help of non-Catholic groups was then enlisted to clean up literature made available to juveniles in the community (112).

Although NODL's literature noted that the list was not to be used for purposes of boycott or coercion, it frequently was used for just those purposes (Haney 92). In other cases, NODL's lists were used by police in communities to clear newsstands of objectionable material, even if such material was not found to be obscene under state law (Gardiner 118). In nearly all cases, a request from the police department did not need to be followed up by legal action. Samuel Black, vice president of the Atlantic Coast Independent Distributors Association and a distributor in Springfield, Massachusetts, told a House committee investigating paperback books and comics in 1952 that when a complaint was filed with the police department, the chief of police gave his company twenty-four hours' notice before any official action was taken. Police censorship was preferable to volunteer censorship groups, Black told the committee, because the latter accomplished little more than generating "personal glory for some people that want to see their names in the press" (House Select Committee Hearings, 38–39).

One of the more drastic forms of action taken was the burning of comic books organized in several communities. An editorial in *Senior Scholastic* February 2, 1949, questioned both the wisdom and effectiveness of such a move, pointing out that book burnings and emotion orgies "partake of the very violence we deplore in bad comic books." It warned: "Flames can be dangerous things. Sometimes they get out of control and destroy priceless literature." Rather than burning comic books, the editorial suggested, communities should strive to give children quality books and magazines at a moderate price ("To Burn" 5). An editorial by Adrian Tielman of Roosevelt College in Chicago, published in the May 1949 issue of *Educational Administration and Supervision,* suggested that comic book burning sent children the wrong messages (300). Such actions, he argued, were "inadequate training for a democracy" (301).

Critics charged that the decency crusades effectively censored not only material available to children but adult reading material as well. The church's position was that while removal of such material might infringe on an adult's "right to read," good citizens should be willing to waive their rights in order to protect children (Haney 95). Other critics argued that the NODL decency code was too sweeping and its standards more severe than most obscenity statutes (Blanchard 193). The comics editor of the New York Herald Tribute Syndicate, Harold Straubing, feared that pressure groups failed to recognize comics were valuable as a means of communication and learning. He added that "nobody bothers to investigate the person who is criticizing; when it comes to the comics, every Carrie Nation who waves a hatchet makes everybody tremble" (McMaster 46).

But decency crusades aroused little protest in specific cities where they were conducted. Since they were usually organized by civic and religious leaders in the community, few would speak out against their work. Also, most adults were not familiar with the content of comic books and were willing to accept the evaluations of the decency crusaders without question, or simply did not care. But perhaps most important, the issue was carefully constructed as one concerning the welfare of children, rather than being a censorship issue. Those who might have argued against censorship and invoked the First Amendment would have seemed to be advocating giving children access to material that community leaders were condemning as bad. Throughout the campaign against comics, the critics insisted the issue was not censorship, although it clearly was, at least in part. The First Amendment, they argued, was not meant to protect corporate greed and irresponsibility at the expense of children. Being able to define the battle against comics in the minds of the public as one of child welfare rather than one of censorship was a major victory for the anti–comic book forces.

NODL had a definite impact in communities with active decency crusades. Retailers relied on the good will of their community to remain in business and were sensitive to public opinion. In testimony in 1952 before a House committee investigating pornography, church representatives reported that 99 percent of the dealers were very cooperative. In addition, the NODL organization provided a model for other civic and religious organizations that sought to rid newsstands of objectionable periodicals and paperback books. For example, in 1954 an organization titled the Citizen's Committee for Better Juvenile Literature was formed in Chicago. One of the committee's stated goals was to work for the elimination of materials seen as detrimental to or having no beneficial value to the intellectual, social, cultural, or spiritual growth of children. Volunteer reviewers read material purchased by the group. A list of materials rated "objectionable" by those volunteers was given to organized teams who visited neighborhood retail outlets and requested that the items be removed (Twomey, "Citizen's Committee" 624–28). The group was the outgrowth of an editorial campaign against comic books conducted by the *Southtown Economist,* a southside Chicago community newspaper.

In fact, many community campaigns against comic books were triggered by newspaper crusades. A series of articles in the *Sacramento Bee* in spring 1954 brought about a move for cooperative action to ban horror-type comic books from newsstands. Quoted in the June 26, 1954, issue of the trade publication *Editor and Publisher,* the *Bee* defended its campaign to ban the comics this way: "This is not a matter of suppression of ideas or of unconventional literature. It is a matter of protecting youth and the community against sewerage. To repeat, this is not a civil liberties issue. It does not involve suppression of ideas" ("Daily is Leader" 38). Another *Editor and Publisher* article published two weeks later noted that the religion editor of the *Dayton Journal Herald* wrote a series on lurid comic books that caused the city manager to order police to check newsstands and bring in examples of objectionable comics ("Religious Editor" 50).

One exposé that received national attention and was widely reprinted was the *Hartford Courant's* four-part series on comic books. The idea for the series came from a column by editorial writer Thomas E. Murphy, who speculated about factors contributing to juvenile delinquency in Hartford, Connecticut. When he discovered that children in troubled areas of the city spent a larger portion of their leisure time reading crime and horror comic books than other children, he wrote a column asking parents, "Do you know what your children are reading?" A series devoted to the problem of comic books followed; the first story ran February 14, 1954. In order to stress the importance of the problem, the *Courant* ran the story above the newspaper's nameplate, a format it had seldom used in its 190-year history. The headline was: "Depravity For Children—10 Cents a Copy!" (Towne 11). The first article was simply a collection of plot summaries gleaned from the comic books that reporter Irving M. Kravsow purchased in Hartford and spent two weeks reading. He warned parents than any child could buy a "short course in murder, mayhem, robbery, rape, cannibalism, carnage, sex, sadism and worse." Kravsow then went to New York to interview publishers for the second article, which appeared February 15 with the headline: "Public Taste, Profit Used to Justify 'Horror' Comics." The third article in the series printed the reactions of educators, religious leaders, and civic officials to comic books. The final story in the series noted that the United States district attorney was warning publishers that they must "clean house." The response was immediate. Emergency meetings were scheduled by service and civic organizations and committees were formed to address the problem (Towne 11).

One of the earliest organizations of this type, the Committee on Evaluation of Comic Books in Cincinnati, formed in June 1948, achieved national status when its work was publicized by *Parents' Magazine.* Since it confined its activities to reviewing comic books, some felt that the committee's work was more thorough and trustworthy than that of NODL (Blanchard 274). The chairman was Jesse L. Murrell, a Methodist minister from Covington, Kentucky. He headed an executive committee of ten and a reviewing staff of approximately 130 individuals. The committee reviewed and rated comic books and published lists of the results. Each comic book story was evaluated in terms of its cultural, moral, and emotional tone and given a rating of no objection, some objection, objectionable, or very objectionable. Only comic books falling into the first two categories were deemed suitable for children. Reviewers included mothers, educators from both public and parochial schools, PTA members, juvenile court workers, librarians, clergymen, and members of the business community. The results were made available to anyone for a nominal fee to cover mailing costs. In addition, *Parents' Magazine* published the committee's list each year.

In the August 1954 report in *Parents' Magazine,* comics rated objectionable or very objectionable in the "cultural" category included those that belittled traditional American institutions; comics that used obscenity, vulgarity, profanity, or language of the underworld; stories expressing prejudice against class, race, creed, or nationality; stories that treated divorce humorously or as glamorous; those that expressed sympathy with the criminal against law and order; and those that made criminals and criminal acts attractive. Books that were rated "morally" objectionable included those in which women were used to glamorize crime; any situation having a sexual implication; figures that were dressed indecently or unduly exposed; stories that provided details or methods of crime, especially if enacted by children; the portrayal of law enforcement officials as stupid or ineffective; and the portrayal of drug addiction or excessive use of alcohol. Comic books rated as "morbidly emotional" and objectionable included any showing kidnapping of women or children; characters shown bleeding, particularly from the face or mouth; use of chains, whips, or other cruel devices; morbid picturization of dead bodies; stories and pictures that had a sadistic implication or suggested use of black magic; portrayal of maiming or disfiguring acts of assault or murder; and people being attacked or injured by wild animals or reptiles. A comic book like *Superman* was rated as having some objection because it depicted criminal acts or moral violations (even if legally punished) and because it featured "sinister creatures" portrayed in a grotesque, fantastic, or unnatural way. A horror title such as *Shock SuspenStories* was rated as very objectionable in six different categories. "Funny animal" books like *Tweety and Sylvester* were about the only titles to receive the no-objection rating.

It is important to note that while crusades against comic books were often begun with the idea of eliminating from the newsstand those comics containing graphic violence or sex, the groups rating comics quickly expanded their goals, monitoring the cultural and moral values depicted in the pages. Rating the violent content of comic books proved difficult. Is it acceptable, say, in a Western comic to show men having a fist fight but not shooting at each other? And must the violence be specific, or is the threat of violence, either spoken or implied by a raised hand or a close-up of a gun, enough to condemn the comic book? Extending the rating system into the areas of cultural and moral values opened the door for a purge that left only the most innocuous comic books on the stands. As will be discussed in more detail in the next chapter, some of the better crime and horror comic books took a stand on social issues of the day. By condemning all references to race as being racist, for example, reviewers effectively closed off all discussion of racism.

The difficulties inherent in reviewing comic book content is made apparent in comparing the work of different groups. Although the Cincinnati committee had the same goals as NODL, their lists often did not agree. In 1949, for example, the Cincinnati Committee rated 29 percent of comics as fully acceptable, and the Catechetical Guild of St. Paul gave an "A" rating to 25 percent of comics using the NODL lists. But on the Catholic list were five comics given a "very objectionable" rating by Cincinnati reviewers (Blanchard 248–49).

Articles in local newspapers frequently provided the impetus for decency crusades, but national media attention to the problem of comic books also launched several campaigns. While the comic book industry ignored local media attacks, national publicity was another matter. After the publication of Marya Mannes' article in *New Republic* in February 1947 (see chap. 1), the publishers formed a trade association, the Association of Comics Magazine Publishers, but it took another national attack on comics to spur the publishers into action.

In March 1948, a debate on comic books was broadcast on the ABC Radio Network program "America's Town Meeting of the Air." The March 2 program generated more than six thousand letters, a record response. *Newsweek*'s March 15 coverage described the discussion as a duel between John Mason Brown, scholarly drama critic of the *Saturday Review of Literature*, author, and lecturer, and Al Capp, "wisecracking cartoonist" who drew "'Li'l Abner." Marya Mannes argued on Brown's side, and George Hecht, publisher of a line of educational comics and *Parents' Magazine,* stood with Capp. The opening statements by Brown and Capp were reprinted in the *Saturday Review of Literature* on March 20. Brown's attack was based on the comic book's contamination of children's culture, a familiar criticism. He argued that comic books were the lowest, most despicable, and most harmful form of trash, designed for readers who are too lazy to read. In a statement that was often repeated, Brown called comic books "the marijuana of the nursery; the bane of the bassinet; the horror of the house; the curse of the kids; and a threat to the future" (Brown 31–32). Capp's defense of the comics centered around arguments that the murder, crime, and violence found in the pages of comic books were no different from that in the newspaper and that comic strips were "as old a form as the written word itself" (Capp 33).

It is important to recognize that in the beginning, the response from the industry and other spokesmen defending comic books was much less organized and much less persuasive than the arguments the critics presented. As noted earlier, attacking community leaders who purported to have the welfare of children at heart was not likely to influence many. Even after the association of comic book publishers reorganized in 1948, the group did not have the funding to launch a public relations campaign of sufficient scope to counter the critics. Other groups that might have spoken out were reluctant to become "tainted" with the negative public image of comic books. Comic strip cartoonists, for example, generally considered comic books the poor step-cousin of the comic strip and most were anxious to disassociate themselves from the medium. Capp's assertion that comics were an art form to be appreciated was probably an argument ahead of its time, coming in a period when few recognized the value of studying popular culture. And when Fredric Wertham entered the fray, comic book defenders had no expert waiting in the wings to put up against the noted psychiatrist.

In March, Wertham released his findings about the effects of comic books to his colleagues in a symposium on comic books he organized for the Association for the Advancement of Psychotherapy and to the public in an article written by Judith Crist for *Collier's*, "Horror in the Nursery." Wertham maintained that comic book reading was an influencing factor in the case of every delinquent or disturbed child he studied (Crist 22).

The symposium, titled "The Psychopathology of Comic Books" was held on March 19, 1948, at the New York Academy of Medicine. Also speaking at the symposium were Gerson Legman, Dr. Hilde Mosse, Paula Elkisch, and Marvin L. Blumberg. Their remarks and a summary of the discussion that followed were published in the *American Journal of Psychotherapy*. All the speakers condemned the comic books, accusing them of being unhealthy escape mechanisms, of teaching children that violence was the only solution to their problems, and of stirring primitive impulses that retarded the development of socially desirable behavior and attitudes. Comics were defended by representatives of the industry who attended the symposium, including Charles Biro, Alden Getz, and Harvey Kurtzman, but they were not given much opportunity by Wertham to present their views (Wertham, "Psychopathology" 490). When criticized for not allowing the industry representatives to speak, he remarked: "I am even more guilty than that: I once conducted a symposium on alcoholism and didn't invite a single distiller" (Wertham, "Comics... Very Funny" 29).

For her article in *Collier's*, published March 27, 1948, Crist illustrated Wertham's points with anecdotal information gleaned from case histories of the children the psychiatrist treated, a technique Wertham was himself to use successfully in later articles and books. Sandwiched between the horror stories of children who acted out the comic book stories they read, however, were several key ideas that would be repeated throughout Wertham's decade-long fight against comic books.

First, Wertham wanted his audience to realize how popular comic books were. He estimated that there were more than sixty million comic books in circulation per month and pointed out that some of his young patients reported reading as many as twenty a week, trading with siblings and friends (Crist 22). Second, he saw himself as "a voice for the thousands of troubled parents who, like myself, are concerned primarily with their children's welfare." Wertham told Crist he had heard parents express anxiety about comic books literally hundreds of times in letters and during conferences (97). Third, he attacked those in his profession who served as consultants to the publishers, noting that many of them were "psychoprima donnas" who did no clinical work with children. He said: "The fact that some child psychiatrists endorse comic books does not prove the healthy state of the comic books. It only proves the unhealthy state of child psychiatry." He refuted the consultants' claims that comic books were simply healthy fantasy outlets for aggression and that children were aware that the world of comic books was one of make-believe (Crist 23). In addition, he rejected the idea that comic books could serve as educational tools: "Not only are comic books optically hard to read, with their garish colors and semiprinted balloons, but they are psychologically bad, turning the child's interest from reading to picture gazing" (Crist 96).

Finally, and perhaps most important, Wertham took the opportunity to press for legislation against comic books. If publishers were unwilling to clean up comic books, he argued, "the time has come to legislate these books off the newsstands and out of the candy stores." He believed that present penal laws in most states could be used to eliminate comic books (Crist 22). He decried the unwillingness of law enforcement to take action: "It is obviously easier to sentence a child to life imprisonment than to curb a hundred-million-dollar business" (Crist 23). Also sharing the blame were mental hygiene associations, child study committees, child care councils, and community child welfare groups who failed to speak out against comics. Countering arguments about the freedom of the press, Wertham said: "We are not dealing with the rights and privileges of adults to read and write as they choose. We are dealing with the mental health of a generation—the care of which we have left too long in the hands of unscrupulous persons whose only interest is greed and financial gain" (Crist 97).

Wertham used the material he prepared for the symposium as the basis for an article on comic books solicited by Norman Cousins, editor of *Saturday Review of Literature*. It was titled "The Comics...Very Funny!" and appeared in the May 29, 1948, issue. It was condensed for the August issue of *Reader's Digest,* and letters to Wertham poured into the offices at both publications, many of them offering help or advice for a national movement to get comic books off the shelves. It also triggered police action against comic books in more than fifty cities (Gilbert 98–99; Wertham, "Comics...Very Funny" 7). The article begins with an extensive listing of anecdotal evidence demonstrating that children were imitating the violent acts they read about in comic books. Illustrations included two comic book panels, one showing a woman being attacked by an ape and another showing a needle about to be plunged into the eye of a helpless woman, and the cover for an issue of *Jo-Jo: Congo King,* with a scantily clad woman in the foreground being pursued by a man dressed in a loincloth riding a water buffalo. These illustrations were labeled "Marijuana of the Nursery" (7), a title no doubt inspired by drama critic John Brown's scathing attack on comics two months earlier. Wertham noted: "Comic books are the greatest book publishing success in history and the greatest mass influence on children...one billion times a year a child sits down and reads a comic book." Next, Wertham listed seventeen of the arguments made in favor of comic books, refuting each one with a sentence or two included in parentheses. Wertham had presented most of these arguments in the *Collier's* article. But he did introduce two new elements: first, he took issue with the idea that only abnormal children are adversely affected by comic books; and second, he disputed the notion that comic books prevent crime and delinquency because the stories always end with the triumph of law enforcement. He concluded by restating his position that "comic books represent systematic poisoning of the well of childhood spontaneity" (29). What was missing from this article is perhaps more important than what was included; nowhere in "The Comics...Very Funny!" was his call for legislation against comic books repeated.

These latest attacks on comic books prompted the ACMP to reorganize in June 1948, and publishers appointed committees on public relations and advertising, censorship, editorial improvements, and research (Smith

1652). On July 1, 1948, the association announced the adoption of a code to regulate the content of comics. The six-point code forbade depiction of sex or sadistic torture, the use of vulgar and obscene language, the ridicule of religious and racial groups, and the humorous treatment of divorce. As *Newsweek* noted in its coverage of the new code, the most detailed provision dealt with the issue of crime: "Crime should not be presented in such a way as to throw sympathy against law and justice or to inspire others with the desire for imitation. No comics should show the details and methods of a crime committed by a youth. Policemen, judges, government officials, and respected institutions should not be portrayed as stupid or ineffective, or represented in such a way as to weaken respect for established authority" ("Purified Comics" 56). The emphasis on regulating depictions of crime reflected concerns about possible links between comic books and juvenile delinquency. Many felt that even children who did not exhibit other delinquent behavior might be enticed into imitating crimes pictured in detail in their favorite comics, and children who did not act on what they read were still getting the wrong message about authority from the stories that glorified criminals.

The ACMP hired a staff of reviewers who read the comics before they were published, and approved comics were allowed to carry the association's seal of approval on the cover. The president of the association, Phil Keenan of Hillman Periodicals, warned the public not to expect overnight miracles, because the improvements would be made to comic books currently in production, and those books would not be put into circulation for several months ("Code for the Comics" 62). Almost immediately, the industry ran into trouble trying to enforce its code. While there had been strong support initially for a trade association, many of the largest publishers broke ranks. Some left the organization because they did not want their companies associated with those publishing what they felt were inferior comics, some because of objections to the code, some because of the time and expense involved in supporting prepublication review, and some because of what ACMP executive director Henry Schultz characterized as "internecine warfare in [the] industry." As a result, only about a third of the publishers actually supported the new code, and that number dwindled until, by 1954, there were only three publishers left in the organization and the prepublication review process had been abandoned.

In August 1948, Wertham attacked comic books and denounced the code at the Seventy-Eighth Annual Congress of Correction of the American

Prison Association. His paper, "The Betrayal of Childhood: Comic Books," was a five-part analysis consisting of case histories, content analysis, an evaluation of effects, an examination of the industry, and a proposal for action. Wertham said that the case histories demonstrated that the behavior of young children was influenced by reading comic books; a study of typical cases "shows that whatever antecedent factors existed, the factor of imitation (as is well-known to parents, even if not to the experts of the comic-book industry) is often very important" (71). He called comic books a "correspondence course in crime" because of their detailed explanations of how crimes are committed and noted that during the first six months of 1948, there was a drastic increase in the number of comic books that capitalized on crime and violence (57).

Then Wertham listed seven ways in which comic books affect children:

1. Comic books may suggest criminal or sexually abnormal ideas.
2. They create a mental preparedness or readiness for temptation.
3. They suggest the forms a delinquent impulse may take and supply details of the latest techniques for its execution.
4. They may tip the scales in the behavior of an otherwise normal child and act as the precipitating factor of delinquency or emotional disorder.
5. They supply the rationalization for a contemplated act which is often more important than the impulse itself.
6. They set off a chain of undesirable and harmful thinking.
7. They create for the child atmosphere of deceit, trickery and cruelty. (58)

Wertham concluded that children who spend time and money on comic books "have nothing to show for it afterwards." If the Pure Food and Drug law can protect children's bodies, Wertham argued, then "surely the minds of children deserve as much protection." He stated that the self-regulation of the industry, represented by the code passed two months earlier, was a "farce" and while he did not advocate censorship, he suggested his solution for legislation was a "democratic" one—the protection of the many against the few (59).

The failure of the industry's attempts at self-regulation in 1948 gave impetus to calls for legislation at the local, state, and national levels. Decency crusades and media campaigns were carried out in towns and cities all across America and were highly effective at the local level in controlling the distribution of comic books deemed unsuitable by the church and civic groups that organized against the comic book menace. But many felt that scattershot efforts at controlling comic books were not enough. One of the proponents of state and federal legislation was Wertham, who was seeking a ban on the sale of all comic books to children under age sixteen.

Some of the strongest support for legislation against comic books came from the National Congress of Parents and Teachers and from the National Education Association. A resolution adopted by the National Congress on September 16, 1948, spelled out a "Plan of Action" against unwholesome comics, motion pictures, and radio programs. The proposal called for studies of the effects of mass media on children and urged the national group to meet with publishers and producers to improve productions. In addition, state groups affiliated with the National Congress were urged to organize local radio listener councils, motion picture councils, and evaluating groups for comics and other publications. In addition, members were asked to review state and local laws and to initiate community action to improve and enforce existing laws ("Plan of Action" 12). Mabel W. Hughes, president of the National Congress, wrote in her editorial in the organization's publication, *National Parent-Teacher,* that comic books deserved not only censure, but censorship (Hughes 3). Her call for censorship was echoed by the editor of the *NEA Journal,* Joy Elmer Morgan, who condemned the exploitation of the immature minds of children by commercial interests. Responding to the comic book industry's charges that censorship undermined press freedom, Morgan wrote: "We fail to see the point. *Freedom* of the press cannot be separated from *responsibility* of the press. Press freedom ... was never intended to protect indecency or the perversion of the child mind" (Morgan 570).

Others, however, felt that legislation against comic books would set a dangerous precedent. *The Nation* went on record in its March 19, 1949, issue as being opposed to legislation directed against comic books, adding: "Comic books are an opening wedge. If they can be 'purified'—that is, controlled—newspapers, periodicals, books, films, and everything else will follow" (319). The trade publication of the newspaper industry, *Editor and Publisher,* also saw the possibility of a dangerous precedent being set with the legislation of comic book content. In an editorial in its December 18, 1948, issue, it called on newspapers to fight laws against comics. The editorial pointed out that various community ordinances made public censors of city officials. It warned that it would be difficult to restrain such officials from extending censorship to other media. It concluded: "For instance, wouldn't it be the next logical step for such censors to forbid the sale to minors of newspapers carrying news stories of crime? Censorship breeds censorship!" ("Censorship of Comics" 36). Not surprisingly, the comic book industry opposed legislation, using the same argument about the dangers of censorship and maintaining that industry self-regulation was the proper course. Henry Schultz, executive director of the industry trade association, noted that self regulation was the "true and lasting solution." Censorship, he argued, "can do naught but lead us down a dark and dangerous road from which there may be no returning" (Schultz, "Censorship" 223–24).

While the ACMP and the comic book industry had seemingly found allies, most of those who defended comic books against censorship did not condone the publication of crime and horror comic books. In fact, if there had been a way to assure such groups that censorship laws would be limited to comic books, they no doubt would have thrown their support wholeheartedly behind such legislation. This conclusion is reflected in the fact that decency crusades in local communities were praised by the very same people who opposed censorship laws. In many ways, the decency crusades were a more insidious form of censorship, since there was no legal recourse against such actions.

Decency crusades, however, had their greatest impact on retailers and on the readers whose selection of comic books was dictated by a small group in the community intent on policing public morality. Such actions had little impact on the industry. Of more concern to publishers, however, was the work of legislators who sought laws to control or ban the publication of comics. The threat of legislation directly affected the economic well-being of the comic book publishing industry. A major hurdle, however, was the constitutionality of any legal remedies targeting comic books.

The legal case of most concern to those drafting state and federal legislation against comic books was a case that dealt, not with a comic book, but an adult crime magazine, *Headquarters Detective, True Cases from the Police Blotter.* Two thousand copies of the magazine were seized in New York under a section of the New York Penal Code that made it illegal to publish, distribute, or sell any book, pamphlet, magazine, or newspaper made up primarily of criminal news, police reports, or accounts of criminal deeds, or pictures, or stories of deeds of bloodshed, lust, or crime. The book dealer was convicted, but after more than seven years of litigation, lower court decisions were reversed by the United States Supreme Court on March 29, 1948, on the grounds that the law was unconstitutional. Similar statutes in eighteen states were overturned by the decision in *Winters v. New York* (Twomey, "Anti–Comic Book Crusade" 16–17; Mitchell "Evil Harvest" 36–37).

The Supreme Court found the laws prohibiting depiction of crime and violence in the media unconstitutional as written, since they violated both the First and Fourteenth amendments. Although obscenity and pornography were not protected under the First Amendment, the Court ruled that crime magazines, while containing little of value to society, were as much entitled to free speech protection as the best of literature (*Winters* 667). The Court also noted that while words such as *obscene, lewd, lascivious, filthy, indecent,* or *disgusting* were "well understood through long use in criminal law," the provisions against crime and bloodshed were unconstitutionally vague because the clause had no "technical or common law meaning." Without a precise definition, it was impossible for an individual to know when he or she was in violation of the law. Therefore, the New York law was also in violation of the Fourteenth Amendment guaranteeing due process.

Gerson Legman, speaking before the Association for the Advancement of Psychotherapy as part of a symposium on comic books organized by Fredric Wertham, noted that the *Winters* decision would make it difficult to pass legislation against comic books. Legman interpreted the Supreme Court decision to mean the court had separated obscenity from violence and ruled that the latter had constitutional protection. He commented that it was hypocritical that after looking at hundreds of pictures in comic books showing half-naked women being tortured to death, critics could only complain that the women were half naked. He added, "If they were being tortured to death with all their clothes on, that would be perfect for children" (476).

The Supreme Court's decision in 1948 set guidelines for media content that are still at issue today. Laws regulating obscenity and pornography are on the books in almost every city and state, but the regulation of violent content in the media, while it spurs periodic public outcry and legislative investigation, ultimately remains the responsibility of the media industries and their self-regulatory bodies. Opponents of crime comics took heart, however, from one section of the *Winters* decision that left the door open for legislators to rewrite state laws. The court noted that states do have the right to punish the circulation of objectionable printed matter not protected by the First Amendment provided that "apt words" were used to describe the prohibited publications (*Winters* 672). In addition, the strong dissenting opinion by three justices gave hope to legislators that a law directed against "objectionable" comic books would be upheld in the future if it contained clear and precise language (Twomey, "Anti–Comic Book Crusade" 18; Feder 21).

In their dissenting opinion, Justices Frankfurter, Jackson, and Burton noted that laws such as the New York statute were an attempt by legislators to deal with the persistent problem of crime and with its prevention. By striking down these laws, they argued, the court had given constitutional protection to publications that, in the court's opinion, had nothing of any possible value to society, but denied to states the power to prevent the evils that such publications cause (*Winters* 676).

One of the first tests of the *Winters* decision as it related to legislation aimed at curbing crime comics was an ordinance passed by the Los Angeles County Board of Supervisors. After studying the *Winters* decision, Los Angeles County Counsel Harold W. Kennedy and Deputy Counsel Milnor E. Gleaves issued a legal opinion with suggestions on how legislation banning crime comics should address the problems of vagueness cited in the Supreme Court decision. They concluded that the three problems facing a city that wanted to draft an ordinance to meet the test of the *Winters* case were: (1) drafting legislation that did not violate the provisions of the First Amendment and its guarantee of the freedom and speech and the press; (2) drafting an ordinance that answered the problems of being vague and indefinite; (3) writing an ordinance that drew on the appropriate statutory power for enforcement. Legislation should make a definite distinction between allowable and forbidden publications and should use technical or common law meaning in defining the crimes that it would be illegal to depict (Rhyne 7–12).

The ordinance passed by the Los Angeles Board of Supervisors on September 21, 1948, excluded newspaper accounts and illustrations of crimes and listed precisely which crimes could not be depicted. Those crimes included: arson, assault with caustic chemicals, assault with a deadly weapon, burglary, kidnapping, mayhem, murder, rape, robbery, theft, or voluntary manslaughter. The ordinance provided for a five-hundred-dollar fine or a six-month jail term for selling crime comics to children under eighteen

(Rhyne 11; "Unfunny Comic Books" 38). County police were responsible for enforcement of the ordinance, although county officials said volunteer groups, such as the various parent-teacher groups who were instrumental in getting the ordinance passed, might be asked to help monitor newsstands. An informal survey taken by the county board ten days after passage of the ordinance revealed that virtually no objectionable comic books were on sale in the area.

The Association of Comic Magazine Publishers, an industry trade group representing about one-third of the publishers, issued a press release October 18 denouncing the Los Angeles ordinance, calling the restrictions "a grievous error which' undermines the principle of press freedom." Henry Schultz, executive director of the association, said the publishers were prepared for "a fight to the finish" on the issue. He added that the ordinance "unwittingly opened the editorial offices of American publications to the menace of press censorship." The association announced it was retaining a Los Angeles law firm to institute legal action to test the constitutionality of the ordinance ("Comics Group Plans to Test" 32; Morgan, "Ubiquitous Comics" 570).

The Los Angeles County ordinance covered only the rural areas of the county, but some groups hoped the California legislature would enact the ban statewide. No retailers were prosecuted under the ordinance, and on December 27, 1949, the law was declared unconstitutional by the California Superior Court. Quoted in the December 31, 1949, issue of *Editor and Publisher,* Judge Harley Shaw commented that under the ordinance, even school history textbooks devoting chapters to Lincoln's assassination or the incident that touched off World War I, the assassination of Archduke Ferdinand at Sarajevo, and that contained illustrations of these events, would be banned. He concluded: "The central question is the validity of a county ordinance which is commonly thought to outlaw comic books. We conclude it runs counter to the state and federal constitutions" ("Ban" 10). The issue here was not the language used in defining which depictions of crime and violence were to be outlawed, but rather the broader issue of how to define a comic book. A major problem that emerged in legislation targeting comic books was how to formulate a legal definition of a comic book narrow enough to exclude other illustrated matter. Although comic books were clearly a separate medium from newspaper comics and other illustrated material, writing a legal definition of comics proved to be quite difficult. Apparently the problem stumped the Los Angeles legal staff; while some called for an appeal of the court decision, no further legal action was taken ("Psychiatrist Charges Stalling" 9).

Although Los Angeles abandoned its attempt to pass legislation regulating comic books, other cities and states considered various ordinances and bills to control or prohibit the publication of objectionable comic books. Nowhere was the effort more sustained than in New York, home to the comic book publishing industry. Between 1948 and 1955, the New York State legislature conducted an extensive investigation of comic books and tried on several occasions to pass legislation controlling comics.[2] The New York legislature, in response to the *Winters* decision, began by passing an amendment to Section 1141, Subdivision 2, of the Penal Law that had been found to be unconstitutional in the *Winters* case. That bill, sponsored by Senate Republican majority leader Benjamin F. Feinberg at the request of the New York District Attorneys Association, was intended to address the court's concern that the language was too vague. The original statute outlawed printed matter "principally made up of criminal news, police reports, or accounts of criminal deeds, or pictures, or stories of deeds of bloodshed, lust or crime." The amended version modified the wording of the statute as follows: " . . . principally made up of accounts or pictures depicting sordid bloodshed, lust or heinous acts." Legislators apparently believed the addition of "sordid" before bloodshed and the changing of "crime" to "heinous acts" would provide a more precise definition of material to be prohibited by the statute ("Comic Book Curb Vetoed" 20).

The comic book industry, naturally, opposed passage of this bill. The head of the Association of Comics Magazine Publishers, Henry Schultz, wrote Gov. Thomas Dewey urging him to veto the bill. In a letter dated April 1, 1949, Schultz argued that the bill was unconstitutional. He also suggested that the legislation was based on the premise that magazines (including comic books) that contained accounts of crime were harmful, and that this assumption was not supported by any valid evidence and "rests entirely upon opinion, emotional and unscientific." Schultz also suggested that the program of self-regulation recently adopted by the trade association was the only practical solution to the problem posed by comic books.

Although the bill passed both houses, it was vetoed April 18, 1949, by Governor Dewey. The primary difficulty with the proposed legislation lay in defining what materials would be prohibited. In his veto memorandum, Dewey cited the case of *Winters v. New York,* noting the bill made little change in the language already held invalid by the highest court in the land. Dewey felt the addition of the adjective "sordid" and the substitution of the words "heinous acts" for the word "crime" did not adequately address the objections in the *Winters* case. He concluded: "The bill is therefore unconstitutional within the language of the *Winters* case and it is disapproved."

In addition to his attempt to rewrite the state's penal code, Senator Feinberg also introduced a proposal, cosponsored by Assemblyman James A. Fitzpatrick, that would have created a comic book division in the state Department of Education to review all comic books and issue permits for publication, similar to the procedure used to license motion pictures. All publishers would be required to apply for a permit before publication. The fee was set at three dollars for each application. Appeals could be made to the Board of Regents. If the permit was denied, the publisher could still publish the comic book, but he would be required to carry a notice on the title page of the comic book that a permit had been denied. In addition, he would be required to file a copy of the comic book with the district attorney in each county where the comic book was to be distributed thirty days in advance of publication ("State Bill" 18; Mitchell, "Evil Harvest" 67; "Comics Censorship Bill" 1160). Such a procedure obviously would have been so expensive and cumbersome for publishers that they would have been unable to publish and sell comic books in the state of New York— no doubt the intention of the lawmakers introducing the bill.

Opponents to the bill warned Governor Dewey and legislators that the Feinberg-Fitzpatrick bill was an attack on the constitutional guarantees of freedom of the press that could extend censorship to the newspapers and set a dangerously repressive precedent ("State Laws" 1244). A *New York Times* editorial published February 25, 1949, noted that a censor who was asked to read all comic books published "would quickly go mad" and opposed the creation of such a position in the Department of Education. Instead, the state should rely on public opinion to bring about needed reforms. Although such a remedy might take longer than imposing state regulation, such legislation was a "dangerous invasion" of freedom of the press (Editorial, 38). Despite this opposition, the bill was approved by the senate February 23, 1949, on a 49-6 vote. Feinberg called the measure a progressive step and a method of regulation that would be free of politics. However, the bill later died in committee in the assembly ("State Senate Acts" 17).

During the legislative debate over comic book regulation, one of the opponents of those bills, Sen. Harold I. Panken, introduced a resolution February 28, 1949, to defer action until a study had been made by a legislative committee. The Joint Legislative Committee to Study the Publication of Comics was created on March 29, 1949, and fifteen thousand dollars was appropriated for its work. The appointment of the joint committee marked the beginning of the first systematic study of the comic book industry by a state legislative body. Serving on the committee were Panken, Sen. Henry W. Griffith, another Democrat who had opposed the Feinberg-Fitzpatrick bill, and assemblymen Joseph Carlino, Lawrence Murphy, and James Fitzpatrick. Carlino was selected chairman of the committee at its first meeting in Albany June 24, 1949 ("State Laws" 1243).

One of the first actions the group took was to ask Committee Counsel Thomas Collins to prepare a memorandum of law regarding the legal issues involved in regulating comic books. In addition, the committee conducted a survey of county court and children's court judges, state district attorneys, probation officers, and city clerks. The legislators asked these officials to submit data on juvenile delinquency and evidence that would indicate there was a connection between juvenile delinquency and reading crime comic books. The committee also requested information on legislation passed in other states.

The results were inconclusive, and on January 17, 1950, the committee announced that no legislation would be proposed (New York Legislative Interim Report 11; "Delays Comic-Book Curb" 23). In its February 1950 report to the legislature, the legislature's comic book committee wrote: "The intensive work done by the Committee and its staff to date convinces it that it lacks sufficient data upon which to form an opinion as to whether the charges set forth in the resolution justify legislative remedies." In order to gather additional information, the committee decided to conduct hearings in order to allow experts on both sides of the debate to testify and present evidence. During 1950, the committee held hearings in June, August, and December (New York Legislative Interim Report 11; "Delays Comic-Book Curb" 23; Mitchell, "Evil Harvest" 67).

At the June hearings, most of the witnesses called to testify before the committee favored some sort of state regulation to curb objectionable comic books. These included judges, assistant district attorneys, child psychiatrists, and representatives of women's groups. These witnesses called for legislation targeting comics books dealing with sex or glorifying crime, horror books, and books full of lust and bloodshed. None of the witnesses had any complaints about books such as the "classic" comics or the Walt Disney types ("Witnesses Favor" 29). Following the June hearings, Lev Gleason, now president of the Association of Comics Magazine Publishers, issued a statement noting that publishers disagreed with the views expressed at the hearing and asking for an opportunity to present the publishers' side of the case before the committee ("Hold Hearings" 65).

Publishers got their turn in August, and they urged the committee to reject the idea of legislation in favor of industry self-regulation, since, in the words of trade association director Henry Schultz, state regulation would be both unfair and unworkable. Harvey Zorbaugh of New York University, who also testified in favor of self-regulation, told the committee that parents should provide more guidance in children's reading ("Comics Publishers Speak" 38; "Oppose State Regulation" 24). In December, psychiatrist Fredric Wertham appeared before the committee to ask for what he labeled as "public health laws" to ban the sale of crime comics to children under fifteen. Wertham cited several cases in which there was evidence crime comic books led teens to commit crimes. He rejected the idea of self-regulation, telling legislators, "The crime comic book industry sees children as a market of child buyers and no more." ("Psychiatrist Asks" 50).

Following its year-long investigation, the New York legislative committee again declined to propose any legislation, but it took a strong anti–comic book stand in its report, published in early 1951. Among the findings of the committee: crime comics impaired the "ethical development" of children and described how to make weapons and commit crimes; comics with sadistic and masochistic scenes interfered with the normal development of sexual habits in children; and crime comics were "a contributing factor leading to juvenile delinquency" (*Report* [1951] 10). Although the committee believed the majority of comic book publishers were "responsible, intelligent and right-thinking citizens with a will to improve their industry," a "small, stubborn, willful, irresponsible minority" of publishers were responsible for the bad reputation of the industry. In addition, the entire industry was "remiss in its failure to institute effective measures to police and restrain the undesirable minority" (9). The committee also condemned the practice of crime comic publishers of hiring legal and public relations counsel "in a deliberate effort to continue such harmful practices and to fight any and every effort to arrest or control such practices" (10).

Legislators stopped short of calling for regulation, however, commenting that they had no wish to burden another industry with regulation and that they would take steps to regulate comics only as a last resort. Instead, the committee urged publishers to adopt a self-regulatory code, noting: "This has been done successfully in the field of entertainment, radio, television, motion pictures, newspaper and magazine publishing. It can be done in the comic book industry" (16–17). The unwillingness of publishers to cooperate with one another was criticized in the committee's report: "The industry must eliminate inter-company distrust and must approach this common problem intelligently and in a spirit of mutual cooperation without curtailing legitimate competition and rivalry for public support of their respective editions." The committee also warned that failure to heed the justified public clamor that comics be improved would mean "the State will be compelled to do it for them" (*Report* [1951] 17; "N.Y. Legislature" 16).

The problem of state regulation also was recognized. In calling for nationwide voluntary regulation, the legislators noted, "It is conceivable that a substantial number of the forty-eight states might pass individual review laws which would destroy the industry entirely because of the difficulty in submitting to so many different agencies" (*Report* [1951] 20–21). However, the committee rejected arguments that such laws would be unconstitutional: "The Committee entertains no doubt of the validity of legislation drawn by counsel if and when enacted." The report added the committee was unimpressed with testimony offered by publishers "as to the impossibility of drafting a bill that could withstand a test in the courts" (20).

The committee urged the largest publishers to take immediate steps to create a self-regulatory association and appoint an independent administrator with no industry connections to act as a reviewer. Such an agency should be in place before the legislature convened in 1952. The committee also encouraged voluntary citizens' community review groups to continue to seek support from newsdealers and distributors in rejecting unsuitable comic books (21). The chairman of the committee, Assemblyman Joseph Carlino, appeared before the Association of Comic Magazine Publishers at the association's third annual meeting held April 26, 1951, to reinforce the committee's call for industry self-regulation. Carlino told publishers, "If the comic book industry cannot adequately police itself, the legislature of this state, I know, will have to take affirmative action." Carlino stressed that he did not want to drive comic book publishing from the state, but added, "If you would like to avoid government interference, get together and you will have no fears from this state in the direction of interference with your business." Harold A. Moore, president-elect of the association, replied: "We have been urging self-regulation for three years. We therefore heartily agree with the assemblyman that the whole industry should be represented in an organization to undertake self-regulation" ("Comics Publishers Warned" 74). Despite the warning, the Association of Comics Magazine Publishers did nothing to revamp its code or beef up enforcement. The largest publishers, who by their position in the industry would have had the power to put some teeth into self-regulation, did not want to associate themselves with companies that were publishing material they considered to be in questionable taste. Rather than seizing control of the trade group, these publishers tried to distance themselves from the rest of the industry.

In 1951, the New York legislative committee met several times to review the progress of the industry toward self-regulation. When no action was forthcoming from the comic book publishers, the committee conducted hearings December 3 and December 4, 1951, in order to determine the "form and content of the regulatory legislation" to be recommended concerning comic books in the 1952 legislative session (*Report* [1952] 11). In his opening statement, Chairman Joseph Carlino commented that it had been the hope of all committee members that objectionable comics would be eliminated without the necessity of governmental control or state legislation. However, the industry had been given the opportunity to correct existing abuses and nothing had been accomplished toward industry-wide regulation (11). He noted the "respectable publishers" had "shirked their public responsibility in failing to perfect effective self control," and concluded: "We must, therefore, go forward and set the pattern in New York state which undoubtedly will be adopted and followed in other states in order that this intolerable condition be eliminated" (11).

Psychiatrist Fredric Wertham once again appeared before the committee, urging them to pass legislation to protect children against the "virus" of comic books. He testified that most of the eighty million comics were the cause of "psychological mutilation" of children. He told legislators that the publishers would not police themselves because the harmless comic books do not sell ("Health Law Urged" 35). Rev. Charles C. Smith, director of the National Organization for Decent Literature office of the Albany diocese, urged the re-passage of the Feinberg-Fitzpatrick bill creating a comic book censorship division in the New York Department of Education. Mrs. Charles S. Walker, legislative chairman of the New York State Congress of Parents and Teachers, pressed legislators for an outright ban of objectionable comics ("Health Law Urged" 35). Ten publishers and representatives of the industry also testified, presenting a solid front against prepublication censorship or an amendment to the penal code that would make selling certain comic books illegal. Some accused committee members of being biased against the industry and of being victims of self-seeking propagandists ("Comics Trade" 37).

The committee rejected arguments made by the publishers that legislation against comic books would be an unconstitutional infringement on press freedom. In their report, the legislators argued that the constitution was never intended "to be a license to endanger the health, welfare, morals, or safety of a considerable number of the public." They noted that the First Amendment was not intended to protect "ruthless individuals" in their quest for profits "at the expense of the health and safety of little children" (*Report* [1952] 14–15). The committee wrote that appeals for self-imposed restraints had "fallen upon deaf ears" and "it is regrettable that the comic book industry has refused to adopt [them]." The committee singled out for criticism the large publishers with their "ostrich-like attitude." Even though the large companies produced wholesome material for the most part, the committee felt those publishers should have taken the lead in forming a regulatory body. Commented the legislators: "With their prestige and position, these major publishers could bring about industry-wide reform for their own preservation and future well-being as well as that of their minor competitors" (17).

The committee recommended passage of six laws targeting the comic book industry, noting that the industry had given them no other choice (18). Two of the proposals submitted for consideration in 1952 to the legislature were similar to earlier attempts at comic book regulation that had failed to win legislative approval or had been vetoed by the governor. The first was an amendment to the state statute that had been invalidated in the *Winters* decision. The proposed amendment would prohibit publication of material "principally made up of pictures, whether or not accompanied by any written or printed matter, of fictional deeds of crime, bloodshed, lust or heinous acts, which tend to incite minors to violent or depraved or immoral acts." It differed from earlier legislation in that it was intended to cover only fictional accounts, and it was worded in such a way that the intent of the law was to protect minors (19). The second bill proposed was for the creation of a comic book division in the New York Department of Education. The mechanisms for prepublication review and the issuing of permits was identical to those proposed in the earlier Feinberg-Fitzpatrick bill (19–21). The rest of the legislation recommended by the committee gave various New York courts jurisdiction to try cases that arose from the violation of the proposed state statute forbidding the publication of fictional accounts of crime, bloodshed, lust, or heinous acts (21–24).

The legislation was formally introduced on February 20, 1952. The *New York Times* reported the industry was expected to put up a "fierce battle" against the legislation. The New York Assembly passed the amended state statute March 13 on a 141-4 vote, and the Senate approved it the following day. But the proposal for prepublication review by the Education Department was killed in committee in both the assembly and the senate. The amended state statute was vetoed April 14, 1952, by Governor Dewey on constitutional grounds, since the minor changes in the law did not cure the basic deficiency of the earlier law.

Opponents of comic books in New York were no closer to seeing laws against comics enacted than they had been when the legislature began its investigation four years ago. Although the committee continued its work, the failure to pass any of the legislation proposed in 1952 destroyed any credibility the committee had. New York was not alone in its inability to pass legislation against comic books. While more than one-third of the states investigated amendments or proposals relating to the distribution and sale of comic books and other literature, most of these proposals were either defeated in committee or never gained sufficient support to pass both houses of the state's legislature (Feder 23). Edward Feder, in summarizing the attempts to draft such legislation, wrote, "It has proved to be a difficult task to write effective legislation of this kind which does not infringe upon constitutional provisions guaranteeing due process and freedom of the press" (Feder 20).

Once the initial threat had passed, the trade association formed by the comic book publishers, the Association of Comics Magazine Publishers, became inactive, largely due to lack of support from most of the major publishers. The association no longer provided any prepublication review of comics under the six-point code adopted by the association in 1948. Instead, the few remaining members adopted a provision by which they agreed to do their own censoring and put the seal on the cover of those comics that in their judgment conformed to the code (Senate Hearings 72).

The work of the New York Legislative Committee to Study the Publication of Comics highlights the difficulties faced by state legislatures around the country wrestling with the idea of passing laws against comics. One problem was the lack of legal precedent for outlawing violent content. While the courts had clearly established that obscenity and pornography did not enjoy First Amendment protection, the Supreme Court's ruling in the *Winters* case struck down laws denying such protection to publications with violent content. Another difficulty was in the legal definition of comic books. Lawmakers were never able to describe comic books in such a way that laws intended to restrict them didn't also apply to magazines and other illustrated material.

The failure of the industry to police itself, however, left publishers vulnerable to further attacks. The impetus for the next wave of criticism was provided by psychiatrist Fredric Wertham. Perhaps as a result of the failure of lawmakers to take action, Wertham again turned to the popular press as a forum for his views about comic books. He collected his articles and lectures describing his research on the effects of mass media violence into a book-length study and Rinehart and Company agreed to publish it. The book originally bore the title *All Our Innocents,* but Wertham's editors changed it to the more evocative *Seduction of the Innocent* (Reibman 17). The book was not published until spring 1954, but excerpts were printed in the November 1953 issue of *Ladies' Home Journal* in an article titled "What Parents Don't Know About Comic Books." Those excerpts were drawn primarily from three chapters of *Seduction of the Innocent*: "What Are Crime Comic Books," "The Effects of Comic Books on the Child," and "The Struggle Against the Comic-Book Industry."

Historian Martin Barker, who examined the campaign against American comic books in Britain, noted that Wertham's book was the most famous and influential investigation of comics ever published. It became the "primer of the American campaign" and has been cited since in almost every study of comics (Barker 57). The book summarized the case against comics, drawing on case studies of children Wertham had dealt with over the years, and it was intended for a popular audience. It was considered for inclusion as an alternate selection for the Book-of-the-Month Club. Wertham maintained later than the Book-of-the-Month Club withdrew its offer and refused to distribute the book because of pressure from the comic book publishers (Wertham, "Curse of the Comic Book" 403). In addition, the bibliographic notes at the end of the book were removed by the publisher after the book was published, which Wertham felt also demonstrated the power of the comic book publishers (Reibman 18).

With his book, Wertham clearly hoped to rekindle interest in the type of legislation for which he had lobbied at the federal and state levels; the book was written primarily to alert parents and others that crime and horror comics existed and were read by children. Wertham believed that most adults had no idea of the content of comic books. Parents assumed that comic books were mostly of the "funny animal" variety. Those who were aware of the existence of crime comics were complacent because of a mistaken belief that such comics were sold to and read by adults, or they thought that by forbidding their children to read such comics they were providing adequate protection. Wertham also provided graphic descriptions of the sex and violence to be found in comic book pages, complete with illustrations.

The illustrations Wertham chose were single panels presented out of context. But they were powerful images nonetheless. One book reviewer described them this way:

> It is a shocking gallery, including a landscape in which the phallic symbolism could scarcely escape an observant six-year-old; a baseball game played with a corpse's head for the ball and with entrails for the base paths; pictures showing men and women being hanged, dragged face down and alive behind cars, branded, having their eyeballs pierced with needles (a favorite motif), and their blood sucked by beautiful female vampires; representations of nudes in all shapes and conditions (this is apparently known in the trade as "headlight" art), usually being bound or beaten, or both; and helpful diagrams illustrating the latest methods of breaking into a house or fracturing an Adam's apple with the edge of the hand. These examples appear in black-and-white, but it is explained that they were considerably more effective in the three-color [sic] originals. (Gibbs 134–41)

The publication of Wertham's article in *Ladies' Home Journal* coincided with the announcement in early 1953 of the formation of the Senate Subcommittee on Juvenile Delinquency. The primary goal of the committee, according to Sen. Robert Hendrickson, would be to furnish leadership and stimulate activity at the state level. The committee was established April 27, 1953, and in preparation for hearings scheduled to begin in November, the committee sent out a questionnaire to about two thousand individuals, including experts, social workers, and representatives of service organizations, church groups, and others concerned with the problems of youth, requesting their opinions about the extent and causes of delinquency (Gilbert 149–50; "Senate Committee" 1). More than 50 percent of those responding to that questionnaire placed some blame for delinquency on films and comic books. In addition, the committee received thousands of unsolicited letters from citizens, and nearly 75 percent of these letters reflected concern over comic books, television, radio, and the movies (Gilbert 150). Most of the letters sent to the Senate subcommittee specifically addressing the comic book issue were written following the publication of excerpts of Fredric Wertham's book. As a result of this pressure to investigate the mass media, the committee scheduled a series of hearings on media effects and delinquency. That investigation began with the comic book industry in April 1954.

Chapter 3

The Senate Investigation

The Senate Subcommittee on Juvenile Delinquency conducted its investigation of the comic book industry in the spring of 1954.[3] The committee held three days of hearings in New York City (the location selected because most of the comic book publishers were based there), called twenty-two witnesses, and accepted thirty-three exhibits as evidence. When it was all over, the comic book industry closed ranks and adopted a self-regulatory code that is still in effect today in modified form.

The driving force on the committee was Sen. Estes Kefauver. Sen. Robert Hendrickson was the chairman of the Senate subcommittee during the period in which the committee held its comic book hearings, but the committee is often referred to as the Kefauver committee, and when the 1954 elections returned control of Congress to the Democrats, Kefauver was given the chairmanship of the juvenile delinquency subcommittee. Under his direction, the committee wrote its report on the comic book industry, issued in March 1955, and continued its examination of violence and sex in the mass media with hearings on film and television. Kefauver, a Tennessee lawyer who was first elected to the House of Representatives in 1939, ran a successful race for a Senate seat in 1948. He rose to national prominence for his investigation of organized crime in the United States beginning in 1950 (Gorman 74). That investigation attracted a great deal of public interest and acquired a prestige probably unequalled by any other congressional probe, and Kefauver used the publicity in his bid for the Democratic presidential nomination. While he lost the 1952 nomination to Adlai Stevenson, Kefauver hoped that the hearings on juvenile delinquency, a much less politically sensitive issue, might provide a platform for another try at the presidential nomination (Gorman 84).

It was during the course of the Senate investigation of organized crime that Kefauver first turned his attention to comic books, gathering information on the comic book industry from a survey sent to judges of juvenile and family courts, probation officers, court psychiatrists, public officials, social workers, comic book publishers, cartoonists, and officers of national organizations who were interested in the issue. That survey was sent out in August 1950. The questionnaires were drawn up with the assistance of psychiatrist Fredric Wertham, who was acting as a consultant for the Senate committee. The survey included seven questions:

1. Has juvenile delinquency increased in the years 1945 to 1950? If you can support this with specific statistics, please do so.
2. To what do you attribute this increase if you have stated that there was an increase?
3. Was there an increase in juvenile delinquency after World War II?
4. In recent years have juveniles tended to commit more violent crimes such as assault, rape, murder, and gang activities?
5. Do you believe that there is any relationship between reading crime comic books and juvenile delinquency?
6. Please specifically give statistics and, if possible, state specific cases of juvenile crime which you believe can be traced to reading crime comic books.
7. Do you believe that juvenile delinquency would decrease if crime comic books were not readily available to children? (Organized Crime Committee, Committee Print 1)

Of those responding to the survey, nearly 60 percent felt there was no relationship between comic books and juvenile delinquency, and almost 70 percent felt that banning crime comics would have little effect on delinquency. Since the report failed to make a strong case against comics, it was issued with little fanfare and the committee took no further action. Despite the fact that the earlier Senate investigation failed to produce any recommendations or action, it provided a starting place when the judiciary subcommittee on juvenile delinquency turned its attention to the mass media.

As is the case with most congressional hearings, staff members for the juvenile delinquency subcommittee conducted an extensive background investigation before the actual hearings began. The groundwork for the comic book hearings was done by Richard Clendenen, executive director of the subcommittee. He was the chief of the juvenile delinquency branch of the United States Children's Bureau and the bureau's leading expert on delinquency. Prior to his position with the Children's Bureau, Clendenen worked as a probation officer in a juvenile court and was an administrator at various institutions for emotionally disturbed children and delinquent children. In 1952, the new director of the Children's Bureau, Martha Eliot, made juvenile delinquency her priority and created a Special Delinquency Project that Clendenen headed. Eliot loaned Clendenen's services to the Senate subcommittee, partly because the subcommittee was underfunded and partly to give her agency a voice in the investigation; Clendenen joined the staff in August 1953 (Senate Hearings 4; Gilbert 57–58, 149). Clendenen began by requesting from the staff of the Library of Congress a summary of all studies published on the effects of comic books on children. He also sent several prominent individuals samples of the comic books under investigation and solicited their opinions on the effects of such material (Senate Hearings 10). He was aware of the work done by the New York Joint Legislative Committee to study comics and that done by the Cincinnati Committee on Evaluation of Comic Books, and their reports were included in the committee's records.

The Post Office Department was given an extensive list of comic book titles, along with the names of publishers, writers, and artists, to investigate. The purpose of the Post Office investigation was to determine whether any of the titles listed had ever been ruled "unmailable" and whether any of the individuals listed had come under Post Office Department scrutiny (Senate Records, "List of Names"). Postal regulations were sometimes used as a censorship tool by the federal government. The Post Office investigation failed to turn up any violations, and that line of inquiry was dropped. The subcommittee staff also conducted interviews with various publishers in order to learn more about the operation of the comic book industry. Publishers were asked to provide copies of the titles they published and circulation figures for each publication. In addition, the staff was interested in finding out about how a comic book was "processed" from the creation of the story idea through its execution, and who reviewed the manuscripts and artwork (Senate Records, "Routine Interview").

Once the preliminary investigations were complete, staff members drew up a list of witnesses. The list was finalized on Wednesday, April 21, shortly before the start of the hearings, and the staff provided committee members with brief background statements for each of the major witnesses, spelling out the position each was expected to take on comic books and delinquency and suggesting the direction that questioning might take. Among the witnesses were experts on juvenile delinquency, including psychiatrist Fredric Wertham, comic book publishers such as William Gaines, and a number of distributors and retailers who were to testify about the distribution and sale of comic books. The committee also heard from witnesses who had been active in other investigations of comic books, including James Fitzpatrick, then chairman of the New York committee to study comics, and E. D. Fulton, who engineered a ban on crime comic books in Canada.

The hearings opened with a statement from Senator Hendrickson, who outlined the purpose and goals of the committee. Hendrickson announced that the hearings would be concerned only with crime and horror comic books, acknowledging that authorities agreed the majority of comics were "as harmless as soda pop." He argued that freedom of the press was not at issue and that his committee did not intended to become "blue-nosed censors." And he claimed the committee approached the issue with no preconceptions; rather, the task of the committee was to determine whether crime and horror comic books produced juvenile delinquency (Senate Hearings 5).

The testimony of the first witness, committee staffer Clendenen, set the tone of the hearings. He began his presentation by showing examples of the crime and horror comics under investigation by the committee. He had originally prepared a show of twenty-nine slides to accompany the plot summaries of several comic book stories, but due to time constraints he discussed only seven comic book titles, accompanied by thirteen slides (Senate Records, "Stories Used"). The slides consisted of both comic book covers and sample panels from individual stories contained in the books. Clendenen told the senators his examples were "quite typical" of crime and horror comics, but in fact he deliberately selected comic book titles that had already been singled out for criticism by Wertham and others. In addition, the plot summaries written by Clendenen emphasized the violence. With most of his examples, Clendenen included a count of how many people died violently in the comic book.

For example, while discussing "Frisco Mary," a story from *Crime Must Pay the Penalty* (March 1954), Clendenen showed two slides, the cover of the comic, which had nothing to do with the story, and a single panel taken from page five of the story, which Clendenen described in his prepared statement as, "Shot of Frisco Mary using submachine gun on law officer" (Senate Records, "Stories Used"). The story is about Mary Fenner, known as "Frisco" Mary, and her gang. Rather than being the victim, like many women depicted in the crime stories, Mary takes charge of the gang and commits much of the violence in the story. In the scene Clendenen selected, Mary leads her gang in a bank robbery, and their crime is interrupted by the arrival of the sheriff. The lawman is shot by the gang member in the getaway car, and Mary steps up to finish off the job in the slide Clendenen presented, where she remarks: "We could have got twice as much if it wasn't for this frog-headed rat!! I'll show him!" She is chided by a fellow gang member for being too trigger-happy. After some careful detective work, police discover the gang's hideout. The police take Mary and her husband, Frank, into custody. The rest of the gang, afraid that Frank will "rat them out," break him out of jail and shoot him down. The police then shoot the gang members, remarking, "Well—that finishes the Fenner gang—and saves the state the cost of a trial." Mary, the sole remnant of the gang, is tried and executed in the gas chamber.

Clendenen's account of the story was as follows:

> One story in this particular issue called "Frisco Mary" concerns an attractive and glamorous young woman who gains control of a California underworld gang. Under her leadership the gang embarks upon a series of hold-ups marked for their ruthlessness and violence. Our next picture shows Mary emptying her submachine gun into the body of an already wounded police officer after the officer has created an alarm and thereby reduced the gang's take in a bank holdup to a mere $25,000. Now in all fairness it should be added that Mary finally dies in the gas chamber following a violent and lucrative criminal career. (Senate Hearings 7)

This story is a good example of the type of crime comics that critics found objectionable. The lead character, Mary Fenner, is extremely violent and kills without hesitation or remorse. Her victims are innocent, unarmed men who are foolish enough to get in her way. There is always a big monetary payoff for the crime, and the gang members escape unscathed (until the end of the story). The police, too, are violent men who do not hesitate to shoot the fleeing robbers in the back and then gloat. This story, like many, justifies the violence by making sure the criminals are punished in the end. But Mary's fate is buried in a caption, without any illustration, at the end of the story, finishing with, "She breathed out her life

Illustration 1. This panel from a story titled "Frisco Mary," published in *Crime Must Pay the Penalty*, shows gang leader Mary Fenner killing the sheriff, who has interrupted a bank robbery. This panel was shown to senators during the first day of the comic book hearings as an example of the violence found in the pages of comic books. Crime Must Pay the Penalty #3 © 1948 by Ace Magazines. (Retouched for reproduction.)

in a California gas chamber—discovering, but too late—that crime must pay the penalty!" After nine pages of glorifying the violence and rewards of the criminal life, the short tag at the end of the story seems almost inconsequential.

Next, Clendenen introduced the survey of literature on comics and juvenile delinquency compiled by the Library of Congress, noting that the expert opinion and findings of the studies reflected a diversity of opinion regarding the effects of crime comics on children. The four experts testifying before the committee reflected that diversity. Two experts who took the position that crime comics were harmful were Harris Peck, a psychiatrist and director of the Bureau of Mental Health Services for the New York City Children's Court, and Wertham, who of course had been campaigning for years for laws against comics. Two experts who asserted that there was little evidence of harm caused by the comics were Gunnar Dybwad, the executive director of the Child Study Association of America, and Lauretta Bender, a senior psychiatrist at Bellevue Hospital. One other group was invited to testify about effects of comics—the comic book publishers themselves. The committee heard from four industry representatives: William M. Gaines, publisher of the Entertaining Comics Group; William Friedman, publisher of Story Comics; Monroe Froehlich, Jr., business manager for Magazine Management Company, publishers of Marvel Comics; and Helen Meyer, vice president of Dell Publications.

The two witnesses whose testimony received the most attention were Wertham and Gaines. In many ways, these two personified the struggle over comic books in postwar America. Wertham played a central role in the comic book controversy, beginning with his attack on comic books in 1948. His credentials were impressive, and he was quickly embraced as a leading expert in the field of comics and juvenile delinquency and was often asked to testify in cases in state and federal courts. Wertham's book summarizing his case against comics, *Seduction of the Innocent,* was published just before the Senate began its hearings on comics, and it was this material on which Wertham based his testimony. Gaines, who inherited his comics publishing business after his father died in a boating accident in 1947, was the most outspoken of the comic book publishers, and the media frequently interviewed him when they needed a quote from an industry representative. Gaines's company, called Educational Comics in 1947, was publishing "kiddie comics" with names like *Bouncy Bunny in the Friendly Forest.* Gaines began to introduce new titles, and by the end of 1949 was publishing six love, crime, and western comics. In 1950, he changed the company name to Entertaining Comics and issued what became known as the "New Trend" comics, launching such horror titles as *The Crypt of Terror* and *The Vault of Horror.* The new titles sold well, and within a year E.C.'s financial problems were over. It was these titles that attracted the attention of critics such as Wertham and, as a result, the subcommittee (Jacobs 60–64; Kurtzman 28).

Wertham testified on the afternoon of the first day of the hearings, followed by Gaines. Gaines originally had been scheduled to appear in the morning, but other witnesses apparently ran on longer than expected, pushing Gaines's testimony until after lunch. After the committee reconvened, however, Wertham appeared to testify, and the committee moved him ahead of Gaines. Gaines later contended that the postponement of his appearance adversely affected his testimony. According to his biographer, Gaines was taking diet pills, and as the medication began to wear off, fatigue set in. Gaines recalled: "At the beginning, I felt that I was really going to fix those bastards, but as time went on I could feel myself fading away...They were pelting me with questions and I couldn't locate the answers" (Jacobs 107).

The committee took a very respectful tone with Wertham, allowing him to make a long statement before beginning its questioning; moreover, most of the questions were meant simply to clarify, rather than challenge, any of his testimony. Wertham began by noting that his was the only large-scale study of comic books, and that he never received a subsidy for his work, nor had he ever accepted a fee for speaking about comic books. Wertham then challenged the subcommittee's definition of the crime and horror comic, arguing for a more encompassing view. For Wertham, it made "no difference whether the locale is western, or Superman or space ship or horror, if a girl is raped she is raped whether it is in a space ship or on the prairie." Wertham singled Superman out, noting that the comic books aroused in children "phantasies [*sic*] of sadistic joy in seeing other people punished over and over again while you yourself remain immune." Wertham called it the "Superman complex" (Senate Hearings 82, 86). Much of his testimony was anecdotal evidence of the harm of comic book reading drawn from his book or from articles, with Wertham describing how children imitated the violence they read about in comic books. For example, he told the senators of this incident in New York State: "Some time ago some boys attacked another boy and they twisted his arm so viciously that it broke in two places, and, just like in a comic book, the bone came through the skin" (Senate Hearings 85).

Wertham also used the hearings to clarify his stand on the effects of comics, stating without any doubt or reservation that comic books were "an important contributing factor in many cases of juvenile delinquency." Even Wertham, whose position on the effects of comic books was more extreme than that of his colleagues, did not say they were the only cause of juvenile delinquency. "Now, I don't say, and I have never said, and I don't believe it, that the comic-book factor alone makes a child do anything," he said. Other environmental factors were at work. But, he added, he had isolated comics as one factor of delinquency and his was "not a minority report" (Senate Hearings 87–90). Underlining where he differed from his colleagues, however, he contended the kind of child affected was "primarily the normal child...the most morbid children that we have seen are the ones who are less affected by comic books because they are wrapped up in their own phantasies [sic]" (Senate Hearings 83).

Despite Wertham's reputation, it was Gaines's testimony that was given wide play in the media—including front-page coverage in the *New York Times*—primarily due to an exchange between Gaines and Kefauver that served to demonstrate in the minds of many the absurdity of the comic book industry's defense of what they published. Asked to defend his stories, Gaines stressed they had an "O. Henry ending" and that it was important that they not be taken out of context. When Chief Counsel Herbert Hannoch asked if it did children any good to read such stories, Gaines replied: "I don't think it does them a bit of good, but I don't think it does them a bit of harm, either." He maintained throughout the hearings that comics were harmless entertainment.

Then Herbert Beaser, Hannoch's assistant, asked Gaines: "Is there any limit you can think of that you would not put in a magazine because you thought a child should not see or read about it?" Gaines said, "My only limits are bounds of good taste, what I consider good taste" (Senate Hearings 103). With that statement, Gaines set himself up for the famous exchange with Senator Kefauver over a comic book cover. While questioning Gaines, Kefauver held aloft a comic book featuring a cover drawn by artist Johnny Craig for a comic titled *Crime SuspenStories* and remarked: "This seems to be a man with a bloody ax holding a woman's head up which has been severed from her body. Do you think that is in good taste?" Having just said that he would publish anything he felt was in good taste,

Illustration 2. This cover of *Crime SuspenStories,* depicting a husband who had just killed and dismembered his wife with an axe, was used as evidence by Senator Estes Kefauver against publisher William Gaines, who testified that he only published comic books that were in 'good taste.' The exchange over the cover was front-page news in the *New York Times* the next day. © 1954 by Tiny Tot Comics, Inc. Used with permission from William M. Gaines, Agent, Inc. 1997.

Gaines had no choice. He answered, "Yes, sir, I do, for the cover of a horror comic."' When Kefauver held up another cover showing a man choking a woman with a crowbar, Sen. Thomas Hennings halted that line of questioning, observing, "I don't think it is really the function of our committee to argue with this gentleman" (Senate Hearings 103).

But the damage was done. Historian Maria Reidelbach notes that public sentiment turned decisively against the young publisher, as television and print news reports widely quoted the "severed head exchange" (28). The front-page story in the *New York Times* emphasized that testimony and carried the headline: "No Harm in Horror, Comics Issuer Says." Such reports helped to confirm what comic book critics had been arguing all along—that comic book publishers were a decadent group out to make a profit at the expense of children, with little regard for the impact their crime and horror comics had on the youth of America. Common sense dictated that full-color comic book covers with gruesome illustrations were definitely not in good taste for children's reading material.

While the "severed head" exchange received the most publicity, it was the discussion of the E.C. story "The Whipping" that really points to the essential difference between the positions that Wertham and Gaines took. In his testimony, Wertham accused Gaines of fostering racial hatred by using the word "spick" several times in one story. The story Wertham summarized for the senators was published in *Shock SuspenStories* No. 14, 1954. In it, a Mexican family has moved into the neighborhood. One man, Ed, becomes enraged when his daughter Amy becomes involved with the son of the Mexican family, Louis Martinez. His efforts to turn his neighbors against the Martinez family fail, so Ed stirs up the men in community by telling them the boy had tried to rape his daughter. The men put on hoods and break into the dark house, putting a large sack over the head and body of the person they find inside, whom they then drag outside and beat to death with a belt. In the next-to-last panel, Louis comes racing into the yard, calling the girl's name. In the last panel, the men learn that they have mistakenly killed the girl, whom the boy had secretly married.

Wertham summarized the story, beginning with the statement, "I think Hitler was a beginner compared to the comic-book industry...They teach them race hatred at the age of four before they can read." He then offered "The Whipping" as an example, noting that in New York City the integration of Puerto Ricans was a "great social problem." He pointed out that in the story, a derogatory term for Puerto Ricans was repeated twelve times. He commented: "It is pointed out that a Spanish Catholic family moved into this neighborhood—utterly unnecessary. What is the point of this story? The point of the story is that then somebody gets beaten to death. The only error is that the man who must get beaten to death is not a man; it is a girl" (Senate Hearings 95).

Gaines was angry at the way Wertham had represented the story, especially since Wertham had to have read the story "to have counted what he said he counted." Gaines told the committee: "Dr. Wertham did not tell you what the plot of the story was. This is one of a series of stories designed to show the evils of race prejudice and mob violence, in this case against Mexican Catholics...This is one of the most brilliantly written stories that I have ever had the pleasure to publish. I was very proud of it, and to find it being used in such a nefarious way made me quite angry" (Hearings 99).

Wertham clearly did misrepresent the story in his testimony. One tactic used effectively by many critics was to take panels and dialogue from comic book stories out of context in order to illustrate a point. But Wertham's misreading of the story may not have been deliberate, because there are actually two stories being told in "The Whipping," one through the images and the dialogue in the word balloons, and another in the captions that accompany the story. The social message about the evils of racism is conveyed by the omniscient narrator through the use of captions. But if a reader skips the captions and skims the dialogue, a much different story is told, where the racism seemingly is justified by the attempted rape of Amy; the fact that it is a trumped-up charge is explained only in the caption. The ending, then, rather than being read as a punishment for racist thinking, simply becomes an ironic twist of fate—a father has been tricked into killing the very daughter he has sworn to protect.

But no one reading the entire story would construe it as one preaching racial hatred. The surprise ending, common in the E.C. stories, was intended to shock the reader with the consequences of racism. The text makes clear the wrongness of intolerance based on different colored skin, facial features, accents, and unfamiliar religions. The whipping also becomes a metaphor for all victims of intolerance. Amy's bound and gagged body is meant to symbolize victims' helplessness, a symbolism made explicit in the caption: "a victim unable to defend himself against that fantasy...

unable to cry out...unable to be heard...a victim like all victims of intolerance."

While Wertham emphasized the beating in his summary, there is actually very little violence depicted in the seven-page story. In one panel, Ed strikes his daughter after she tells him she will continue to see Louis. On the final page, we see one of the hooded figures who objected to the continued beating struck across the face with a belt by Ed. In the last panel, Louis cradles the body of his dead wife, Amy. The blows struck by Ed are suggested, rather than shown. Instead, the violence in this story is found, not in the images, but in the words that accompany the drawings. The beating, which takes place across four panels, is described this way: "The strap...rose and fell...again and again...Savage, wild, angry angry strokes fell upon a gagged victim...and the victim fell beneath the onslaught and lay still and unmoving in the cool grass." The conventions of graphic storytelling invite the reader to fill in the action between the panels, as the words work with the images to create a sense of brutal violence that neither words nor pictures alone could invoke.

If this story indeed had a social message against racism, with little graphic violence, why was it singled out as an example of a "bad" comic? Much of the protest had to do with the way the moral of the story was delivered. Rather than depicting "good" behavior being rewarded, "The Whipping" and other stories like it showed "bad" behavior, which was only punished in the very end of the story. Comic book critics believed that the only tales suitable for children were those providing positive role models, heroes whose behavior was above reproach. In "The Whipping," the protagonist was flawed. He appears normal, a lonely figure standing below a streetlamp, described in the caption as a middle-aged, balding man, a typical American father. But the image is deceiving; the narrator explains Ed has been corrupted by racial hatred. As a father, he is a figure of authority; but his eighteen-year-old daughter has defied his authority, and he can only reestablish his power over her by striking her, as shown in the two flashback panels on the first page and in the image repeated in reverse angle on page four. Also disturbing is the image of Amy—blonde and shapely—that serves to emphasize the "whiteness" of her character. Her full figure radiates a sexuality that heightens the tension, not between Louis and Amy, who are almost never shown together, but between father and daughter. The girl's mother, shown in only one panel, cooking at the

Illustration 3. The story "The Whipping," reprinted from *Shock SuspenStories* #13, was used by both psychiatrist Fredric Wertham and publisher William Gaines to discuss the kinds of "messages" that comic books delivered to their young readers. Wertham suggested the racial slurs were inappropriate in reading material for children and incited racial hatred, while Gaines urged the senators to consider the social message being delivered about racism. © 1954 by Tiny Tot Comics, Inc. Used with permission from William M. Gaines, Agent, Inc. 1997.

AND THEN HE REMEMBERED THE BEGINNING OF IT...SIX MONTHS AGO...WHEN THE SPANISH CATHOLIC FAMILY MOVED INTO THE HOUSE DOWN THE BLOCK...

SPICKS! FROM *DOWNTOWN!*

THEY'LL *ALL* BE MOVIN' UP, NOW! THE *NEIGHBORHOOD'LL* BE *RUINED*.

...HOW HE AND TWO OF HIS NEIGHBORS HAD GOTTEN TOGETHER.

WE GOTTA *DISCOURAGE* 'EM. WE GOTTA *KEEP* 'EM WHERE THEY *BELONG!*

LET *ONE* OF 'EM *OPEN THE GATE,* AND THEY'LL *ALL POUR THROUGH!*

WE GOTTA *SHUT IT...* BEFORE IT'S *TOO LATE...*

...HOW THEY'D DECIDED...

WHAT WE NEED IS A *VIGILANTE SOCIETY. YOU* KNOW! A GROUP THAT *PROTECTS OUR INTERESTS!*

WE COULD *ALL BELONG!* NO ONE WOULD *KNOW* OUR IDENTITY...

WE COULD WEAR *HOODS...*

...AND WE COULD *STOP* THOSE DIRTY SPICKS IN THEIR *TRACKS...*

THEN IT'S *AGREED?* WE FORM A *GROUP* AND WE *DRIVE 'EM OUT OF THE NEIGHBORHOOD?*

YEAH!

HE REMEMBERED HOW THE THREE OF THEM HAD APPROACH-ED OTHER MEMBERS OF THE COMMUNITY...

WHEN WE GET *ENOUGH GUYS,* WE'LL BURN A *CROSS* ON THEIR LAWN. IF *THAT* DON'T *CONVINCE* 'EM, WE'LL *RAID 'EM* ONE NIGHT AND TAKE 'EM OUT AN' *WHIP 'EM.* WHA'D'YA *SAY,* GEORGE?

I...I DON'T *KNOW,* BOYS. I'M *ALL FOR* KEEPING THEM *OUT OF THE NEIGHBOR-HOOD...* BUT A *HOODED SOCIETY?* I DON'T *KNOW...*

...AND HOW, ALTHOUGH THE SPARK WAS THERE, THEY'D BEEN UNABLE TO FAN IT INTO A ROARING FIRE...

CRIPES! WHAT'S THE *MATTER* WITH YOU GUYS? DO YOU WANT TO SEE *YOUR KIDS* PLAYIN' WITH *THEIR KIDS...*YOUR *DAUGHTERS* GOIN' OUT WITH THEIR *SONS?*

AW, *THEY* BEEN KEEPIN' PRETTY MUCH TO *THEM-SELVES,* ED. BESIDES... IT'S *ONLY ONE FAMILY!* THEY'RE NOT *HURTIN'* ANYBODY!

2

YES, THE SPANISH PEOPLE HAD MOVED IN! AND, ALTHOUGH HE AND HIS FRIENDS HAD TRIED HARD TO WHIP THE NEIGHBORHOOD INTO ACTION, THEY'D REMAINED... UNMOLESTED...

I TELL YOU, IT'S A *CRYIN' SHAME!* A BUNCH OF *YELLOW-BELLIES,* THAT'S WHAT THE *REST* OF THE GUYS AROUND HERE ARE...

YOU'LL SEE! THEY'LL WAKE UP!

YEAH! WHEN IT'S *TOO LATE!*

HE REMEMBERED HOW HE'D COMPLAINED TO HIS WIFE...

CAN YOU *IMAGINE? ME* AND *WILLIE* AND *PHIL* ARE THE *ONLY* GUYS THAT WANT TO *DO* ANYTHING. THE *REST* OF THE MEN IN THE NEIGHBORHOOD ARE *SCARED STIFF.*

PERHAPS IT'S *BETTER* THAT WAY, ED. MAYBE YOU'LL *KEEP OUT OF TROUBLE...*

HE REMEMBERED HOW AMY, HIS DAUGHTER, HAD COME HOME ONE NIGHT AND ANNOUNCED HAPPILY...

THE *CUTEST FELLOW* MOVED INTO THAT HOUSE DOWN THE BLOCK. HE'S *SO* GOOD-LOOKING...

YOU MEAN ONE OF THOSE *SPICKS...*

... AND HOW SHE'D LOOKED AT HIM AS IF SHE'D SEEN HER FATHER FOR THE FIRST TIME...

DADDY! THAT'S NOT A *NICE WORD...*

THEY AIN'T *NICE PEOPLE!* YOU KEEP *AWAY* FROM HIM, YOU HEAR?

...HOW SHE'D CROSSED HER ARMS DEFIANTLY...

I'LL MAKE FRIENDS WITH *WHOEVER I PLEASE,* DADDY! WHEN *I* MEET A BOY, I'M NOT *INTERESTED* IN WHAT *COUNTRY* HIS ANCESTORS CAME FROM...

WELL, *I AM,* AND I'M *TELLIN'* YOU TO *KEEP AWAY FROM SPICKS!*

AND THEN HE REMEMBERED HOW, MONTHS LATER, HE'D COME HOME LATE FROM THE OFFICE ONE NIGHT... AND AS HE'D PASSED *THAT HOUSE,* HE'D SEEN...

AMY!

DADDY! I...I...

THEY'D BEEN *KISSING*...ON THE STEPS.... *HIS DAUGHTER,* AND ONE OF *THEM*...ONE OF THOSE *SPICKS*...

DADDY, I WANT YOU TO MEET *LOUIS*...LOUIS *MARTINEZ.* LOUIS...THIS IS *MY FATHER...*

I'M VERY PLEASED TO *MEET* YOU, MR...

GET HOME, AMY! GET HOME THIS MINUTE!

3

HE REMEMBERED HOW HE HAD FELT HIS BLOOD RUN HOT...POUNDING INTO HIS FACE...CARRYING WITH IT THE COLOR OF HIS FURY...ANGRY RED...PURPLE RAGE...

I...I HAVE TO *GO* NOW, LOUIS. *GOOD-BYE*...

I'LL...*SEE* YOU, AMY!

ALL THE WAY HOME, HIS RAGE HAD SEETHED WITHIN HIM. HE'D KISSED HER! HE OF THE OLIVE SKIN AND THE RAVEN HAIR HAD DARED TO TOUCH HIS WHITE WHITE DAUGHTER. BY THE TIME THEY'D REACHED THE HOUSE, HE'D EXPLODED...

I *THOUGHT* I TOLD YOU TO *KEEP AWAY* FROM *SPICKS!* IS *THIS* THE WAY YOU *OBEY YOUR FATHER?* ANSWER ME!

LOUIS IS VERY *SWEET*, DADDY! I *LIKE* HIM A *LOT!*

HE'D SHOUTED AT HER...

I DON'T CARE! I *FORBID* YOU TO *SPEAK* TO HIM AGAIN! DO YOU *HEAR?*

I'M *EIGHTEEN*, DADDY! I'M *OLD ENOUGH* TO *DECIDE FOR MYSELF* WHO I *SPEAK* TO...

AND THEN, HE'D SEEN RED. HE'D LASHED OUT, STRIKING HER...

AS LONG AS *YOU'RE* LIVING IN *MY* HOUSE, *I'LL* DECIDE WHO YOU'LL SPEAK TO...

O WWWW W W!

AND SHE'D CRIED AND SOBBED...

BUT I *LOVE* HIM, DADDY! DON'T YOU *UNDERSTAND?* I *LOVE* HIM!

NO DAUGHTER OF *MINE'S* GOING TO RUN AROUND WITH NO *GREASY MEXICAN*...

HE'D TRIED TO DISCOURAGE HER. HE'D THREATENED HER. BUT TO NO AVAIL. ONE NIGHT, AMY'D COME HOME AFTER THREE IN THE MORNING...

YOU WERE OUT WITH *HIM* AGAIN, *WEREN'T* YOU? *THAT MARTINEZ!* THAT *SPICK!*

I WAS OUT WITH *LOUIS*, YES!

AND SO, HE'D MADE UP HIS MIND...

I'VE GOT TO GET *RID* OF THAT MARTINEZ. I'VE GOT TO *MAKE* THAT BLASTED SPICK FAMILY *MOVE AWAY!* BUT *HOW? HOW?*

THE *OTHER* GUYS AROUND WON'T *HELP!* THEY'RE NOT EVEN *ANGRY!* THEY'RE... THEY'RE...

..AND THEN HE'D *THOUGHT* OF A *WAY* TO *GET* THE NEIGHBORHOOD MEN ANGRY... ANGRY ENOUGH TO *ACT*...

4

So HE'D GONE TO THEM...ONE AT A TIME. HE'D PICKED THE ONES WITH DAUGHTERS, FIRST. THEY'D BE THE EASIEST TO RILE. AND HE'D EMOTED HIS WELL-PLANNED STORY...

THAT'S RIGHT! LAST NIGHT, AMY, MY DAUGHTER, CAME HOME *CRYING HER EYES OUT.* I TRIED TO *MAKE* HER TELL ME WHAT *HAPPENED.* AT FIRST SHE *WOULDN'T.* SHE SAID SHE WAS *TOO ASHAMED...*

HE'D GONE FROM HOUSE TO HOUSE, ASKING FOR THE MEN, SPEAKING TO THEM ALONE, TELLING THEM EACH HIS SHOCKING NEWS...

...THEN, I FINALLY *GOT IT OUT* OF HER. SHE WAS PASSIN' THAT *SPICK* HOUSE LAST NIGHT, AND THE *BOY*...THAT *LOUIS...*HE GRABBED HER...

WHAT?!

...ANGERING THEM...FRIGHTENING THEM... STIRRING THEM INTO ACTION...PRODDING THEM TOWARD VIOLENCE...

...HE *CALLED* MY LITTLE GIRL *FOUL NAMES.* HE *DID* THINGS WITH HIS *HANDS.* HE PROBABLY WOULD HAVE DONE *WORSE* IF SHE HADN'T FOUGHT HIM OFF...

FOR GOD'S SAKE, ED!

AND THIS EVENING, HE'D GOTTEN THEM ALL TOGETHER ...SHOCKED MEN TO WHOM HE'D TOLD HIS SHOCKING LIES...

SOME OF YOU HAVE *DAUGHTERS* OF YOUR *OWN!* ARE WE GOING TO *WAIT* UNTIL SOMETHING *WORSE* HAPPENS? ARE WE GOING TO LET THEM START COMIN' *IN* HERE UNTIL IT ISN'T *SAFE* FOR OUR *WOMEN-FOLK* TO WALK THE STREETS *ALONE?* ARE WE...

WHAT ARE WE WAITING FOR?

So THEY'D AGREED AT LAST TO ACT...TO BAND TOGETHER... TO HIDE BEHIND PILLOW CASE HOODS AND BED-SHEET ROBES AND DRIVE THE INTRUDER FROM THEIR STREET...

WE'LL MEET AT *TWO A.M....*ON THE *CORNER.* BRING *STRAPS... CLUBS...ANYTHING!* WE'LL *TEACH THEM...*

LET'S GO! WE'VE ALL GOT *WORK* TO DO!

AND NOT A *WORD...* TO *ANYONE...NOT EVEN THE WOMEN!*

NOW HE STOOD BELOW THE GLARING STREET LAMP, HIS ROBE AND HOOD WITH THE CRUDELY CUT EYE-HOLES IN ONE HAND, A BURNED DOWN CIGARETTE IN THE OTHER, PEERING INTO THE BLACKNESS...LISTENING...

IT'S *ALMOST TIME!* THEY *SHOULD* BE HERE...ANY MINUTE...ANY MINUTE...

AND THEN THEY STARTED TO APPEAR...THE OTHERS... THE ANGRY MEN...WITH THEIR WHIPS AND BLACKJACKS AND ROPES AND SACKS...AND THEIR BEDSHEET COSTUMES, WHITE AND PURE...LIKE THIS WHITE AND PURE THING THEY WERE ABOUT TO DO...

EVERYBODY'S HERE!

OKAY! LET'S PUT ON OUR HOODS...

AND *REMEMBER!* NO TALKING! NO NAMES!

5

THEY MOVED THROUGH THE DESERTED STREETS, LIKE GHOSTS...PHANTOM FIGURES ON A PHANTOM MISSION. FOR ISN'T THE BASIS OF MOST HATRED AND INTOLERANCE BUT FANTASY...

THEY ARE THE DELUSIONS OF THE BIGOT...THE EXAGGERATIONS OF THOSE WHO DESIRE TO EXAGGERATE...THE CONCEPTIONS OUT OF DARKNESS OF THOSE WHO WOULD THROW US *INTO* DARKNESS AS THESE MEN NOW PROBE IN DARKNESS...SEARCHING FOR THEIR FANTASY ENEMIES ... THE OLIVE SKIN...THE DARK HAIR...THE ACCENT...

WHITE GHOSTS IN THE DARK NIGHT...DRAGGING THEIR VICTIM OUT OF HIS BED...OUT OF THE SECURITY OF HIS HOME...OUT INTO THE DARKNESS...

THE FICTION OF DIFFERENTLY COLORED SKIN...THE ABSURDITY OF ODDLY SHAPED FACIAL FEATURES...THE ILLUSION OF STRANGE ACCENTS...THE MYTH OF UNFAMILIAR RELIGIONS... ALL THESE ARE THE FANTASIES OF HATE...

AND FROM THE DARKNESS, TOO, COME THE SCREAMS OF THE PERSECUTED...THE ANGUISHED CRIES OF PAIN OF THOSE WHO ARE HOUNDED DOWN BY THESE FANTASIES...

THE MIDDLE-AGED MAN...THE SLIGHTLY BALDING ONE...THE MAN WITH THE GRIM FACE, NOW HIDDEN BEHIND THE WHITE MASK...THE ONE CALLED ED...THE PERPETRATOR...THE CREATOR OF THE FANTASY...STEPPED FORWARD, UNROLLING HIS STRAP...

6

THE STRAP...THE WEAPON OF HIS DELUSION...
THE REVOLVER OF HIS HATE... THE PUNCTUATOR
OF HIS FICTION...ROSE AND FELL... AGAIN AND
AGAIN...BRINGING DOWN UPON HIS FANTASY THE
REALITY OF PAIN...

DIRTY...UHH...LITTLE...
UHH...SPICK...

SAVAGE, WILD, ANGRY ANGRY STROKES FELL UPON A GAGGED
VICTIM...A VICTIM UNABLE TO DEFEND HIMSELF AGAINST THAT
FANTASY...UNABLE TO CRY OUT...UNABLE TO BE HEARD...A VICTIM
LIKE ALL VICTIMS OF INTOLERANCE...

UHH...UHH...UHH...

ALL RIGHT, ED!
THAT'S ENOUGH!

THE WHIP-WIELDER SWUNG OUT,
STRIKING THE OBJECTOR ACROSS
HIS HOODED FACE, AND THE PAIN
WAS FELT BENEATH THE COVERING...

I TOLD
YOU! NO
NAMES!

YOU...
@#!XX!!

THE OBJECTOR MOVED OFF, WHIMPER-
ING... STUNG BY HIS OWN WORK...
SUFFERING THE PAIN OF HIS OWN
MISSION. HE'D OBJECTED, YES! BUT
HE'D OBJECTED *TOO LATE*. THE
WHIP-WIELDER RETURNED TO HIS
VICTIM...

UHH...UHH...UHH...

AND THE VICTIM FELL BENEATH
THE ONSLAUGHT AND LAY STILL AND
UNMOVING IN THE COOL GRASS...

ED! HE...HE'S
DEAD!

YOU...
YOU
KILLED
HIM!

SHUT
UP!
LET'S
GO!

THE SCREAM CAME FROM DOWN THE BLOCK. THE FIGURE
DARTED TOWARD THEM...THE FIGURE OF A BOY WITH
OLIVE SKIN AND BLACK HAIR...

AMY! AMY!

LOOK!

IT'S...
HIM!

OH,
GOD...

THE BOY KNELT BESIDE THE STILL FIGURE AND TENDERLY
REMOVED THE SACK AND GAG AND KISSED THE WIDE
STARING EYES AND WHITE DEAD FACE AND HE CRIED
QUIETLY...

WE...WE WERE MARRIED...
SECRETLY! SHE WAS WAITING
FOR ME...TO GET HOME...
FROM WORK...SOB...

AMY! AMY! OH
LORD! I'VE
KILLED MY
DAUGHTER!

THE
END   7

stove, is a plump, matronly woman who does not evoke any sexual feelings, unlike Amy. The contrast between "white" and "nonwhite" and the sexual tension are reinforced on the next page with this caption: "All the way home, his rage had seethed within him. He'd kissed her! He of the olive skin and the raven hair had dared to touch his white white daughter."

What made this comic objectionable to the adults who read it was not the violence, nor the racist language, but the suggestion that the evil was perpetrated by a figure of authority whom children have been taught to respect, and that the innocent are made to pay for the actions of the flawed protagonist. The incest subtext, which may have been lost on the young readers, was almost certainly another aspect of the story to which its critics were reacting, whether or not they consciously acknowledged the sexual feelings aroused by the daughter.

Not all of Gaines's stories offered such a direct social message, and Gaines tried to draw a distinction between the "messages" that were deliberately incorporated into the stories and the suggestion on the part of the committee that children might be picking up on other unintentional messages about the use of violence to solve problems. In defending his story "The Orphan," where an abused child kills her father and frames her mother for the murder in order to go live with a kindly aunt, Gaines said: "No message has been spelled out there. We are not trying to prove anything with that story. None of the captions said anything like, 'If you are unhappy with your [mother], shoot her.'" (Senate Hearings 101).

The key here is that these unintentional messages found in the comics—messages about violence, the victimization of women, or the making of criminals into heroic figures—lay at the heart of the dispute between Gaines and Wertham. While no one comic book told children what to believe, Wertham argued that the exposure over time to the same types of messages built up a social context in which children learned to accept, if not to imitate, the violence. Wertham argued that learning did not take place only in the schoolroom, but painlessly through the entertainment children absorbed daily. Gaines, on the other hand, truly felt his comics offered harmless entertainment that had little lasting impact on the children who read them. Wertham, he suggested, simply failed to understand the conventions of horror and the delicious thrill of being frightened by a comic book story. In his testimony, he remarked: "Some may not like them. That is a matter of personal taste. It would be just as difficult to explain the harmless thrill of a horror story to a Dr. Wertham as it would be to explain the sublimity of love to a frigid old maid" (Senate Hearings 98). There was—and still is—no empirical evidence to prove either point, despite Wertham's claims to the contrary. But common sense was on Wertham's side in the debate. The senators and the American public were inclined to accept Wertham's argument at face value that the mayhem and monsters found in the pages of comic books simply could not be considered appropriate reading material for children.

After the exchange about comic book covers and about the "messages" contained in comic books, the committee turned its attention to a full-page E.C. advertisement entitled "Are You a Red Dupe?" The ad, introduced by Clendenen earlier, further eroded Gaines's credibility with the committee. It depicted the censorship in Russia of "Panisky Comicskys" (clearly a reference to *Panic*, a comic book published by E.C. that had been banned in Massachusetts) and showed a man being hanged for publishing comic books. Below this illustration, the ad stated that there was a movement in America to suppress comic books. In bigger type, the ad claimed: "The group most anxious to destroy comics are the communists!" As evidence, the ad quoted a story from the *Daily Worker* dated July 13, 1953, about the way comic books were "brutalizing American youth, the better to prepare them for military service in implementing our government's aims of world domination..." At the bottom of the ad was the following call to action: "So the next time some joker gets up at a P.T.A. meeting, or starts jabbering about the 'naughty comic books' at your local candy store, give him the once-over. We're not saying he is a communist! He may be innocent of the whole thing! He may be a dupe! He may not even read the 'Daily Worker'! It's just that he's swallowed the red bait...hook, line and sinker!"

The ad was the brainchild of Gaines and E.C. business manager Lyle Stuart. Said Gaines later: "It was all pretty dopey. I made the ad out of devilishness. It was supposed to be a spoof, but it didn't come off that way." The ad ran in all of E.C.'s comic books, and Gaines sent a tearsheet of the ad to anyone who wrote him attacking his comics (Jacobs 104–5). (What Gaines could not have known at the time he created his ad was that in Britain, the Communist Party would later become the leading organizer of the campaign against American crime and horror comics [Barker 23]). Clendenen, in his testimony, interpreted the ad as saying that "anyone who raised any question whatsoever about the comics was also giving out Red-inspired propaganda" (Senate Hearings 59). Kefauver, more than the other committee members, reacted very negatively to being accused, however indirectly, of being a Communist. At the time of the hearings, Kefauver was beginning his campaign for reelection, and charges were being made by his opponent in the Senate race that Kefauver was "coddling Communists," charges that received heavy media play around the country (Gorman 176).

Gaines left the hearings knowing that he had done more harm than good for the industry. His biographer noted that Gaines was "in a state of shock" and "took to his bed for two days with a painfully knotted stomach, most likely psychosomatic" (Jacobs 110). The comic book industry's case was not helped by the experts selected by the committee to present the other side and testify in defense of comic books, Dybwad and Bender. Dybwad began his testimony by noting that the Child Study Association of America had conducted a study of comic strips in 1937 and surveys of comic books in 1943 and 1949. When Herbert Beaser, chief counsel to the subcommittee, asked Dybwad for an opinion about the effect of crime and horror comics on children, Dybwad refused to take a stand. He felt widespread distribution of such literature was symptomatic of larger problems within society, but he could say little about individual effects. He personally knew of no case where reading comic books had been linked with a criminal offense, and while he wouldn't deny that there might be a connection, "so far I have not seen the clinical evidence" (Senate Hearings 127). Bender, considered an expert on emotionally disturbed children, was the final witness to testify about the effects of comics. Unlike many others, she did not find the horror comics shocking, but rather "unspeakably silly." She added: "The more an artist tries to show horror and the more details he puts into the picture, which most poor artists do, the sillier the thing becomes, and the children laugh at it." Children who identified with comic characters would discard a comic if it caused them anxiety (Senate Hearings 153).

But Kefauver discredited the testimony of both Dybwad and Bender by pointing out that the comic book studies for the Child Study Association were done by Josette Frank, who was also employed as a consultant by National Comics, a leading comic book publisher, and that Bender worked for that same publisher. The National Comics Editorial board had been in operation since around 1941, and members were chosen for their professional standing and personal integrity. The practice of including such experts on an editorial board was common among comic book publishers, who used the credentials of their board members to demonstrate their adherence to high editorial standards (Organized Crime Committee, Committee Print 151).

While some comic book companies used these editorial boards to deflect criticism of their publications, National published none of the material under attack by the critics. It was the oldest comic book publisher in the country and one of the largest, and its best-known characters were Superman, Batman, and Wonder Woman. The company published two crime comics, *Gang Busters* and *Mr. District Attorney,* that were adaptations of popular radio shows, and one horror comic, *House of Mystery.* All three titles were so tame that they continued to be published even after the Comics Code of 1954 went into effect; censors could find nothing offensive about them (Benton, *Comic Book* 104). While National may have used their experts in an attempt to defend the type of comics they published and distance themselves from publishers of crime and horror comics, it is doubtful that National had any interest in defending publication of crime and horror comics.

Frank had initially been contacted by National in 1941 to write reviews of children's books, reviews that National published in its comic books. Frank said she was chosen because of the publication of her book *What Books for Children* in 1941. She reviewed approximately three hundred children's books and was paid what she described as "the usual review rates." National dropped the book review feature when wartime paper shortages forced publishers to cut back. In addition to reviewing children's books, Frank occasionally was asked to comment on upcoming projects. She suggested the formation of an editorial advisory board, and that board worked out a "statement of standards" for National's writers and artists. Frank noted she was also paid a fee for serving on the editorial board (Organized Crime Committee, Committee Print 187). Bender had been a member of the board since 1944 "with the full knowledge and approval of New York University," receiving a monthly fee of $150 for her services. She wrote to the New York Academy of Medicine to check on the appropriateness of serving on National's board and was told that her services were "entirely in conformity with the rules and regulations" of the academy. The executive secretary of the academy, Dr. Iago Galdston, added: "I personally think that you are in a position to render a valuable public service by supervising these comic magazines" (Organized Crime Committee, Committee Print 184).

The exposure of Frank and Bender as "paid apologists" for the industry was the focus of press coverage for the second day of the hearings. The headline in the *New York Times* read: "Senator Charges 'Deceit' on Comics." The story summarized Kefauver's charges that the Child Study Association of America deceived the public in presenting reports on comic books by failing to note that some of the experts it employed were at the same time being paid by the comic book publishers. The *Times* coverage continued: "Senator Kefauver charged that reports on comic books—which opposed censorship but urged self-regulation by publishers and more active interest by parents—had 'minimized' the crime and horror book problem. He contended this was the effect of publisher retainers" (Kihss 29).

The subcommittee could have called numerous experts to testify, so the selection of these two witnesses suggests they were deliberately included to give the committee the opportunity to discredit the defenders and strengthen the argument that comic books were harmful. The committee also worried about the credibility of their "star" witness, Wertham. The background statement prepared by the Senate staff noted that Wertham represented the "extreme position among the psychiatrists" (Senate Records, "Background Statement"). The staff recommended careful questioning of Wertham to bring his views more in line with the moderates who criticized comics books. Clearly, this task would be aided by making sure the opposing view lacked legitimacy. Wertham himself probably had a hand in engineering the exposé of Frank and Bender. Hendrickson had contacted Wertham in late 1953, when plans were first being formulated for hearings on comics. At that time, Wertham asked to be subpoenaed, and historian James Gilbert noted the request was "probably so he could make charges against comic-book consultants" (150). And Wertham attacked both Frank and Bender in his book *Seduction of the Innocent.*

The final publisher to testify, Helen Meyer of Dell Comics, used the hearings to distance herself from other publishers. Dell had never published crime and horror comics, was anxious to publicize that fact, and denied any association with the publishers who did (Senate Hearings 198). Meyer pointed out that Wertham was ignoring the "good" comics in order to make a stronger case against the bad comics. She denounced the Association of Comics Magazine Publishers, saying the organization intended to use Dell Comics as "an umbrella for the crime comic publishers." She concluded: "We abhor horror and crime comics. We would like to see them out the picture because it taints us."

Most of the rest of the testimony concerned distribution. Seven people involved with distribution, ranging from distributors to wholesalers to retailers, testified. In fact, the two-day hearing in April was extended to a third day in June because the committee was dissatisfied with the information about distribution and the problem of so-called tie-in sales, by which retailers were forced to carry unwanted publications in order to get their shipments of desired titles (Senate Hearings 200). Distribution was explained in great detail in the subcommittee's 1955 report. Comic publishers were represented by one of thirteen national distributors, each handling different lines of comics. The distributor coordinated activities with the printer to assure that the correct number of copies would be shipped to appropriate wholesalers. The wholesalers, in turn, took publications received from distributors and sorted them into bundles that would be distributed to newsstands, drug stores, and other retail outlets. The retailer might return unsold copies to the wholesaler, who in turn shipped them back to the distributor, who then returned the comic books or their covers to the publisher for credit (Senate Report [1955] 5–7). As noted in chapter 2, one technique of the anti–comic book crusaders was to persuade retailers not to carry objectionable titles. Often, the campaigners were told that the retailer had no choice in what he sold. Testimony by retailers and newsdealers indicated that tie-in sales were a common practice in the industry. Distributors and wholesalers, however, denied that such practices existed, insisting that no retailer ever had to sell a comic book that he or she did not want to handle.

The subcommittee also was interested in what self-regulatory and legislative measures had been taken and how effective such measures were. Schultz, executive director of the industry trade association, described the industry's effort to regulate itself beginning in the late 1940s. As noted earlier, that effort had failed, largely due to the expense of a prepublication review process and the lack of support by many of the major publishers. Testimony on legislative measures were given by two witnesses, E. D. Fulton, a member of the House of Commons of Canada, who discussed the Canadian law banning the sale of crime and horror comics, and James A. Fitzpatrick, who was chairman of the New York legislative committee to study comic books. Fulton noted that the law to ban the sale of crime and horror comics had proven ineffective in Canada. After it passed, that type of comic was replaced by what Fulton termed "salacious" material, and within the year, the crime and horror comics were back on the stands as well. Canadian law enforcement officials proved reluctant to prosecute retailers and distributors under the law, and the publishers were American and therefore not subject to Canadian law (Senate Hearings 160–61). Fitzpatrick called upon the subcommittee to consider federal regulation against comic books as the most effective way to prohibit the sale of such material to children. He also suggested strengthening postal regulations (Senate Hearings 208–11).

Senator Hendrickson concluded the third and final day of testimony by noting that the committee would continue to collect information about comic books and would study the issue carefully before drawing up conclusions and recommendations. The thrust of the subcommittee's report was foreshadowed by Hendrickson's closing remarks: "I think I speak for the entire subcommittee when I say... [a] competent job of self-policing within the industry will achieve much" (Senate Hearings 310).

In fact, the intention of the hearings from the beginning was to force (or frighten) the publishers into adopting a self-regulatory code like that of the film industry. While declaring itself neutral in the debate over media effects, the committee looked for evidence to challenge the contention by experts that comics had little or no effect on most children; this it did through a very selective examination of the material and by discrediting those who testified in defense of comics. This tack was in keeping with the pattern of other congressional investigations, where the committee perspective was determined before the actual work began and the investigations served as little more than a dramatization of the committee's point of view (Moore 242). Gorman sees a strong parallel between the crime hearings and the hearings on juvenile delinquency. He writes that both featured a "parade of witnesses" who were seeking a solution to "an extremely complicated problem by attacking what seemed to them to be a few simple causes" (198).

The Senate committee clearly never intended for its investigation to be a fact-finding mission. The legislators were more interested in appearing to do something about a problem that had captured the public's attention than in truly exploring issues of media effects. And from the beginning, the senators and their staff realized that no legislation could possibly result from the hearings. Any government attempt to pass censorship laws would be met with the same constitutional questions faced by state lawmakers. The only possible solution to the problem was to encourage the publishers themselves to take responsibility for the problem and to act.

What was lost, quite deliberately, in the hearing process was the defense of comics presented by Gaines and others. One argument that fell flat with the committee was that comic book publishing was a business, providing consumers with what they wanted. The comic book industry, publishers argued, did not "seduce" readers away from more wholesome fare by some secret process, but simply put on the market what readers were interested in buying. Monroe Froehlich, business manager for one of the publishers, argued that the industry did not create the demand for weird comics. He concluded while his company would like to produce comics with "worthwhile" editorial matter, "nobody would buy such comics" (Senate Hearings 175). Gaines made the argument that children, like adults, should have freedom of choice. He asked: "What are we afraid of? Are we afraid of our own children? Do we forget that they are citizens, too, and entitled to select what to read or do? We think our children are so evil, simple minded, that it takes a story of murder to set them to murder, a story of robbery to set them to robbery?" (Senate Hearings 98). Fears about media effects, however, had long centered on the vulnerability of the young audience, and Gaines's argument failed to persuade the committee. Gaines also argued that violence in comic books was no different from the violence described in newspapers, which also were available to children, and he pointed out, "Once you start to censor, you must censor everything" (Senate Hearings 100). Publisher William Friedman followed up on Gaines's argument, suggesting that by targeting comic books, the senators seemed to be making "a whipping boy" out of comics and ignoring other forms of media violence (Senate Hearings 149). Finally, Gaines's strongest argument, that there was no real evidence that comic books did any harm, was buried in the exchanges over comic book covers and Communists.

The Senate Subcommittee on Juvenile Delinquency issued its interim report in March 1955. The delay between the end of the hearings and the publication of the report was partly due to the elections of November 1954. It was also due to disputes between the Kefauver subcommittee and the committee that controlled printing of congressional reports over the use of illustrations. Although illustrations were not usually included in Senate reports, members of the subcommittee felt that the subject matter required illustrations and they met with the Joint Committee on Printing in August 1954 to get approval for the proposed illustrations (Kefauver Papers, "Report on Comic Books").

A draft of the report was initially submitted to all subcommittee members on November 13, 1954, and revised at a meeting of the subcommittee on November 26. The report was approved at the end of December and sent to the printer on December 29. At that time, the committee staff was notified that the illustrations Kefauver and the others wanted included in the report were "unsuitable for reproduction in a Senate document" and the matter would have to be taken up by the Joint Committee on Printing, even though approval had already been granted. The request for illustrations was delayed until the new Joint Committee on Printing was appointed. The Government Printing Office was instructed to go ahead with the printing job without illustrations; they could be inserted after the galley proofs were checked (Kefauver Papers, "Report on Comic Books").

In a letter to the chairman of the Joint Committee on Printing, Kefauver wrote, "I understand that there is some reluctance to depart from precedence and publish a report which includes illustrations." He added that without illustrations, the report on comic books would be very difficult to follow "and would fail to accomplish its desired end, of leading toward an improvement in the type of comics which all of our children now are subject to" (Kefauver to Jenner). The chairman of the Joint Committee on Printing, Sen. William Jenner, replied that the matter would be scheduled for the next meeting of the committee "sometime" in February.

It is not clear whether the Joint Committee on Printing denied Kefauver's request or whether the Subcommittee on Juvenile Delinquency elected not to wait for the printing committee's decision, but the report was published in March without illustrations. Kefauver edited the third section of the report, which included specific examples of material dealt with at the New York hearings, to provide more detail in the descriptions of the individual stories. For example, the last two sentences describing the plot of a story titled "With Knife in Hand" originally read: "The doctor then commits suicide by plunging a scalpel into his own chest. His wife also dies on the operating table for lack of medical attention." Kefauver changed the text to read: "The scene then shows the doctor committing suicide by plunging a scalpel into his own abdomen. His wife, gasping for help, also dies on the operating table for lack of medical attention. The last scene shows her staring into space, arms dangling over the sides of the operating table. The doctor is sprawled on the floor, his hand still clutching the knife handle protruding from his bloody abdomen. There is a leer on his face and he is winking at the reader, connoting satisfaction at having wrought revenge upon his unfaithful spouse" (Kefauver Papers, Galley Proofs). By adding the more descriptive, graphic language, Kefauver hoped to compensate for the lack of illustrations. Illustrations had been used by

Illustration 4. This illustration is from *Strange Tales #28,* from a story titled "With Knife In Hand," about a doctor who commits suicide rather than help his dying wife, who has been unfaithful. It was selected for inclusion in the Senate subcommittee's report on its investigation of the comic book industry. When Senator Estes Kefauver was denied permission to use illustrations in the report, he revamped the descriptions in the text to add more emphasis to the violence depicted. Strange Tales #28 © 1954 by Marvel Entertainment Group, Inc. (Retouched for reproduction.)

comic book critics to draw attention to their case, and the Senate report was not as powerful a document without them.

The interim report was written by Kefauver, who had replaced Hendrickson as chair of the committee at the end of 1954, and despite the report's emphasis on the violent nature of comic books, it reflected the inconclusive nature of the testimony about direct links between comic books and juvenile delinquency. "Surveying the work that has been done on the subject, it appears to be the consensus of the experts that comic-book reading is not the cause of emotional maladjustment in children," the report said (Senate Report [1955] 16). While citing the need for further research, the report called for immediate action without waiting for further evidence, concluding that the nation "cannot afford the calculated risk involved in the continued mass dissemination" of crime and horror comics to children. It added that the absolute right of the comics industry "to produce what it pleases unless it is proven 'beyond a reasonable doubt' that such a product is damaging to children are unjustified." The report ended by calling for "precautionary measures" until more research could be done (Senate Report [1955] 23–33).

With that settled, it remained only for the report to make recommendations for solutions. The senators did not call for federal censorship. Rather, the committee placed responsibility for censoring comic books primarily on publishers. The report stated:

> Within the industry, the primary responsibility for the contents of each comic book rests squarely upon the shoulders of its publisher...the publishers of children's comic books cannot discharge their responsibility to the Nation's youth merely by discontinuing the publication of a few individual titles. It can be fully discharged only as they seek and support ways and means of insuring that the industry's product permanently measures up to its standards of morality and decency which American parents have the right to expect. (Senate Report [1955] 29)

Although the senate subcommittee came to no conclusion about comic books and juvenile delinquency and failed to propose any legislation, the hearings themselves prompted the industry to do what several years of criticism and threats at the local and state level had failed to do—adopt a strict self-regulatory code to which most of the publishers would adhere. The industry formed the Comics Magazine Association of America in fall 1954 and implemented a code. As will be discussed in chapter 5, the publicity generated by the Senate hearings prompted the comic book industry to put into place a vigorous program of self-censorship and that program, combined with pressure from the distributors, wholesalers, and retailers, brought sweeping changes. One immediate effect of the comics code was that crime and horror comics disappeared from newsstands, thus helping diffuse anti–comic book sentiment among the public.

Forcing the comic book industry to police itself had been the goal of the Kefauver committee from the beginning, but the development and implementation of a comics code was due in large part to the efforts of Fredric Wertham, whose campaigns against comics put the controversy on the national agenda. There were many comic book critics, but Wertham's credentials as a psychiatrist made him a credible, high-profile source capable of generating and sustaining national attention for his cause.

Chapter 4

Fredric Wertham and the Comics Crusade

Fredric Wertham is given the credit — or the blame — for "cleaning up the comics" in the 1950s, but he was not pleased with the outcome of the Senate hearings. The establishment of a self-regulatory code administered by the comic book publishers fell far short of the legislation he had pushed for since the end of World War II. To understand his role in the comic book crusade and his dissatisfaction with the effect he had on the outcome, one must place Wertham's attack on comics in the larger theoretical framework of his ideas about violence and society.

Wertham's work, especially his book *Seduction of the Innocent,* is often cited as an early example of media effects research, and social scientists today criticize Wertham for his lack of scientific methodology and for his failure to offer quantitative evidence to support his findings. For example, Lowery and DeFleur describe his project as a qualitative content analysis supported by clinical case studies and psychological testing. They suggest that Wertham was claiming that comic books had relatively uniform effects, which was "clearly a version of the old magic bullet theory." They add that the major weakness of Wertham's position is that it was not supported by scientifically gathered research data and that Wertham presented no systematic inventory of comic book content. They write, "Without such an inventory, the conjectures are biased, unreliable, and useless." They conclude that Wertham's book proposed a simplistic model of "direct and immediate relation between cause and effect" (262, 264). Patrick Parsons suggests that Wertham's criticism was a "crude social learning theory model which either implicitly or explicitly assumed unmediated modeling effects, often accompanied by an equally simple Freudian interpretation of comic content" (82). Other detractors echo some, if not all, of these criticisms.

Moreover, even Wertham's motives are sometimes questioned, with some implying that he acted more out a desire for personal recognition and gain than any genuine concern for children.

These critics, however, misinterpret Wertham's work. Despite the fact that Wertham singled out comic books as a factor in juvenile delinquency, he was very careful to point out that there was no direct, linear relationship between reading comic books and delinquent behavior; comic books did not "cause" juvenile delinquency (although many of Wertham's critics and his followers clearly believed he meant just that). His argument was much more complex. His project was to explore the relationship between culture and individuals, and his belief was that the social and cultural matrix in which individuals existed had been largely ignored by psychiatry in its efforts to understand individual behavior. Wertham's goal was to establish a social psychiatry in which an understanding of the role of culture necessarily played a prominent part. When Wertham wrote of the "mass conditioning" of children by comic books, he never suggested that the medium had uniform effects. "A child is not a simple unit which exists outside of its living social ties," he wrote (*Seduction* 118). Comic book reading was just one of a number of factors that needed to be considered when studying children's behavior. His point was that comic books were part of the social world of children and should not be dismissed as harmless entertainment. He stressed that children did not learn only in school, but from play, from their entertainment, and from their social interactions with adults and with other children. He wrote: "A great deal of learning comes in the form of entertainment, and a great deal of entertainment painlessly teaches important things" (*Seduction* 89).

Wertham was not interested in a social science approach, with its emphasis on individual effects, in his study of comics. Rather, his aim was to understand the ways in which mass media shaped society. He maintained that psychiatry's goal should be to understand social influences affecting individual behavior. Historian James Gilbert has argued, quite rightly, that Wertham's views were consistent with the theories of mass culture and mass society that preoccupied American intellectuals during the 1950s (111). Wertham shared many of the concerns of the scholars of the Frankfurt School who settled in the United States in the 1930s and whose critique of American mass culture was quite influential in the intellectual community. Wertham was no stranger to their ideas and philosophy; he knew Theodor Adorno well and was familiar with the work of other critics in the same tradition, such as Arno Mayer and Siegfried Kracauer, and Gilbert argues the assumptions Wertham put forth are better understood from this perspective (234). A close reading of *Seduction of the Innocent,* coupled with an understanding of where this book fits into Wertham's larger body of work, supports this position.

Comic books presented Wertham with an ideal vehicle for his work on children, violence, and society, and his credentials as a leading psychiatrist enabled him to publicize his work in the popular media and thereby influence public opinion. He proved very effective in generating public outrage over the content of comic books and capitalizing on it to further his own agenda of social reform. A brief review of his career reveals why Wertham was quickly embraced by the media and the public as an expert in the controversy.

Frederic I. Wertheimer was born in Germany March 20, 1895. Wertheimer earned his medical degree in Germany and did postgraduate work in Paris and in London. In 1921 and 1922, he served as an assistant to Emile Kraepelin, a distinguished psychiatrist. Wertheimer emigrated to the United States in 1922 when he was invited by Dr. Adolf Meyer, director of the Phipps Psychiatric Clinic at Johns Hopkins Hospital in Baltimore, to take a position at the clinic (Reibman 13; Rothe 634). He changed his name to Wertham after becoming a U.S. citizen in 1927, and in 1948, he changed the spelling of his first name to Fredric (Nisbet 29).

Wertham served for eight years as director of the Phipps Clinic, where he was chief resident in psychiatry and assistant in charge of outpatients of the Mental Hygiene Clinic. He also taught psychotherapy and brain anatomy at Johns Hopkins Medical School. During this time, he met and married Florence Hesketh, an artist doing biological research. Together they wrote a monograph, "The Significance of the Physical Constitution in Mental Disease," published in 1926 under the name Wertheimer. In 1929, he became the first psychiatrist in the United States to receive a fellowship from the National Research Council. He used his funding to begin research that he eventually used as the basis for his first book, *The Brain as an Organ.* It was published in 1934 and became a standard medical textbook (Reibman 12; Rothe 634). Also while at Johns Hopkins, Wertham developed the mosaic test, where patients assembled colored pieces of wood into a freely chosen design that could then be evaluated by psychiatrists. It became an important diagnostic tool in his later work in forensic psychiatry (Reibman 13). He was greatly influenced by Meyer, who developed the first standardized method of taking case histories of mental patients (Campbell 716). Meyer emphasized that mental disorders needed to be understood in relation to the patient's environment, and his detailed case studies led to a study of the home and of the organization of a patient's social life (Campbell 723).

Wertham left the Phipps Clinic to take a position as senior psychiatrist in the Department of Hospitals of New York City in 1932. He also became an assistant professor of clinical psychiatry at New York University. That same year, he organized and became director of the psychiatric clinic connected with the New York Court of General Sessions (later the Supreme Court of New York) (Rothe 634). It was the first clinic of its kind, providing psychiatric evaluations of every convicted felon (Hitzig 10). Between 1933 and 1936, he was successively the psychiatrist in charge of the alcoholic, children's, and prison wards of Bellevue Hospital. From 1936 to 1939, he served as the director of the Mental Hygiene Clinic at Bellevue. In 1940, he became director of psychiatric services at Queens Hospital (Reibman 13; Rothe 634).

During the 1930s, Wertham's interests shifted from brain physiology to forensic psychiatry. He was frequently called upon to testify in cases involving violent crimes, and his experiences led him to develop what would be a lifelong interest in the causes of violence. He was involved as an expert witness in several sensational murder cases in the 1930s; they provided material for three books, *Dark Legend* (1941), *The Show of Violence* (1948), and *A Circle of Guilt* (1956).

In 1938, Wertham published an article that set the tone for much of his later research. It appeared in the *Journal of Criminal Law and Criminology* and dealt with the relationship of the legal system to psychiatry, suggesting that the two must work more closely together in order to prevent crime rather than just punish the criminal. He also discussed the role of the mass media in educating the public for crime prevention, suggesting that a self-censorship of newspapers could "instruct the public instead of alarming it." He urged newspapers to use restraint in covering sensational crime stories: "Is it so impossible for the majority of decent people and the newspapers to arrive at a mutual agreement so that readers, especially immature ones, will not see day after day the lurid details of a murder illustrated by countless photographs of a beautiful nude model?" Immature readers, especially children, needed to be protected from society, Wertham argued. That, not psychiatric treatment, was the first step in crime prevention. He concluded his article: "Let us not *begin* by dissecting and delving into the minds of children. Let us first correct and improve the circumstances under which they grow up" (Wertham, "Psychiatry" 852–53). This article is important because it reflects Wertham's early concern with children, violence, and the effects of the mass media. Peter Nisbet, in his study of Wertham's writings, noted: "For the next thirty years, Wertham returned again and again to this fundamental topic: the importance of social factors in the study of violence, whether that violence be a murder, juvenile delinquency, or Nazi genocide" (25).

Also in the 1930s, Wertham began his fight against a system that denied minorities proper access to psychiatric care. While still at Johns Hopkins, he became friends with Clarence Darrow because Wertham was one of the only psychiatrists who would agree to testify on behalf of indigent blacks (Rothe 635). When he moved to New York in 1932, he began to search for a way in which to provide needed psychiatric services to blacks and low-income people. He proposed setting up a free clinic in Harlem, but he was unable to interest city officials, foundations, or private charities in the project. Some accused him of political motives rather than humanitarian ones, while others accused him of trying to establish a segregated institution (Ellison 302). It was not until March 8, 1946, that the Harlem-based clinic opened its doors in a church basement (Hitzig 10). By the end of 1947, its staff consisted of fourteen psychiatrists, twelve social workers, and other specialists and clerical workers, all volunteers. The suggested fee for services, if the patient could afford it, was twenty-five cents ("Psychiatry in Harlem" 50). The Lafargue Clinic was named after Dr. Paul Lafargue, a Cuban-born black French physician, politician, social reformer, and philosopher (Reibman 15). It was the only psychiatric clinic in Harlem and the only center in the city where both blacks and whites could receive treatment (Ellison 295). It survived until 1957, when the retirement of Rev. Shelton Hale Bishop, the pastor at St. Philip's Episcopal Church where the clinic was based, along with implementation of complex new government regulations, persuaded Wertham to close the clinic (Gilbert 96).

The treatment of children was emphasized at the Lafargue Clinic because more than half of the delinquent children to enter New York City's juvenile justice system were from Harlem. Wertham estimated about one-fifth of his patients were children ("Psychiatry in Harlem" 50). One Lafargue social worker explained that the goal of the staff was to find children who were maladjusted before they became delinquent, noting that the courts usually didn't bother much with the "Negro kids," sending them to institutions such as the State Institution for Mental Defectives, which made hardened criminals of them (R. Martin 800). It was Wertham's work with the children at the Lafargue Clinic that stimulated his interest in comic books. He first became aware of comic books while director of the Bellevue Hospital Mental Hygiene Clinic. He noted: "My assistants and I studied children very carefully and off and on we made the observation that children who got into some special trouble were especially steeped in comic-book reading. But at first we did not put these observations together" ("Curse" 394).

It was at the Lafargue Clinic that the psychiatrist, working with Dr. Hilde Mosse and other associates, first began a systematic study of the effects of comic books on children with a technique Wertham would come to call the "clinical method," using detailed case histories to draw general conclusions (Gilbert 27). His subjects were a cross-section of children he saw at his clinics, children referred to him from public and private child-care agencies and by the courts, and children he saw in his private practice. Wertham integrated his study of comic books into his routine work on children and their mental hygiene. He was disturbed by the harsh treatment given delinquent children, whom he saw as victims of a system that did nothing to protect children from a harmful environment and influences but then found fault with the children, rather than examining "the invasion of that child's mind from the outside" (*Seduction* 244). The "invasion" about which Wertham wrote was the result of the commercialization of children's leisure time, and he argued children were vulnerable to influences from the comic book industry, an industry that had apparently supplanted the family as a means of transmitting values and beliefs.

After a two-year study, Wertham concluded: "So far we have determined that the effect is definitely and completely harmful." That remark was published in the article on his research, written by Judith Crist, titled "Horror in the Nursery," which appeared in *Collier's* March 27, 1948 (22) (see chap. 2). That article, along with a symposium organized the same month for his professional colleagues, marked Wertham's entry into the campaign against comic books. As noted in chapter 2, his attacks prompted the industry to adopted a six-point self-regulatory code that year. Although the 1948 comics code was relatively ineffective in curbing the excesses of the industry, Wertham turned his attention for a while to other projects, situating his battle against comic books in the larger context of his study of violence with the publication of *The Show of Violence* in 1949. Drawing on a number of the sensational murder cases with which he had been involved, Wertham explored the relationship between psychiatry and the legal system, laying out in detail for the first time his case for the development of what he called social psychiatry (8). His position, which essentially called for psychiatrists to take a more active role in social reform, set him outside the mainstream of his profession.

Most psychiatrists focused on individual rather than social causes in their search for explanations of juvenile delinquency. This pattern was established by the child guidance movement of the 1920s, which created clinics for treatment of juvenile delinquency and other childhood problems and created programs for training child psychiatrists (Levine and Levine 143). The professional functioned as "an agent of deviancy control," and there was rarely a discussion of environmental factors as they related to mental health. The nuclear family was presumed to be the socializing agent, and the theories and clinical methods developed focused on the problems of individuals (245). In his synthesis of work done on children and juvenile delinquency in the 1940s and 1950s published by the American Orthopsychiatric Association in its journal, Dr. Benjamin Karpman said: "[Psychiatrists are] practicing therapists engaged in treating individual delinquents. They are not in a position to prescribe what shall be done in order to prevent delinquency. The therapist cannot remedy, except in a few individual instances, unsatisfactory familial situations; and there is little or nothing he can do about deplorable social and economic conditions" (338).

It was precisely this attitude among his colleagues that Wertham attacked in his book *The Show of Violence.* It was not a new argument for him. In a two-part review of current books about psychiatry written in 1945 for *The New Republic,* Wertham wrote: "It is not the individual but the social which is the distinctly human. If we do not realize that, we do not deserve to be called psychiatrists. We remain merely veterinaries of the mind" ("Who Will Guard" 580). In writing *The Show of Violence,* Wertham hoped that "the courageous and practical psychiatric study of criminal cases will have a healthy reverberation on psychiatry itself for the development of a long-overdue social psychiatry" (Wertham, *Show* 25). He criticized psychiatrists for being too concerned with the inner conflicts in man. He wrote, "They have not yet learned sufficiently how closely these are connected with the outer conflicts in society," arguing that individual and social factors are not mutually exclusive opposites (243–44).

In addition to attacking psychiatry for its individualistic focus, Wertham also argued against the predominant theories about the innate aggressiveness of mankind as a cause of violence, asserting, "People like to be nonviolent." He looked instead to the "social medium" where personal growth takes place as the source for violent acts (253). He believed that civilization could progress to a point where crime and violence would be eliminated. He added, "It is easy to laugh at that as a Utopia; but there is no proof that hostility and violence are an ineradicable part of human nature. To accept that as a dogma would mean being unscientific about the present and nihilistic about the future" (*Circle of Guilt* 59). It was this theory about human personality and violence that led Wertham to reject arguments made by other psychiatrists that comic books had a cathartic function, allowing children to release their hostilities in harmless fantasy. He felt comic books created a callousness to violence: "The lack of respect for human life can begin in childhood in the comparative indifference to torture, mutilation, and death so rife in comic books. The comic books are obscene glorifications of violence and crime, of sadistic and masochistic social attitudes" ("Wertham on Murder" 52).

Wertham was also highly critical of the popularization of psychiatry after World War II, which he felt contributed to the growing feeling that individual, not social, action was the solution to all problems. He labeled the myriad self-help books written by both laymen and psychiatrists "peace-of-mind literature." The attraction of such books, he noted, was that they offered simple, pat answers to complex problems. The approach taken by the authors suggested that the capacity for happiness exists within each individual. He wrote: "The influence of the environment in producing worry, tension or anxiety is either completely disregarded or accepted as inevitable. There are no social forces, no social history, no social interaction, no social responsibility...The lesson is, clearly, that it is not the social scene but its isolated inhabitant that needs to be analyzed" (Wertham, "Air-Conditioned Conscience" 27). This type of "escape literature" meant that individuals could "escape from social responsibility." He concluded, "One can extract from these books a new concept, never before so fully elaborated—the concept of an air-conditioned conscience" (27). He felt that psychoanalysis was being abused and used "at random for almost everything." He argued, "Social problems are social problems, and you cannot psychoanalyze them out of existence" (Wertham, "What to Do" 206).

The Lafargue Clinic was one example of the way in which Wertham put his own beliefs about social psychiatry into action. Another was his work on the psychological effects of school segregation. At the request of the NAACP, the Lafargue Clinic undertook a study of black and white Delaware school children and concluded that segregated school systems were psychologically harmful (Wertham, "Nine Men" 497). Wertham's testimony in 1951 was a major factor in the decision to outlaw school segregation in Delaware, and his research and testimony in the Delaware cases became part of the legal argument used in the landmark school desegregation case, *Brown v Board of Education of Topeka* (Reibman 15).

Although his next major attack on comic books in the popular press did not come until 1953, Wertham remained active in the battle against comic books. The 1948 articles had stimulated an interest in legislation against comic books at the state, local, and national levels, and Wertham was called upon to give expert testimony. He spoke several times before the New York Joint Legislative Committee to Study the Publication of Comics, formed in March 1949 to make recommendations about legislation (see chap. 2). Wertham also convinced Sen. Estes Kefauver, head of the Special Senate Committee to Investigate Organized Crime, to investigate the comic book industry. The results failed to provide strong evidence of a relationship between comic books and delinquency, and the Kefauver committee dropped its inquiry into comic books (see chap. 3). Wertham denounced the "Kefauver-Dewey charter" that he felt had granted the comic book industry the right to print whatever it wanted without regulation or control (*Seduction* 389). Discouraged by this lack of action on the part of state and federal lawmakers, Wertham again turned to the popular press as a forum for his views about comic books. He collected his articles and lectures describing his research on the effects of comic book violence into a book-length study and Rinehart and Company agreed to publish it. *Seduction of the Innocent* was released in 1954.

Wertham's book, while it drew on his research, was not intended to be a scholarly presentation of his ideas. He used his book as a vehicle to make his case against comics in hopes he could once again mobilize public opinion in support of his proposed ban on the sale of comic books to children. The book was not an objective overview of the comic book industry but a deliberately sensationalized portrait of the worst that comic books had to offer. The chapter titles, the illustrations and the stories drawn from his case studies were intentionally provocative. For example, chapter seven, subtitled "Comic Books and the Psychosexual Development of Children," is called "I Want to Be a Sex Maniac!" The illustrations included were several panels emphasizing the sex and violence found in the pages of comics. Wertham even reproduced the cover from the July/August 1949 issue of "Crime Detective Comics" showing a psychiatrist bound and gagged as his office is being robbed. Wertham's caption: "Caricature of the author in a position comic-book publishers wish he were in permanently." And the narrative is supplemented with the kinds of anecdotal evidence drawn from his case studies and other reports that had proved so effective in earlier magazine articles.

Wertham's first goal was to alert parents to the fact that crime and horror comics existed and were read by children. He began his book by noting that the comic book industry gained a hold with its crime and horror comics before parents and others were aware of the shift in content. By the time the issue of harm was raised, Wertham suggested, "the conquest of American childhood by the industry was already an accomplished fact" (*Seduction* 220). He argued that the problem of crime comics was too widespread to be handled on an individual basis. The problem was a social one and children needed help, not at the family level, but on a larger scale. Such reasoning supported Wertham's call for legislation.

Wertham also shared some of the cultural elitism of the Frankfurt School in his rejection of the suggestion that comic books were a form of children's culture that could be likened to fairy tales or figures from folklore. "Comic books have nothing to do with drama, with art or literature," Wertham wrote. In fact, echoing earlier critics, Wertham believed that comic books prevented children from developing an appreciation for good literature. If fed a diet of stories in which the solution to all problems is "simple, direct, mechanical and violent," children will be unable to advance to more complex works that cannot be reduced to the elements of a comic book plot, he argued (*Seduction* 241).

While Wertham's main concern was violence, he also studied the way race and gender were depicted in comic books. In a discussion of the "jungle" comic books, Wertham wrote that while the white people in these comics were blond, athletic, and shapely, the natives were usually portrayed as subhuman or even ape-like. Such portrayals, where the heroes were always "blond Nordic supermen," made a deep impression on children (*Seduction* 32). Wertham noted that such images acted to reinforce attitudes of prejudice at the individual level, but they also worked at the broader social level, labeling as "minorities" what really constituted "the majority of mankind" (100). Children, he argued, were presented with two kinds of people: one is the tall, blond, regular-featured man or pretty young blonde girl, and the others fall into the broad category of inferior people. The social meaning attached to such representations becomes clear, according to Wertham, when children are asked to identify the villain in a story and invariably choose the character who is nonwhite, of an identifiable ethnic background, or one who in some other way deviates from the norm. Children take for granted these standards about race; in other words, such representations become normalized. And where nudity was found in comics, it was generally nonwhite women who are portrayed this way. Noted Wertham: "It is probably one of the most sinister methods of suggesting that races are fundamentally different with regard to moral values, and that one is inferior to the other. This is where a psychiatric question becomes a social one" (105).

The issue of gender is linked to violence in Wertham's study, since women are generally victims in comic books. Wertham believed the blending of sensuality with cruelty was a particularly disturbing aspect of comic book ideology that had a great deal of resonance with the disdain for the opposite sex that young male readers often had. In many comic books, women were portrayed as objects to be abused or to be used as decoys in crime settings. Women who did not fall into the role of victim were generally cast as villains, often with masculine or witchlike powers. These plots suggested that men had to present a united front against such women. Wertham commented, "In these stories there are practically no decent, attractive, successful women" (191). Wertham also objected to the genre known as romance or love comics. Such comics moved from the realm of physical violence against women to psychological violence in which the main female character is often humiliated or shown to be inadequate in some way.

Wertham's ideological analysis, while relatively unsophisticated, would not be out of place in the company of media scholarship today that addresses many of these same issues. Another area in which Wertham might be considered a pioneer is that of audience analysis. The "clinical" method of taking lengthy case histories based on interviews with subjects has parallels in the field of anthropology, where researchers investigating culture conduct extensive field interviews. The ethnographic methods of anthropology have been adopted by some modern media scholars as a way to study media audiences, and in many ways, Wertham was engaging in similar research. He was interested in talking with a large number of children in an effort to discover how they made meaning out of this cultural product and the way they used comic books in their everyday lives.

Of course, as noted before, by the time Wertham wrote *Seduction of the Innocent,* his agenda was clearly defined and his book was meant to serve that agenda. Therefore, the material presented from conversations with children, rather than being analyzed in any systematic way, was carefully selected to support Wertham's conclusions about comic books, and the dialogue he quotes seems quite contrived. This type of audience study, where researchers analyze what readers or viewers say, introduces a different set of interpretive problems that Wertham never acknowledged and probably never recognized. Even so, his insistence that the effects of comic books could be best understood by analyzing how the readers themselves made sense of what they were reading suggests that on one level, Wertham rejected the theoretical perspective he is accused of perpetrating—that the readers were passive consumers.

One assertion that Wertham made about his readers was that they did not remember entire stories, but only fragments, so the claims by publishers that the criminals always got caught and punished in the end was empty reassurance. Wertham offered this young boy's summary of the stories he liked: "They have a lot of girls in them. There is a lot of fighting in them. There are men and women fighting. Sometimes they kill the girls, they strangle them, shoot them. Sometimes they poison them. In the magazine *Jumbo,* they often stab them. The girl doesn't do the stabbing very often, she gets stabbed more often" (*Seduction* 55). In another example, Wertham cited a comic featuring Hopalong Cassidy in which a barber threatens another man with a razor and Hopalong Cassidy attacks the barber and saves the man. Comments Wertham: "I have talked to children about this book. They do not say this book is about the West, or Hopalong Cassidy, or about a barber. They say it is about killing and socking people and twisting their arms and cutting their throats" (*Seduction* 309).

One way in which Wertham asserted comic books did have a direct influence on children was the way in which children made use of comics in their everyday lives by imitating the criminal acts they saw in comic books. He wrote: "Comic books and life are connected. A bank robbery is easily translated into the rifling of a candy store" (25). He devoted a great deal of time to discussing examples of such acts of imitation. While this might seem to contradict his position that comic books in and of themselves did not cause juvenile delinquency, Wertham was using these examples as a way to articulate how children's actions simply mirrored the violence of their environment. Children who were exposed to a steady diet of comic books and other violent material learned that such behavior was socially acceptable and put those lessons into practice. Wertham shifted the blame from the individual to the environment: comic books didn't make children delinquent, but were part of a cultural matrix that normalized delinquent behavior in the minds of children. This is what Wertham meant when he spoke about the "moral disarmament" of children. He explained: "It is an influence on character, on attitude, on the higher functions of social responsibility, on superego formation and on the intuitive feeling for right and wrong" (91). He concluded: "Inculcation of a distorted morality by endless repetition is not such an intangible factor if one studies its source in comic books and its effect in the lives of children" (95).

Wertham's generalized critique of mass culture focused on the way that mass culture mediated between the child and his environment. He identified the problem as a social one that extended far beyond the publication of comic books. He wrote of the "cult of violence" that originated in social life, of which comic books were one manifestation. Juvenile delinquency reflected the social values of society, and comic books were not a mirror of a child's mind but "a mirror of the child's environment." He added: "The very fact that crime comics are socially tolerated shows how much expression of hostility we tolerate and even encourage" (*Seduction* 117). But these broad criticisms of society were expressed in a fragmentary way throughout *Seduction of the Innocent,* rather than being explicitly outlined. This may have been deliberate on Wertham's part. As Gilbert points out, Wertham's arguments were a popularization of "some of the most radical European criticisms of mass society." However, those intellectuals were not willing "to confront the practical question of controlling the mass culture" (108, 121). Wertham, with his emphasis on social reform, deemphasized the intellectual roots of his argument in order to ally himself with the conservative groups who seemed to be most willing to take action against comic books.

Wertham's efforts to stir action against the comic book industry did not go unnoticed by the publishers, but Wertham painted a portrait of a powerful, well-organized propaganda machine determined to silence him and other critics by any means possible. Comic book publishers, Wertham believed, deliberately set out to deceive the American public by employing psychiatrists as experts in defense of the industry. Comic books, he argued, would have been driven from the market without such propaganda efforts: "Were it not for the confusion spread so adroitly by the comics experts, the good sense of mothers would have swept away both the product and the pretense" (*Seduction* 268). He also contended that the affiliation of some comic book publishers with national magazines kept the magazines from publishing articles critical of comics (258). And, he argued, publishers used copyright laws to forbid reproduction of the drawings, further weakening the critics of comics (318). In the same way, Wertham saw arguments of freedom of expression as a smoke screen that "draws people's attention away from the real issue and veils the business in an idealistic haze" (325).

There is no evidence to support Wertham's claim of an organized industry-wide attempt to generate public support for comic books and silence the critics. The defense of comics by the industry was scattered at best and largely ineffectual. Henry Schultz, during his tenure as director of the Association of Comics Magazines Publishers, made an effort to combat the negative publicity being generated about comic books as part of his responsibilities as the leader of the publisher's trade association. But the organization was underfunded from the beginning and did not have wide support in the industry, so no organized public relations campaign was possible. Individual publishers took it upon themselves to counter some of the critics, in some cases employing psychiatrists and other experts on their editorial boards and testifying at legislative hearings. These publishers almost certainly singled out Wertham as a target in their efforts, since he was the best known and most influential of their critics, and that may be why he believed the industry was more organized in its defense than it actually was.

The publication of *Seduction of the Innocent,* along with the publicity generated by the Senate hearings, did prompt the comic book industry to take action. Following the conclusion of the hearings, the industry leaders began to meet to explore forming a new association to replace the defunct Association of Comics Magazine Publishers and to establish a new code. As will be discussed in detail in following chapters, in October 1954, the Comics Magazine Association of America was established, and it adopted a code to be administered by a comic-book "czar" who would oversee an operation similar to the film industry's Hays Office. The publishers also launched a campaign to discredit Wertham. James Reibman notes: "To Wertham, a card-carrying member of the liberal intelligentsia, such animosity and misunderstanding were particularly painful. He did not believe in censorship but in protection of those whose extreme youth made them prey to manipulation and influence" (18).

The adoption of self-regulation did not stop Wertham's criticism of the comic book industry. He denounced the code: "Whenever people begin to show signs of doing something themselves about controlling crime comics, the publishers come out with a 'code' or something to divert attention and avert action." He warned those concerned about children's mental health that "it is the duty of anyone concerned with children to avoid falling for this latest stunt of Superman" ("Curse" 403–4). He argued that comic book czar Charles Murphy was not a censor but an employee of the comic book industry and had no real power to enforce a censorship code (404). Wertham read the comics that carried the new code "Seal of Approval" and observed that they contained the same harmful ingredients, including murders, race prejudice, torture, crimes, and pornographic sadism. He concluded, "That is why a law to protect children is necessary" ("Reading" 613).

When *Saturday Review* asked Wertham to write a follow-up to his 1948 article, "The Comics...Very Funny," he wrote a scathing indictment of the comics code titled "It's Still Murder: What Parents Still Don't Know about Comic Books." In it, he condemned the Senate Subcommittee on Juvenile Delinquency for rejecting legislation against the comic book publishers. He claimed that the connection between crime comics and juvenile delinquency was now "well established," and added, "It is easy to build up a straw-man argument that comic books are the 'sole factor' and then demolish it. But nobody every claimed that they are" (12). He continued, "Of course there are other evil influences to which we expose children. That does not mean we should take for granted, and do nothing about any one injurious factor. The comic-book pest, which we can isolate, is one of the worst and most far-reaching" (46). He provided several examples where material published in code-approved comics violated the provisions of the industry's code, and argued, "Surely this is not a counter-measure, but a cover-up continuation of the cruelty-for-fun education of children" (48). He concluded his article by once again urging legislative action: "The comic-book publishers, racketeers of the spirit, have corrupted children in the past, they are corrupting them right now, and they will continue to corrupt them unless we legally prevent it. Of course there are larger issues in the world today, and mightier matters to be debated. But maybe we will lose the bigger things if we fail to defend the nursery" (48). The CMAA reacted to that article by threatening to sue Wertham for libel (CMAA Files [minutes, 26 April 1955]).

Wertham continued to explore the connections between mass media and violence in society, publishing *A Circle of Guilt* in 1956 and *A Sign for Cain* in 1966. *A Circle of Guilt* was a case history of Frank Santana, a New York Puerto Rican teenager accused of murder in a gang-related shooting. *A Sign for Cain* was a more scholarly effort and was Wertham's attempt at a broader social history of violence. It relied less on anecdotal material and focused instead on the broader theoretical issues glossed over in earlier books. In *A Circle of Guilt,* Wertham reproduced a conversation between himself and Santana where the youth talks about the "creeps," his name for horror comics. Santana read about five "creeps" a day and at one time had between two hundred and three hundred in his collection (86). Wertham believed that Santana's actions could be explained in part by the influence of these comic books. He wrote, "Reading creeps was part of Santana's Americanization . . . One lesson we instilled in him by way of comics and movies is that violence is not a problem but a solution. It is a method to be used" (93). When Wertham visited Santana's home to talk to the boy's mother, he asked if he could have Santana's comic books. He was handed twenty-three comic books, nine in Spanish and fourteen in English. Of the latter, all but three had the seal of approval of the comic book industry. Wertham explained he took the comic books because "I intended to offer them all in evidence so the jury could judge for themselves what influence they had on the boy's mind" (102). He never got the chance, because Santana agreed to a plea bargain in the case and was given a lengthy prison sentence. Disturbed by the outcome, Wertham said he wrote *A Circle of Guilt* in order to take Santana's case before "a larger jury" (203).

In *A Sign for Cain,* Wertham devoted one chapter to the mass media and one to juvenile delinquency. He began the chapter on the mass media with this statement: "To discuss violence without referring to mass media is as impossible as to discuss modern mass media without referring to violence" (193). Of all the mass media, comic books were the worst, Wertham argued, because they had little aesthetic value and had their greatest impact on the youngest children (194). In this chapter, Wertham once again sought to refute the many arguments that had been offered in support of the mass media: that they affect only the abnormal child; that they provide a healthy outlet for aggression; that they teach that good triumphs over evil; and that it is impossible to gauge the harm done by mass media because it is one factor among many. In his chapter on juvenile delinquency, he repeated his now-familiar call for understanding delinquency as a social rather than an individual problem. He wrote that children needed a simple understanding of their problems as they see them, a clear and unmistakable condemnation of violence, an easing of social pressures not only on the family level but also on a wider sociological level, and protection against unhealthy environmental influences (297).

In these two books, Wertham also argued that the emerging social scientific approach to studying media effects was misguided. He dismissed the argument about complex causes of juvenile delinquency as "convenient pluralism," and noted that people got sidetracked by looking for "ultimate causes" while missing the problem at hand. He also attacked the theoretical position "that we must measure the intensity of every causal factor quantitatively and that it shall all be put in statistical form." He concluded, "So a large part of these scientific-sounding writings, speeches and pronouncements have fundamentally the purpose of not finding causes but of denying them" (*Circle of Guilt* 77). He called for a multidisciplinary approach to studying media effects, involving sociology, psychiatry, psychology, economics, biology, and history, adding: "Not everything that is valid can be quantitatively measured and caught in the net of statistics" (81). Wertham was suspicious of much of the media effects research being done, arguing that many scholars interested in mass communication formulated research questions based on their interest in the mass media industry rather than an interest in children. Wertham felt that the media industry's economic influence on society was so great that "investigators and writers are influenced, whether they realize it or not, to veer toward apologetic views" (*Sign for Cain* 204). He argued, "The contrast between the immensely powerful mass media and the individual family *and child* is one of the most essential facts of our present social existence" ("Scientific Study" 307).

Wertham critiqued the two most common methods used by media researchers, the questionnaire and the experimental method, claiming that such research methods gave only partial and often highly misleading results. He wrote, "From their results, the real, concrete child as he exists in our society does not emerge" (*Sign for Cain* 205). He argued that survey research, while it sounds objective, is very subjective, rigid, and based on arbitrary presuppositions. It assumes that what is not in the questions is irrelevant. Experimental methods are artificial and study only immediate effects while ignoring long-range consequences. He concluded, "The only method that permits us to arrive at carefully developed, valid results is the clinical method, which permits us to study the whole child and not just one facet" (206–7). He added that clinical study allowed for a thorough examination and observation, follow-up studies over a considerable period, analysis of early conditioning, and study of physique and of social situation. Such an approach "aims at a longitudinal view of his life, at an understanding of psychological processes." He cautioned: "You cannot question or interview a child as if he were a job applicant. You must gain his confidence and show him that you are really interested" (207).

Wertham continued to argue that studying long-term effects of the mass media should be of primary concern. He felt that the most significant effect of continued exposure to media violence was that people were conditioned to accept violence. In writing about the coverage of the Vietnam War on television, Wertham said: "The audience so conditioned from childhood on finds the Vietnam fighting pictures really tame stuff and is easily manipulated with regard to violence by the huge public relations establishment that has been constructed at the top of the military set-up . . . [TV newscasts] really are war commercials ("Is TV Hardening Us" 51).

He was highly critical of the 1972 Surgeon General's report on the effects of television violence, accusing the government of suppressing and censoring the clinical evidence that demonstrated adverse effects of television violence, brutality, and sadism. Suggesting that such programming affects only children already predisposed to violence, he argued, put all the blame on the child and the audience. Media effects research that ignored established clinical research methods in favor of methodologies that examine behavior could not account for the influence on mental attitudes. Wertham concluded: "From a psychiatric as well as human point of view the Surgeon General's Report and his statements are a betrayal of children and their parents, of responsible science, of public health, and of the people's trust in their governmental medical leadership" ("Critique" 219).

In the 1950s, Wertham had been more ambivalent about television. While he condemned the violence that he saw, even in children's programming, he still believed that television would rise above its beginnings to become a medium of "entertainment, information and instruction" (*Se-*

duction 383). Wrote Wertham in 1953, "Television has a spotty past, a dubious present and a glorious future" (*Seduction* 369). He embraced the technology as a "miracle of science" while dismissing comic books as "a debasement of the old institution of printing" (*Seduction* 381). What was wrong with television, he argued, was that comic books had set the tone for programming and had tainted children's culture. He wrote: "If you want television to give uncorrupted programs to children, you must first be able to offer it audiences of uncorrupted children" (*Seduction* 383). By the 1970s, Wertham had concluded that there was little potential in any mass medium and he made a case for those forms of communication that existed outside of the mainstream media, articulated in his study of fan magazines (or "fanzines") called *The World of Fanzines: A Special Form of Communication*, published in 1973. He defined fanzines as uncommercial, nonprofessional, small-circulation magazines that had been ignored by scholars because they were so unconventional. The fanzine, he wrote, offered "genuine human voices outside of all mass manipulation" (*Fanzines* 35). He praised the content of the fanzines, which he felt offered action without violence, possible because they functioned outside the market and the profit motive: "Sensationalism for the sake of sales, which big mass media publications sometimes indulge in, is foreign to them" (*Fanzines* 74). The communication system in the United States, he wrote, was "influenced by the spirit of our consumer society" and stressed salesmanship and large circulation numbers, leaving what he called "communication gaps and empty spaces" for publications such as fanzines (*Fanzines* 129). Fanzines represented a way in which people could escape the commodification of culture.

This survey and analysis of Wertham's work and his lifelong concerns with children, media and violence demonstrates that his crusade against comics was an example of the practice of social psychiatry that he so wholeheartedly believed should be the responsibility of his profession. His call for a ban on the sale of comic books to children was his way of trying to make a difference in a society that he saw as hostile to the healthy mental development of children. One does not have to agree with his conclusions about media, violence, and society to understand Wertham not as a naive social scientist but as a social reformer. But Wertham ultimately failed. Instead of comprehensive legislation restricting the sale of comic books, legislators and community groups embraced the idea of a comics code, rejecting Wertham's argument that the solution to the problem of comic books was a social, not an individual, responsibility.

Chapter 5

Creation and Implementation of the Comics Code

The idea of a self-regulatory code was nothing new for the comic book industry. The publishers had already made one attempt, through the trade association known as the Association of Comics Magazine Publishers, to police themselves following Wertham's first assault on the industry in the late 1940s. In addition, a number of the companies had their own editorial codes, often formulated with the help of child guidance experts. But such measures were not enforced strictly enough to satisfy comic book critics, and under the threat of government action (whether real or imagined) the industry once again set out to appease public opinion with a self-regulatory code. Not all publishers cooperated. William Gaines, publisher of the controversial E.C. comics, proved to be a thorn in the side of the new association, and Dell Comics refused to have anything to do with the association or the code. But by and large, the industry strategy was successful in convincing the public that the "comic book problem" was solved.

As noted in chapter 2, the impetus for the adoption of the comic industry's first code in 1948 came from Fredric Wertham's attack on comic books published in *Collier's* and in the *Saturday Review of Literature* in the spring of 1948. The comic book industry responded by announcing on July 1, 1948, that it had adopted a regulatory code, similar to that of the film industry, to be enforced by the ACMP. While it may have been modeled on the film code, the ACMP code was nearly identical to an in-house code adopted by Fawcett several years earlier. The six points of the code dealt with sex, crime, torture, language, divorce, and ridicule of religious and racial groups (see "The ACMP Code").

When the code was announced, the comics trade association launched a membership drive and also distributed copies of the code to local societies, civic groups, and comics distributors (Senate Hearings 70). The code was the work of Henry Schultz, the attorney for the Association of Comics Magazine Publishers, whose credentials included membership on the New York City Board of Higher Education and chairmanship of the board of trustees of Queens College. In its coverage of the code, the *New York Times* noted in an article December 6, 1948, that an advisory committee was selected to assist Schultz. It included Dr. Charles F. Gosnell, New York state librarian, John E. Wade, retired superintendent of schools of New York City, and Ordway Tead, chairman of the Board of Higher Education of New York City. The committee warned against the dangers of censorship and released the following statement: "Censorship would be a dangerous and an illegal method of dealing with the situation...As in any of the other media, the way forward is the strengthening of the process of self-regulation within the industry" ("Librarian Named" 37).

Initially, the association hired office staff to review the comics "in the boards" (the phrase used to describe the original pages submitted before being reproduced for publication), and while the association originally considered appointing a commissioner to oversee the code, that task fell to Schultz. The money for the reviewers was raised by a "screening fee" charged by the association for each title submitted by a publisher. For titles with a circulation of 500,000 or more, the publisher paid one hundred dollars; for titles with a circulation of 250,000 to 500,000, the publisher paid fifty dollars; there was no fee for screening titles with a circulation under 250,000. One large publisher, Dell Comics, noted that under the proposed fee schedule, it would cost them three thousand dollars a month to participate in the screening system (Senate Hearings 70–71).

As in the later association, membership was open to publishers, distributors, printers, and engravers. Initially about a third of the publishers joined. These included: Premium Service Company, Famous Funnies, Hillman Periodicals, Parents' Institute, Lev Gleason Publications, McCombs Publications, The Golden Willow Press, Avon Periodicals, Ace Magazines, Orbit Publications, Superior Comics, and Consolidated Magazines (Senate Hearings 70–71). The president of the ACMP, Phil Keenan of Hillman Periodicals, whose company published titles such as *Crime Detective, Real Clue,* and *Western Fighters,* warned the public not to expect changes overnight. Because of early deadlines, improvements would not be noticeable immediately ("Code for the Comics" 62).

Almost immediately, however, the association ran into trouble. Many of the largest publishers refused to join the association because they felt their in-house codes were adequate and because they did not want to be affiliated with some of the more marginal publishers in the industry. Some publishers found subscribing to the code too expensive and dropped their membership. Others objected to the changes being mandated by Schultz's office. And still others simply went out of business, not because of the code standards but because of the highly competitive and glutted comic book market. It was not long before the ACMP could no longer afford the staff necessary for prepublication review of comic books, and the code review system gradually was abandoned.

In the early 1950s, the remaining members adopted a provision agreeing they would do their own censoring and decide for themselves which comic books were eligible for the association's seal (Senate Hearings 70–71). By the time the Senate conducted its comic book hearings in April 1954, that membership had been reduced to only three publishers and a handful of distributors and printers. When Schultz appeared before the Senate subcommittee, the association staff consisted of Schultz and a general secretary, with a budget of fifteen thousand dollars a year. The association published a newsletter that collected newspaper clippings critical of the industry and circulated it to members of the industry. In addition, the association members still met occasionally to discuss industry and business concerns (Senate Hearings 77).

Schultz attributed the failure of the association to the lack of support from the larger publishers. Schultz, testifying before the Senate subcommittee in 1954, commented: "The reason it has not succeeded, I think, is the failure or refusal of some of the larger and better publishers who, while they themselves do not publish comic books which might be in this category, did not recognize their responsibility to the total industry by staying with the organization in its inception and formulating practices and rules which would have become a bible for the industry" (Senate Hearings 77).

Even before the formation of the ACMP and the adoption of a code in 1948, most of the larger comic book publishers had an in-house code in place. These codes were often drawn up with the assistance of advisory boards composed of educators and psychiatrists who were paid a consulting fee for their services. The comic book publishers used these boards of experts to help stave off criticism of their publications.

One of the oldest codes in existence was that adopted by National Comics Publications. Jack Liebowitz, vice president of National, noted that the company had adopted its code "long before there was any criticism of comic magazines generally." The eight-point policy suggested that the company could provide "interesting, dramatic, and reasonably exciting entertainment" without resorting to objectionable devices such as portrayal of the female figure in exaggerated form. In addition, the code specified: "Good people should be good, and bad people bad, so that no confusion can exist in the reader's mind. Heroes should act within the law, and for the law." The code also contained several guidelines for depicting crime and violence, including: "No character may be shown being stabbed with a knife or subjected to a hypodermic injection. Acts of mayhem are forbidden. The picturization of dead bodies is forbidden" (Organized Crime Hearings, Committee Print 150–51). Beginning in 1940, National appointed an editorial advisory board that included the following experts: Dr. Lauretta Bender, associate professor of psychiatry, School of Medicine, New York University; Josette Frank, consultant on children's reading, Child Study Association of America; Dr. W. W. D. Sones, professor of education and director of curriculum study, University of Pittsburgh; and Dr. S. Harcourt Peppard, director of the Essex County Juvenile Clinic, Newark, New Jersey. While the board had no censorship powers, they made recommendations to the editors (Organized Crime Hearings, Committee Print 151).

Fawcett Publications had a seven-point code developed by a three-person board. The board included Sidonie Gruenberg, director of the Child Study Association of America; Professor Harvey Zorbaugh, psychologist and director of the Clinic for Gifted Children of New York University; and Professor Ernest G. Osborne, a psychologist and president of education and executive officer of the community center of the Teachers College, Columbia University. Fawcett's code was essentially the same code later adopted by the ACMP, with provisions dealing with portrayal of crime and law enforcement, nudity and depiction of the human body, and vulgar language. It forbade scenes of sadistic torture, ridicule or attack on any religious groups, and humorous or glamorous treatment of divorce. The final provision outlawed the use of dialects or devices "in a way to indicate ridicule or intolerance of racial groups" (Organized Crime Hearings, Committee Print 128–29). Lev Gleason Publications, while it did not have an in-house code, had employed police officers as consultants, including Mary Sullivan, former chief of the Women's Bureau of the New York Police Force (Organized Crime Hearings, Committee Print 137).

Once the ACMP code was in the works, other companies saw the wisdom of implementing an in-house review. Beginning June 1, 1948, Marvel

Comics Group hired Dr. Jean A. Thompson, a psychiatrist and consultant to the Board of Education of the City of New York. She prepared a code that was distributed to the company's art and editorial departments. Between June 1, 1948, and November 30, 1949, every comic book title published by Marvel was submitted to Thompson for review. Marvel was forced to dispense with Thompson's services in late 1949 when the company experienced some financial difficulties (Organized Crime Hearings, Committee Print 118–19).

The Marvel code contained a "Statement of General Purpose" along with guidelines for content of stories, use of language, artistic depiction of the body and of crime and horror, and recommendations for handling sensitive subjects such as religion, alcohol, gambling, and divorce. Like most media codes, the Marvel code specified that stories should not glorify the criminal or crime, should praise law-enforcement officers, and should always show the criminal being properly punished. Vulgarities of speech were to be avoided because they were too quickly and easily imitated by children. Horrible and sadistic scenes were to be avoided, including scenes of wounding with severe bleeding. A final caution read, "Avoid showing that which may subject the child to nightmares" (Organized Crime Hearings, Committee Print 123–24).

But neither the in-house codes nor the ACMP's attempt at industry self-regulation were enough to silence the criticism of the industry following the Senate subcommittee's investigation of comic books. Publishers conceded something more was needed. William Gaines, publisher of E.C. Comics, took the credit for setting events into motion that would result in the creation of a new trade association for the industry. Dismayed by the way the Senate hearings had gone in April, he sent out a letter to most of the major comic book publishers. It began, "If fools rush in where angels fear to tread, then I suppose E.C. is being pretty foolish. We may get our fingers burned and our toes stepped on." In his letter, Gaines suggested several strategies to battle the growing support for comic book censorship. Gaines began to meet individually with the major publishers. The comic book publishing business was highly competitive, and the men who ran it were not friends with one another, but they saw the wisdom of what Gaines was proposing and agreed to a meeting (Reidelbach 28; Stuart).

Gaines's idea was to hire experts in the field of juvenile delinquency to do research on the effects of comic books, and he had in mind the husband-and-wife research team of Sheldon and Eleanor Glueck of Harvard.

They began working the field of juvenile delinquency with an important study in the 1930s, *One Thousand Juvenile Delinquents*. In it, they suggested that family disintegration was the most important factor in juvenile delinquency. The Gluecks' two postwar works, *Unraveling Juvenile Delinquency* and *Delinquents in the Making,* developed their theories about family environment rather than external influences as a cause of delinquency (Gilbert 132–33). It was clear from the Senate subcommittee hearings that little scientific research had been done on the effects comic book reading had on children. Gaines believed that a research study done by the Gluecks would provide a definitive answer to the question of effects, vindicate the comic book industry, and allow business to continue as usual. Gaines also hoped to interest the American Civil Liberties Union in the industry's censorship fight (Reidelbach 28).

The other publishers, however, were not interested in looking at what they perceived as a long-term solution. They desired more immediate action in order to stem the tide of negative public opinion. Their solution, modeled on what had worked for other media—especially the film industry—was to adopt a code. While the exact wording of the code would need to be worked out, the consensus was that the horror and terror books would have to be sacrificed as proof that the industry meant business. As Gaines noted years later: "And it was always an ironic thing to me that I was the guy who started the damn association and they turned around and the first thing they did was ban the words weird, horror and terror from any comic magazine... those were my three big words" (Gaines interview).

The association held an organizational meeting on August 17, 1954, at the Biltmore Hotel in New York.[4] Thirty-eight publishers, engravers, printers, and distributors attended. Elliott Caplin acted as chairman of the meeting, stressing that time was of the essence since government officials, citizen committees, and newspapers all over the country were talking about the comic book industry. John Goldwater, publisher of Archie Comics, reported on the activities of the Special Committee on Organization. That committee recommended that the association be empowered to establish and enforce a code governing the industry in both editorial and advertising content of comics magazines; that a symbol or seal be designed; and that a public relations campaign be undertaken to inform the public, wholesalers, and newsstand dealers about the new steps taken for self-regulation. These recommendations were incorporated into the CMAA's official bylaws (CMAA Files [minutes, 17 Aug. 1954]).

Those attending the organizational meeting discussed establishing a $200,000 budget, with half of that sum allotted to public relations efforts. Monroe Froehlich, Jr., presented a fee schedule that listed the contributions of various members, based on the number of titles each company published, printed, or distributed. The organizational committee, consisting of Goldwater, Caplin, and Froehlich, had already drafted a code ("Comics Publishers Organize" 3). But Caplin was concerned that it should not be made public until the individual whom the CMAA selected as code administrator had an opportunity to review the code and make recommendations. Those at the organizational meeting approved the principal of establishing a code and agreed to eliminate horror and terror comics. In addition, they agreed that although crime comics would not be eliminated, special consideration should be given in the code to the format of crime comics (CMAA Files [minutes, 17 Aug. 1954]).

The Comics Magazine Association of America became a legally recognized entity on September 7, 1954, when it was incorporated. The articles of incorporation listed six directors: Elliott Caplin, Toby Press; Allen Hardy of Allen Hardy Associates; Harold A. Moore, Famous Funnies; Stanley Estrow, Stanhill Publications; Jack Liebowitz, National Comics; and Monroe Froehlich, Magazine Management Company. The attorney for the association was Henry Schultz, who had served as the executive director of the Association of Comics Magazine Publishers, founded in the late 1940s. Taking their cue from what had proved successful for the film industry, the comic book industry sought a "czar" with the proper credentials to administer their new code.

Leo Holland of the Independent News Company, a distributor subsidiary of National Comics, announced on August 21, 1954, that a search for the czar was under way, noting that the office would be modeled after Hollywood's self-censoring office. The logical choice for the post was Fredric Wertham, the longtime critic of the industry, but Wertham turned the offer down (Gilbert 107). Given Wertham's feelings about the publishers and the comic book industry, it is surprising the industry even approached him with an offer, although enlisting him as a comic book censor would have been a great public relations coup. On September 16, the industry appointed Judge Charles F. Murphy to a two-year contract with an annual salary of seventeen thousand dollars (CMAA Files [letter to Murphy, 1 Oct. 1954]). He took his post October 1, 1954. The publishers also promised a code would be completed by November 15 (Harrison 1).

Prior to taking the job, Murphy had served for nine years as a New York City magistrate. He was active in a number of programs aimed at preventing juvenile delinquency. Murphy, 44, was married and had three children. He said of his job: "I have been given a free hand by the Association to act and make decisions in the public interest. I am using this free hand forcefully." About the code, he commented, "It is, I assure you, the strongest code of ethics ever adopted by a mass media industry and incorporates recommendations made from all quarters" (CMAA "Fact Kit"). The comic book publishers intended Murphy to be nothing more than a figurehead; one industry representative called him "a not-very-bright political hack who was selected mostly because of his religious faith," and the public relations firm hired to handle the CMAA's campaign described him as "a practical man who would recognize the problems of selling comic books in a declining market" (Gilbert 107; Finn 175).

Murphy took the job very seriously, however. The comic book publishers had structured the comics code authority, the code enforcement arm of the Comics Magazine Association of America, to be independent from the other operations of the association in order to give their comics czar credibility. Although Murphy's salary was paid by the publishers, it was understood that he could work free of interference from individual association members. However, the publishers intended for him to ignore all but the most obvious code violations. Instead, Murphy had his staff review the material carefully and demand changes for any infraction of the code, however minor. Murphy did not need to be as strict as he was; there was little oversight on the part of the public as to how well the code was being enforced. Most critics saw the code as a cut-and-dried document, but in fact, it required a great deal of interpretation, and that job fell to Murphy. He failed to understand that all that the publishers required was the appearance of self-regulation to appease most critics. His strict interpretation of the code set him against the publishers. His zeal was one reason that his contract was not renewed by the association at the end of two years (Goldwater interview).

The code adopted by the Comics Magazine Association was formulated in consultation with the public relations firm of Ruder and Finn. The firm's name appears across the bottom of the galley proofs of the code sent to the Senate Subcommittee on Juvenile Delinquency. In creating a public relations campaign for the new trade association, David Finn wrote later: "The purpose of such efforts is not to create an atmosphere in which the reforms demanded by critics will be made; it is to find a way to make the smallest possible concessions necessary to end the controversy" (Finn 174). As an avid reader of comic books in his own childhood, Finn sided with his clients' view that Wertham's position "was psychologically, sociologically and legally unsound" (175). Finn worked closely with Schultz, whom he called "an outstanding figure in the field of civil liberties," and together they stressed in their public relations campaign the "evils of censorship" implicit in any proposed legislation. The industry's new program of self-regulation, designed around its refurbished code of ethics, was the only practical solution (175).

Elliott Caplin, one of the members of the special organizational committee that drafted the first code, recalled that he relied heavily on the Hays film code in formulating the comics code (Caplin interview). A side-by-side comparison of the film code and the comics code shows that the comics code was organized along the same lines as the film code, and much of the language of the film code was incorporated into the comics code. In addition, the ACMP code and the in-house codes drawn up by individual publishers clearly influenced the 1954 comics code.

The comics code consisted of forty-one specific regulations that CMAA President John Goldwater, one of the publishers of Archie Comics, labeled as "problem areas" in comic books. He added: "Taken together these provisions constitute the most severe set of principles for any communications media in use today, restricting the use of many types of material permitted by the motion picture code and the codes for the television and radio industries" (Goldwater, *Americana* 24).

It is not surprising that the bulk of the comics code dealt with the two topics which had brought the ire of the public down around the heads of the publishers: crime and horror. Part A of the code was devoted to regulating the content of crime stories and Part B was aimed at horror comics (see CMAA Code 1954). Crime comics could continue to be published under the guidelines drawn up by the comic book trade association, but all such titles had to adhere to strict rules concerning the presentation of such stories. Without ever admitting that depiction of crime led young readers to become juvenile delinquents, the code nonetheless placed an emphasis on portraying crime in a negative light, on creating respect for established authority, on depicting commission of crime in such a way that young readers would not be tempted to imitate what they read, and on making sure that the excess violence was purged. Many of the twelve guidelines governing crime comics were simply different ways of stating these principles. Part B was much shorter, simply because horror comics were to be eliminated almost entirely. By the time the code was adopted in 1954, the popularity of crime comics had already peaked, to be replaced with elements of horror and terror. By sacrificing the horror comics, publishers hoped to demonstrate their sincerity of purpose in self-regulation.

The sections of the comics code dealing with dialogue, religion, costume, and marriage and sex were of secondary concern to critics who objected to the violence depicted in comics, but many of the conservative critics were actually more offended by depictions of sexual liberty than by violence. The code's moral provisions were meant to answer the criticisms of the Catholic Church's Legion of Decency and other groups pushing for wholesome juvenile comics (Gilbert 105). The publishers were anxious to make sure that comic books would be offensive to no one, and they followed the broad outline of the film code in these areas. For example, the film code forbade the use of obscenity and profanity. The comics code went one step further, adding a warning about use of slang, since it was felt that good grammar should be used in comic books in order to promote the medium's educational value. There were also regulations for how advertising in comic books was to be handled. Despite promotional campaigns directed at companies which sold products such as breakfast cereal, the comic book industry was not very successful in generating income from these "legitimate" advertisers. Instead, their advertising consisted mainly of items sold by mail order companies. The comics code also left a loophole for the code administrator with this catch-all provision: "All elements of techniques not specifically mentioned herein, but which are contrary to the spirit and intent of the Code, and are considered violations of good taste or decency, shall be prohibited." This gave the code administrator broad powers of censorship that went far beyond the explicit prohibitions.

Under these guidelines, it was clear that code-approved comics would tone down the violence and the sex. Beyond that, however, the code spelled out ways in which comic book content would also uphold the moral values of society. There was never to be any disrespect for established authority and social institutions. Good always triumphed over evil, and if evil had to be shown, it was only in order to deliver a moral message. Content would foster respect for parents and for honorable behavior. With these provisions, the publishers were playing to the conservative critics who were just as concerned about morality as they were about violence, or perhaps more so.

The enforcement of the new code was the responsibility of the Comics Code Authority office under the direction of Judge Murphy. It was based on a system of prepublication review. The entire contents of a comic book had to pass through the office before it could be printed. All comic books approved by Murphy's office were entitled to publish the "Seal of Approval" on their cover. At the beginning, the code was administered by Murphy and five trained reviewers, all women. The five included: Sue Flynn, a publicist for thirteen years with the Department of Agriculture and the Voice of America; Marj McGill, a recent graduate of Albertus Magnus College who had done social work while going to college and who had specialized in juvenile delinquency; Esther L. Moscow, librarian and researcher; Dr. Joan Thellusson Nourse, professor in the Department of English at Hunter College and a lecturer and writer on the theater; and Dene Reed, an editor in the story department in Metro-Goldwyn-Mayer for a number of years ("Comics Czar" 47; New York Hearings [1955] 27–28). In a press conference held in December 1954, Murphy said that the staff had excised more than 5,656 drawings and rejected 126 stories during the short time the code had been in effect. The staff examined artists' sketches and suggested changes to deemphasize terror and violence and edited the word balloons in order to delete sexual innuendo and unnecessarily strong language. Murphy told reporters that more than a quarter of the changes involved reducing "feminine curves to more natural dimensions" and having clothing cover "a respectable amount of the female body" ("Comics Czar" 47).

Material was submitted on "boards," the basic drawings that were completed before plates or engravings were made for publication. If a page was approved, it was stamped by the reviewer. If not, it was returned to the publisher with a list of corrections to be made. Pages were photographed to ensure that changes were not made by publishers once approved artwork left the code office. The reviewers examined an average of nine books a day, a total of more than 260 pages (CMAA "Fact Kit"). While testifying before a hearing conducted in February 1955 by the New York legislative committee that had been studying comic books since 1949, Murphy described his job as "a time consuming, back-breaking, ulcer producing, artery-hardening job. I hope I can last out the two year of my contract." He explained that rather than hiring editors, artists, and writers who were familiar with comic book techniques, he felt that choosing reviewers who were not "steeped in the habits and traditions of the old comic book technique" would enable the reviewers to bring a fresh approach to the job. He interviewed more than one hundred individuals for the job and selected five women "because I felt that they were more sensitive to the situation."

It is interesting that comic book censorship was judged to be a woman's task. Certainly the idea was tied in with notions of motherhood and the fact that in postwar America, caring for children was primarily a mother's responsibility. Enforcing standards in children's reading material was an extension of the mother's role. Also, women could be expected to be more stringent in their censorship duties, since women were judged by society to be the weaker sex, more emotional, and thus more easily upset by objectionable content. In addition, the code could be seen as an effort to feminize and domesticate the unruly world populated by comic book characters. In place of violence and rampant sexuality, there would be order and respect.

Murphy showed the New York committee examples of the types of material rejected by the staff. In one adventure story, a drawing of a woman carrying a spear was changed; in the final version, the spear was taken out. In another, a hunter in the jungle is surrounded by lions, with the mouth of the lion "predominant." That drawing of the lion was replaced because the staff thought it was too ferocious, "and you have now the Metro-Goldwyn-Mayer reproduction, the smiling lion." In another story, a bony hand lifting a chess piece was thought to be too gruesome, and the hand was changed to "the ordinary hand as we know it." Comic book westerns also were modified. In one panel, a character was being kicked. The staff required the publisher to remove that panel. In another, a drawing showing a man with an arrow through him was deleted, since the code was interpreted to mean that arrows, hatchets, or bullets were not to be shown piercing the body.

Legislators remained unconvinced by Murphy's display; the chairman noted that "the committee is still concerned over the fact that the product, by and large, still continues to present themes of violence." Murphy answered that the cleanup of the industry could not be accomplished overnight, and that comic books carrying the code seal were just starting to be released on newsstands because it took two to three months for comics to be published once they were reviewed. Murphy saw his job as a process of reeducating publishers: "I think we are both agreed, and were at the time, that you just could not go in like Carrie Nation and destroy an industry and a business which employs thousands and thousands of people—destroy it overnight—that it was a question of education. You had to re-educate the writers and editors and artists with respect to what I thought the Code meant" (New York Hearings [1955] 72). Murphy believed the code was successful. In a speech before the annual meeting of the Association of Towns of the State of New York in February 1956, he noted his office had examined 15,000 stories and dealt with the resulting "interpretive problems" faced in enforcing the code. He concluded, "But regardless of difficulties, the code has been enforced, and the public everywhere is voicing approval" (Murphy, "Role" 245).

The association's public relations firm also believed the new code had accomplished what the industry had set out to do. The code allowed the critics to believe that they had won the battle. At the same time, the code prohibited only the most extreme forms of violence. David Finn later wrote: "It was clear that the change would create no serious obstacles to the continued publication of the same basic material which had always characterized their product. It was also clear that the industry had solved its problem without coming to grips with the basic social issues implicit in its business" (176).

While the role of the code administrator was often seen in a negative light by editors, writers, and artists, Murphy tried to stress that the trade association was also "very much interested in encouraging new and progressive developments in the field" ("Role" 248). The creation of the CMAA marked the first time the comic book publishers had come together with any show of solidarity. They could have used the new organization to address other industry issues, such as distribution and retail sales, to much greater effect than they did. Efforts at cooperative marketing strategies aimed at helping comic books compete with television and targeting comics at new audiences to expand readership could have had a tremendous impact on economic health of the industry. Instead, the publishers poured most of the resources of the organization into the code and the public relations blitz that accompanied it.

Support for the new organization was not unanimous in the industry. Dell Comics, whose sales amounted to about a third of all comics sales, refused to join. George Delacorte explained that Dell had resigned from the earlier association because members refused to adhere to a strict code.

In a statement issued after the CMAA was formed, Delacorte said: "I could not allow the Dell Comics name to be used as an umbrella for some of the inferior products we deemed then, and deem now, unsuitable and unpublishable for our children...If one publisher outside the Association can do nearly half the entire comic book business without resorting to publishing any 'questionable' comic, then the twenty-eight members of the new group doing the other half can benefit from the high example set for them" (New York Hearings [1955] 90–91). Helen Meyer, executive vice president of Dell Publishing Company, testified before the New York legislative committee in February 1955. She told the committee that in response to pressure to join the association, the company had decided instead to launch a "Pledge to Parents" campaign. Beginning March 1955, the pledge would be printed in all comics published by Dell and would read: "The Dell trademark is, and always has been, a positive guarantee that the comic magazine bearing it contains only clean and wholesome juvenile entertainment. The Dell code eliminates entirely, rather than regulates, objectionable material. That's why when your child buys a Dell Comic you can be sure it contains only good fun. 'Dell comics are good comics' is our credo and our constant goal" (77). But Meyer suggested that the association be given a chance to prove itself. After six months, she told legislators, it will be obvious whether the publishers are really sincere about eliminating comics with violence (95).

Another publisher that refused to join was Gilbertson Publications, which published *Classics Illustrated*. Gilbertson maintained that its adaptations of literary classics were not comic books. The third publisher who initially did not join the association was William Gaines of E.C., who tried to continue to distribute comic books without the association seal. He did discontinue his horror line and began publishing a line called "New Direction" comics. Those titles included: *Piracy, Valor, Impact, Extra, Psychoanalysis, M.D.*, and *Incredible Science Fiction*. But wholesalers would not handle the material; it was simply returned, often with bundles of comics unopened. Gaines did join the association, but disputes with the reviewers, along with poor sales on the new titles, drove E.C. out of the comic book business entirely in 1955.

Between 1954 and 1956, several of the major publishers of comic books went out of business, but the best-known "casualty" of the code was Gaines's E.C. Comics. Gaines, who would rebuild his company as publisher of *MAD* magazine, inherited E.C. from his father Max, who has been called by many the father of the modern comic book. In 1947, the elder Gaines was killed in a boating accident, and his twenty-five-year-old son took over a company that was $100,000 in debt. William Gaines, then an education student at New York University and newly divorced, moved in with his mother, finished his studies, and took over as head of the failing Educational Comics (Reidelbach 10–12).

One of Gaines's first moves was to beef up his father's line of kiddie comics. He hired a new artist, Al Feldstein, and by the end of 1949 the company was producing crime and western comics (Jacobs 73). His next step was to create, in 1950, a new line of horror comics. The company changed its name from Educational Comics to Entertaining Comics as *Crypt of Terror, Haunt of Fear,* and *Vault of Horror* joined the E.C. lineup. The new magazines sold well, and within a year E.C.'s financial problems were over (Jacobs 74–75). The E.C. horror line, like all successful comic book ideas, was copied by other publishers, and by 1954 there were more than forty horror titles a month being published (Benton, *Horror Comics* 25).

As a "pioneer" of the horror genre, Gaines was targeted by critics of the medium in the comic book controversy. One such attack came in an exposé on the comic book industry in the *Hartford Courant,* published in February 1954, two months before the Senate subcommittee's investigation of comic books (see chap. 2). Six weeks after running the exposé, the *Courant* reported it was still receiving letters on the subject, all favorable. The only unfavorable letter the newspaper received was from Gaines himself, who accused the *Courant* of presenting a biased picture. *Editor and Publisher* noted: "The same publisher hit back by running full page ads in his comic books declaring that the group most anxious to destroy comics are the Communists," referring to the editorial cartoon that had angered the Senate subcommittee. The magazine also printed the *Courant's* response: "Thus do the sellers of literary sewage justify their profits from the debauch of youth...But the jig is now up for the panderers of dirty comic books, and this Red scare is a frantic rear-guard action from a discredited and soon-to-be deactivated phase of publishing. Their end is in sight and they know it" (Towne 11).

Gaines's unwillingness to bow to the inevitable made him vulnerable to continued attacks. When his fellow publishers ignored his suggestions on how to deal with the industry's problems, he struck out on his own, attacking the Senate subcommittee and launching a letter-writing campaign by E.C. readers in summer 1954, before the CMAA was organized, in an effort to keep his company afloat. After his appearance before the Senate subcommittee, Gaines received a routine letter from its chairman, Senator Hendrickson, thanking him for his testimony. He fired back a reply, telling Hendrickson that the approach of the committee was neither impartial nor scientific and that its treatment of him had been unfair. He complained that he had been scheduled to testify in the morning, was told he would be the first witness in the afternoon, and was "shunted aside" when Dr. Wertham showed up and forced to wait until 4 p.m. before he testified. He noted that his four-minute statement was rudely interrupted, commenting, "I need not tell you that this was far from the kid-glove patience accorded Dr. Wertham—who spoke for hours on end—much of his contribution being obvious gush designed solely to increase the sale of his book." He continued: "The headline-seeking carnival staged by your Committee has given fuel to those in our society who want to tar with the censor's brush. As a result, my business together with the entire comics industry has been severely damaged. Since this was so obviously an objective of your Committee, I trust it will give you some satisfaction" (Gaines to Hendrickson).

In a draft of a reply that was never sent, Senator Hendrickson wrote: "For some time I had before me your letter attacking the integrity of the Subcommittee to Investigate Juvenile Delinquency and charging it with bias in its investigation of the comic book industry. Had opportunity offered, I would have replied to it on the floor of the Senate." Hendrickson noted he did not believe Gaines spoke for the entire industry: "While you are falsely charging us with attempting to wreck an industry, other publishers and distributors are giving concrete evidence of the sincerity of their concern for youth by discontinuing the publishing and distribution of objectionable comics" (Hendrickson to Gaines [draft]).

The speech to which Hendrickson alluded was drafted but never delivered. In that speech, Hendrickson wrote: "Recently, I received a vicious letter from one of the so-called comic book publishers who attacked the integrity of this subcommittee and who charged, among other things, that we are out to destroy the comic book industry." He summarized the testimony Gaines had given at the hearings, concluding: "This is the calm, deliberate thinking of a so-called 'comics' book publisher who attacks a United States Senate Subcommittee that is under mandate to explore and shed light upon possible causes of juvenile delinquency in the United States."

Next, Hendrickson took Gaines to task for encouraging youngsters to write to the subcommittee in defense of comics. The senator wrote:

> Now, I do not object to youngsters writing to their Congressmen. In fact, I welcome it. But I do object to his inferring in this bulletin to thousands of young people that Congressional investigations are conducted because 'November is coming.' And I most strongly object to his deliberately misinforming these youngsters as to the opinion about crime comics of authorities in this field, including Doctor Robert H. Felix, Director of our National Institute of Mental Health. It's malicious, Mr. President, to attempt to discredit the integrity of the Senate in the eyes of American youth. (Hendrickson papers)

Hendrickson concluded the draft of his speech by saying that no attack upon the subcommittee "by a publisher whose own product evoked consternation and revulsion at our hearings" would deter the committee from continuing its investigation into any facet of the media that may be contributing to the "juvenile delinquency scourge."

The "bulletin" to which Hendrickson referred was *The Fan-Addict Club Bulletin,* which was started in November 1953 and mailed to nine thousand charter members. The bulletin, as described by one historian, was "friendly, newsy, and innocuous. Births and marriages among E.C.'s staff and free lancers were announced, and a trading post for old E.C. comics was set up." In the June 1954 issue of the bulletin, mailed to the seventeen thousand subscribers, the address of the subcommittee was printed and fans were urged to begin a letter-writing campaign (Reidelbach 24, 28).

The bulletin began: "THIS IS AN EMERGENCY BULLETIN! This is an appeal for action!" In describing the threat, the bulletin noted: "The congressmen get frightened...November is coming! They start an investigation. This wave of hysteria has seriously threatened the very existence of the whole comic magazine industry." That hysteria, the newsletter argued, was caused by a small minority who oppose comics, adding: "The voice of the *majority*...you who buy comics, read the, enjoy them, and are not harmed by them...has not been heard!" The bulletin urged readers to write "a nice, polite letter" and encouraged youngsters to get their parents to write or add a P.S. to the letter "as the Senate Subcommittee may not have much respect for the opinions of minors." The appeal was signed "Your grateful editors (for the whole E.C. Gang)." (Box 168 National Archives). The same plea was published as an editorial that ran in the E.C. line, and the *Bulletin* and editorials generated an estimated three hundred to four hundred letters from children, teenagers, and adults (Hendrickson to Levy).

The subcommittee kept a separate tally of those who mentioned the E.C. Fan-Addict Club in their letters. The list compiled included the name of the letter writer, state of origin, his or her age (if known), whether the letter favored or opposed horror comics, and relevant comments (usually who else in the family or neighborhood favored horror comics). On the list were 217 names of people writing in support of horror comics and twenty-seven who were opposed to horror comics, but liked other comics ("Survey of E.C.").

The major themes of these letters were that comic books do not cause juvenile delinquency, that crime comics actually teach children that crime is bad, and that readers of comics should decide for themselves what to read. While there are a smattering of postcards in the files, most of the messages are long, handwritten letters. In some cases, a parent obviously wrote or typed the letter for the child to sign, and many parents followed the suggestion in the editorial, adding postscripts to their children's letters. Occasionally, a letter would be signed by an entire neighborhood group of children. The letters were mailed to the subcommittee in two waves. The first group came in response to the call to action in the *Bulletin* and was from younger readers. The second wave resulted from the editorials in the E.C. line of comics and included many adult readers.

Many of the letters rephrased the information given in the editorial, quoting the experts and attacking the so-called "do-gooders" who wanted to rid the country of comic books. But other letters were more clearly the opinions of the writers. One young man from Idaho wrote the subcommittee: "Please do not crucify my favorite pass-time [*sic*] . . . How can anyone truthfully say that reading a magazine actually gives them an urge or an idea to kill? With all of the 'love magazines' being printed, I am surprised we aren't all professional lovers, if that's the case" (Beard letter). One mother offered her own explanation for the anti–comic book sentiment: "I think that the only thing they have against these comics is just that they can't get the kids to help around the house because they are too interested in the comics and that the mothers get tired of picking up a bunch of books" (Thomas letter). A young woman wrote that the comic books were the only entertainment that she and her young daughter could afford, and "the most enjoyment for us is to go to be early in the evening and read a funny book or two" (Scheffer letter). A thirteen-year-old boy asked the senators to "let the kids read what they want and what they like" and concluded, "Besides, if you do take them off [the stands], you'll have every kid in the country on your back" (White letter). The impact of the Senate investigation was mentioned in quite a few letters by readers who were no longer able to find the comics they used to read on the newsstands; retailers had removed the controversial titles from their racks.

The letter-writing campaign, however, was a lost cause long before the letters even reached the Senate subcommittee. Two days before the announcement of the formation of the new trade association, knowing the CMAA would mean the end of his E.C. horror comics, Gaines announced he was discontinuing his line of comics "because this seems to be what American parents want." In reality, Gaines was told by his wholesalers that they simply would not handle the controversial E.C. horror titles any longer. To take their place, Gaines introduced seven titles he labeled his "New Direction" comics (Jacobs 112–13; Reidelbach 30). Distributors, however, aware of Gaines's notoriety, refused to handle the E.C. line without the "Seal of Approval" on the cover, and Gaines joined the association.

Gaines's New Direction comics were not selling well, due in large part to distribution problems, his relations with the CMAA were strained, and Gaines never really reconciled himself to publishing the type of comic book allowed under the guidelines of the code. His relationship with the CMAA was stormy and short-lived. Gaines was clearly unhappy with the way the association was being run. He met individually with several of the publishers but they were apparently unwilling to buck the association. Gaines pushed for greater accountability on the part of the association; the association agreed to meet more frequently "so members could be apprised of the activities of the association" (CMAA Files [minutes, 26 Apr 55]). He publicly attacked the association, despite having an agreement with the CMAA not to do so (CMAA Files [minutes, 23 June 55]).

In August 1955, E.C. business manager Lyle Stuart wrote a letter to James Bobo, then general counsel to the Senate Subcommittee on Juvenile Delinquency, asking the senators to investigate the CMAA, claiming the "autocratic, self-appointed group has subverted the good intentions of the Kefauver Committee into a monopolistic instrument" and suggesting that the association was working to destroy small publishers. Stuart told Bobo in his letter that there were publishers willing to testify about what the association had done to squeeze them out of business (Stuart to Bobo).

The letter to Bobo was inspired, in part, by the latest dispute between Gaines and the CMAA reviewers, a disagreement that was to drive Gaines out of the comic book publishing field. The dispute centered around an issue of *Incredible Science Fiction,* a title that had survived from his previous line with a name change (it was formerly entitled *Weird Science-Fantasy*). As Gaines remembered it, one of the stories was rejected, and Gaines decided to reprint another E.C. story in its place, called "Judgment Day." The story had an antiracism theme and dealt with a planet of robots who had applied for admission to the pre–*Star Trek* version of a galactic federation, but the society of robots who lived on the planet had a policy of segregation based on what color the robot was. The hero of the story, who gets back into his spaceship, decides the robot planet is not ready to join the rest of the galaxy. In one panel, the character removes his helmet and the reader discovers the hero is black. Perspiration dots the character's face.

The code reviewers, citing the code provision that "ridicule or attack on any religious or racial group is never permissible," apparently decided that a perspiring black character somehow violated code guidelines. Gaines, who said he had already decided to leave comics publishing and was simply printing the last of the work completed for his company, fought for the story: "We had to take the perspiration off his forehead. Swear to God. That's what the code said. No sweat on this man's face. Needless to say we wouldn't. And I threatened to go to court. And I raised such a stink they said, oh, all right. So I got it through. And that was the end of the code as far as I was concerned" (Gaines interview).

Another version of the story suggests that Gaines was unable to get code approval of the story and simply printed the comic with the code seal anyway (Benton *Comic Book* 115). A third account of the dispute, given in the letter from Stuart to Bobo, suggests that the story was turned down by Murphy because it conflicted with the code administrator's religious beliefs. Stuart wrote: "Just today we had a story turned down. It was a harmless story for a science-fiction magazine. But in the story an automaton thinks and talks. Nobody is hurt. There is no violence. But the story was turned down because to suggest that an automaton can think is contrary to Judge Murphy's religious beliefs that only man was granted a soul and the ability to think by his Creator" (Stuart to Bobo).

Gaines's departure from the CMAA was noted in the CMAA Board of Directors' minutes of December 14, 1955, this way: "On motion by Mr. Liebowitz, it was decided to accept the oral resignation of Entertaining Comics, made on October 25, 1955, and the executive secretary was instructed to notify this firm of this decision" (CMAA Files [minutes, 14 Dec. 55]).

There is no question that Gaines was made a scapegoat both by comic book critics and by the industry itself. The eccentric young publisher had, in the eyes of the other publishers, done a lot of damage to the comic book industry in refusing to take a conciliatory tone in his dealings with the public, and his headline-grabbing performance during the Senate hearings was a public relations disaster for the industry. Perhaps more on the mark, Gaines had taken a small, financially ailing company and built a highly profitable business that many of his fellow publishers envied and tried, without nearly as much success, to imitate. Driving Gaines out of business with the comics code was good publicity, and if other publishers also fell victim to the code, those who survived would certainly be in a stronger economic position. The comic book market was glutted in the 1950s, and pruning out the undesirable elements made good business sense. The Senate subcommittee turned a deaf ear to Gaines's complaints because they had little sympathy for the publisher and little concern for the economic hardships brought about by their investigation into the industry. The senators were all too happy to point to their accomplishments once the code was in place and to wash their hands of comic books.

Other publishers also left the field, though with less fanfare than E.C. One was Comic Media, which had started in 1951 with two romance comics and had expanded into westerns, war comics, crime titles, and horror comics, including *Horrific* and *Weird Terror.* Notes comic book historian Mike Benton, "The covers of both books often featured either a corpse's face or a leering maniac's head that had been shot, stabbed, or otherwise colorfully disfigured" (*Comic Book* 100). In late 1954, the company discontinued its horror titles and sold its romance and western titles to other companies. Fiction House, which specialized in offering readers half-dressed heroines in exotic locations, found themselves put out of business by the code as well. Their last title was *Jungle Comics* No. 163, cover-dated summer 1954 (Benton, *Comic Book* 119–20).

Several more companies ceased publishing in 1955, including some that had been in business since the late 1930s, and for the first time, no new publishers entered the comic book business. Eastern Color Printing Company, the first company to publish comic books, went out of business. Its problem was not the code, but the depressed state of the industry due to the bad publicity generated by the Senate hearings and the controversy more generally. United Features, another long-lived company, decided to leave the publishing business in 1955 as well, selling its top three titles to St. John Publishing and canceling the rest (Benton, *Comic Book* 112, 150). Stanley Morse, who published comics under four company names, also shut down in 1955. His line, too, had depended heavily on titles that would no longer pass muster (Benton 54). Sterling Comics, which was started in 1954 right before the advent of the code with two crime-and-horror titles, tried to make the transition with watered-down horror and mystery stories, but failed (Benton, *Comic Book* 145–46).

Other companies went out of business for reasons unrelated to the code. Star Publications went out of business in 1955 when Jerry Kramer, one of the partners in the company, died. The other partner, L. B. Cole, went on to work as an art director for *Classics Illustrated* in the 1950s and Dell Comics in the 1960s (Benton, *Comic Book* 145). The next year was not any brighter. Several more publishers went out of business, including Ace Magazines, Avon Comics Group, and Quality Comics Group. These three were the casualty of an industry-wide depression that had more to do with the upheaval in the distribution side of the business than the code.

The leading distributor of comic books in the United States was the American News Company. The company was the target of an antitrust suit brought against it by the Department of Justice in 1952. The company distributed magazines to most of the estimated 110,000 retail magazine outlets in the United States. In addition, its wholly-owned subsidiary, Union News Company, owned and operated newsstands at railroad stations, bus terminals, airports, subways, parks, hotels, and office buildings. American News had approximately four hundred branch offices throughout the United States. Its subsidiary, Union, was the largest magazine retailer in the country.

The lawsuit charged that American and Union had conspired to monopolize the national independent distribution of magazines, primarily because Union refused to sell or display magazines that were not distributed through its parent company and because it forced publishers who wished to have their magazines sold at Union outlets to sign contracts giving American exclusive national distribution rights (*U.S. v. American News*). Under the consent decree in 1955, Union News agreed to buy, sell, and display magazines on the basis of its own interests, not giving preferential treatment to magazines distributed by American News Company (Peterson 92). As a result, American News Company lost many of its mass-circulation clients to other distributors and pulled out of national distribution in August 1955 (Peterson 93). This left many of the comic book companies without a national distributor.

Although there were thirteen national distributors of comics in the mid-1950s, American was by far the largest. At the time it ceased operations, American distributed nearly three hundred comic book titles, more than half the output of the comic book industry (Senate *Interim Report* [1955] 45). While some of American's clients, such as Archie Comics and Dell Comics, were able to find other outlets (or, in Dell's case, start their own distribution company), many of its clients went out of business during that period. Martin Goodman's company, which weathered the storm to become Marvel Comics—the industry leader in the 1980s—was also hurt by the demise of American. Goodman, who had split with Kable News Company to start his own distribution company, Atlas, decided in the post-code period to sign a deal with American. When American abruptly ceased national distribution, Goodman was forced to sign a distribution deal with DC Comics, which limited the company to only eight titles, a mixture of war, western, romance, and teen titles (Daniels *Marvel* 80–81).

In 1956, the strongest comics companies were Dell, National (DC), Harvey, Charlton, and Archie. Dell Comics was the largest comics publisher in the world during the 1950s, selling more than three hundred million comic books annually. Its line of Disney character comics and other comics aimed at the younger audience was so wholesome that the company successfully resisted the pressure to join the Comics Magazine Association (Benton *Comic Book* 109).

The CMAA was never able to get Dell Comics to change its position on the code, but not for lack of trying. The subject was hashed out at an executive committee meeting May 9, 1957, and it was decided that the CMAA president should address the problem in the next newsletter. John Goldwater's editorial in the July 1957 *CMAA Newsletter* noted that while 90 percent of the industry supported the code, "the continued omission of two publishers from their ranks is a source of concern" to the members, who "recognize a danger to the stability of its structure inherent in such division." He suggested that the example set by those publishers who refused to join might influence other publishers "to avoid the discipline and expense of code supervision, thus creating a risk that neither the public nor the industry can afford." He added that the division created confusion in the public and reduced the stature and stability of the industry. He concluded: "All comics publishers, without exception, owe it to themselves and to the public and the industry... to share in the responsibility of keeping the Code and its enforcement machinery strong... [Publishers] can exercise this responsibility only by joining the Comics Magazine Association of America" (Goldwater, "Editorial"). When this strategy failed, CMAA Vice President Jack Liebowitz suggested at the board's July 11 meeting that a more personal, informal approach to Dell might work. Dell, however, remained firm in its decision not to join the association.

For National Comics, which had never published anything but the tamest crime and horror comics, it was business as usual after the implementation of the code. Harvey dropped its horror titles and introduced a number of characters aimed at a very young readership, including Baby Huey, Little Dot, Hot Stuff, Casper, and Richie Rich, who at one time had thirty-eight separate titles devoted to his adventures, more than any other American comic-book character (Benton *Comic Book* 127). Charlton Comics, which weathered the comic-book recession because it also published other types of magazines, bought up titles as other publishers went out of business in the mid-1950s, including a line of romance, western, and horror comics from Fawcett Comics. Charlton published dozens of western, romance, science fiction, adventure, and war comics during the late 1950s (Benton, *Comic Book* 98–99). Archie was the leading publisher of the popular teen comics, and the company continued to add Archie titles throughout the 1950s. The clean-cut world of Archie and his gang posed few problems for code reviewers (Benton, *Comic Book* 95).

The comics code of 1954 succeeded where earlier efforts had failed because it represented a concerted effort on the part of the publishers to act. Negative publicity provided the Comics Magazine Association of America the enforcement mechanism that earlier attempts lacked—the distributors. Their refusal to carry most non-code comics gave publishers no alternative but to join the association and abide by its rules. The impact of the code was not felt until 1955–1956, since most of the comic books on the newsstands in early 1955 were actually created prior to the implementation of the code. But gradually the type of comic book that had caused so much trouble for the industry disappeared, and what remained were romance, teen, and funny animal comics. But dissatisfaction with the code was expressed by the member publishers of the Comics Magazine Association tion almost as soon as the ink on the code was dry, and between 1954 and 1989 the publishers would rewrite the comics code twice to bring the code in line with the changing social and business climate.

Chapter 6

Evolution of the Comics Code

The comics code adopted in 1954 has been revised twice, once in 1971 and again in 1989. The need for a new code was dictated by changes in society, in the industry, and in the audience. However, each change in the code reinforced the idea that comic books were intended for the child reader and should contain nothing that would be inappropriate for young readers. Restrictions on violence, sex, and language, while modified, remained at the heart of the code.

The first few years following the adoption of the Comics Code in 1954 were a time of upheaval in the industry. As noted in the last chapter, many publishers left the field, and those who remained were forced to cope with the effects of negative publicity, the implementation of the new code regulations, problems in distribution, and a need to find new ways to attract an audience whose leisure time was increasingly dominated by television. Charles Murphy and his five reviewers proved to be quite strict in their interpretation of the code, and many comic book editors, writers, and artists chafed under the new restrictions.

At the first annual meeting of the association, held June 14, 1955, at the Roosevelt Hotel in New York, the publishers suggested that the code be reevaluated. Later that year, at the board of directors meeting December 14, 1955, a proposal was made that the association form a committee to evaluate the present status of the code. Although no action was taken by the association at either meeting, similar requests would be heard at many of the CMAA's annual meetings. While there were other factors at work, many of the publishers blamed the code for the downturn in the comic book market.

The depressed market in the mid-1950s affected the new trade association as well. By the end of 1955, the CMAA was struggling financially. Attorney Henry Schultz volunteered to take a reduction in his salary, and the association proposed eliminating one of the five staff reviewers, although Murphy was opposed to that move, asserting that it would cut into the time he had available for public relations work. At their meeting November 15, 1955, the executive and budget committees approved a 1956 budget of $104,200. Murphy objected to the budget restrictions, and he reminded the committee that he had been promised autonomy to run the Code Authority office. The publishers replied in a letter dated February 28, 1956, that Murphy would have to work within the CMAA's budget. Conflicts over the enforcement of the code, coupled with Murphy's frustration with his budget limitations and complaints from the publishers that he was not returning artwork in a timely manner, led to Murphy's decision to resign. He announced his intentions in a letter to Goldwater dated May 9, 1956, stating that he would be returning to private law practice when his contract expired in October. The move came as a surprise to the CMAA directors, but Murphy would not be dissuaded. In June, the board authorized a search for a new code administrator.

The person Schultz had in mind was Arthur DeBra. A graduate of Union Theological Seminary, he was director of exhibitor-community relations for the Motion Picture Association of America (Gilbert 172). He was active in the short-lived committee that had been funded by the Justice Department in 1946 to study the prevention and control of juvenile delinquency, serving on a panel designed to study the influence of radio, film, and publications on youth. He also was a member of a committee formed by the American Bar Association in 1948. The committee's primary goal was to find funding for scientific research on media effects. Although its organizer, Arthur Freund, approached several researchers, including the Gluecks, he was unable to secure funding for the project, and it was abandoned (Gilbert 86–87). It was quite possible that Schultz met DeBra at that 1948 conference, because Schultz may have attended as a representative of the new Association of Comics Magazine Publishers.

Although DeBra had told Schultz he could not take the position until January 1, 1957, at the earliest, he recommended that the CMAA hire Mrs. Guy Percy Trulock as code administrator and Jesse Bader as chairman of a citizens' advisory committee. Trulock had served as president of the New York City Federation of Women's Clubs, an organization of more than five hundred women's clubs with 250,000 members, and was also vice president of the Women's Press Club. In the February 1957 issue of the

CMAA newsletter, the association noted that she brought to the code administrator's job "a wealth of experience in civic and community projects of benefit to the public." Jesse Bader, of the Protestant Motion Picture Council, was given the task of organizing the National Advisory Committee on Comic Books. The association newsletter commented, "Her distinguished record in the religious field, and her broad contacts throughout the world among religious and community leaders assures the industry of the most responsible guidance." These appointments were approved by the CMAA at its meeting September 12, 1956 (CMAA Files [minutes, 12 Sept. 1956]).

Schultz assured association members that DeBra had "tremendous contacts among women's organizations" and "was convinced he could get Dell to join the Association, and that he also expected to get comic editors of newspapers to come in" (CMAA Files [minutes, 19 Oct. 1956]). But DeBra wanted the title of president and to have the code authority report to him, a move the current president, John Goldwater, understandably opposed at the association's October 1956 meeting. Discussion continued throughout the end of the year about DeBra's appointment. Goldwater suggested making DeBra executive vice president, and Schultz noted that would mean rewriting the bylaws of the association. Apparently the publishers were never able to arrange things to DeBra's satisfaction. In addition, the comic book industry continued to decline, which may also have affected DeBra's decision to delay his move from the MPAA to the CMAA. In February 1957, board meeting minutes note that DeBra's starting date had been pushed back to April 1957, and in May the board of directors learned that "due to the present situation in the industry" DeBra had decided to wait until fall. Two months later, the board of directors decided to defer DeBra's appointment "indefinitely."

Without DeBra's direction, the publishers felt Bader's job was unnecessary, and at their meeting in July 1957 they voted to terminate her position. Trulock continued on as code administrator until she resigned for health reasons on September 3, 1965. After that her duties were performed by the executive director of the association, Leonard Darvin, who was appointed officially as code administrator on October 1, 1965. Darvin, an attorney who specialized in trade associations, joined the CMAA at the invitation of Schultz, who was looking for an assistant for Judge Murphy. Darvin was hired initially as a consultant to aid in running the day-to-day operations of the trade association outside of the code administrator's office and to oversee the finances of the CMAA. In short order, he was named the executive director of the association. After he became code administrator, Darvin said he saw his job as handling both industry relations and public relations: "The real thing, the whole thing in my opinion, was to see the code was properly enforced so the kids wouldn't be hurt by reading comics and [there would not be] books written against us and people making speeches against us" (Darvin interview).

His concerns were well founded. Although the adoption and enforcement of the comics code silenced much of the criticism against comic books, the attack by Wertham on the industry published in *Saturday Review* in April 1955 under the title "It's Still Murder" demonstrated that the comic book publishers were still vulnerable despite their comics code.

That vulnerability was further demonstrated by the adoption of laws in two states regulating comic books. The first was the Comic Book Act passed by the state of Washington in 1955. The act made the sale or possession of comic books with the intent to sell without a prior license a crime and required dealers to furnish the supervisor of the Division of Children and Youth Services of the state with three copies of every comic book before distribution or sale. The second was an ordinance adopted by Los Angeles County, a rewrite of an earlier attempt to regulate comics in the late 1940s (see chap. 2). The ordinance prohibited the sale or circulation of a crime comic book to children under eighteen. The ordinance specified which crimes could not be depicted and attempted to provide a specific definition of comic books: five or more sequential drawings accompanied by narration. It also provided broad exemptions, including accounts appearing in newspapers, accounts that depicted actual historical events, and accounts of events from sacred scriptures of any religion.

Both laws were found to be unconstitutional in court challenges. In a decision handed down in February 1958 by the Washington Supreme Court, *Adams v. Hinkle,* the court noted that the licensing requirement punishes a person "not for selling something which may be considered harmful, but for selling without a license. This device is prior restraint in its most abhorrent form." Because the statute covered all comic books, not just those crime comic books judged to be harmful, and because the license was required for all sales, not just sales to minors, the court ruled the Comic Book Act was void on its face. In addition, the sections of the act that prohibited comic books devoted to content described generally as "deeds of violent bloodshed, lust, crime or immorality" were so vague and indefinite that they failed to meet the procedural due process require-ments. The court held that the language in the Comic Book Act was not sufficiently different from that held to be unconstitutional in *Winters v. New York*. Finally, the exemption of newspapers from the prepublication license was held to be in violation of equal protection guarantees. On this final point, Justice Finley dissented, stating that such a position would preclude any further attempts at comic book regulation, arguing that a comic book and a newspaper were not the same thing and that such an exemption was not unreasonable.

In *Katzev v. County of Los Angeles,* the Supreme Court of California ruled in June 1959 that the ordinance prohibiting the sale or circulation of a crime comic book to children under eighteen violated provisions guaran-teeing free press, equal protection, and due process of law. The court ruled that the distribution of crime comic books was protected by the constitu-tion until such time as it could be demonstrated that comic books consti-tuted a clear and present danger. The decision read: "The record fails to show that there is a clear and present danger that the circulation of crime comic books in general will injure the character of persons under the age of eighteen years and inculcate in them a preference for crime" (310). In addition, the Los Angeles ordinance was found to be too broad because it made illegal the circulation of any comic books which contained fictional, nonreligious accounts of crime, and it failed to draw any distinction be-tween various accounts of crime. The ordinance exempted many crime, horror, or sex comic books simply because they were not fictional or did not contain accounts of the enumerated crimes.

Just as in *Adams v. Hinkle,* the court found that the exemptions in the ordinance were "arbitrary and unreasonable" and that the ordinance de-nied plaintiffs equal protection because it drew an "irrational line" between true accounts of crime, even though disgustingly portrayed, and all fictional accounts of crime. The decision stated: "The ordinance ignores the impor-tant factor which might support some comic book legislation, namely, the manner of depiction and the approach of the comic book" (310). Finally, the ordinance was found unconstitutional because it failed to establish a clearly defined standard of guilt. The court noted that the definition of a comic book, while embracing what is commonly known as a comic book, also went further. Illustrated books would be included, as well as accounts that used photographs. Thus, fairy tales or folk tales would fall within the scope of the ordinance, although that was clearly not the intent of the ordinance. Such ambiguity left distributors unable to determine if they were in violation of the ordinance.

In many states where legislation was adopted, however, there were no challenges to the law because prosecutors could find no violations, demonstrating the effectiveness of the code in eliminating certain types of material from the newsstands. In Wisconsin, for example, a law prohibiting the publication, sale, and distribution to minors of crime and horror comic books was signed into law in 1957. The law defined comic books as "any book, magazine or other printed matter consisting of narrative material in pictorial form" and forbade depictions of "acts of indecency, horror, terror, physical torture or brutality." The statute also exempted the portrayal of historical or current events and literary works "of recognized merit." Shortly after the law was passed, the district attorney's office in Dane County examined a sample of forty or fifty comic books distributed in the area and found none to be in violation of the law, noted an article in the December 1957 CMAA newsletter. In fact, that statute was to remain on the books until 1987, when it was repealed because legislators felt the materials prohibited were covered in a newly created statute that forbid sale of materials harmful to children.

Although the laws restricting the sale of comic books, where challenged, were found to be unconstitutional, attempts to pass such legislation reinforced the publishers' belief that a strong self-regulatory code was the best way to stave off such attacks against the industry. Not only would the code enable the industry to monitor comic book content in order to avoid publishing the type of comic book that might be targeted under such laws, but the code also demonstrated the publishers' willingness to act responsibly, reassuring groups that might otherwise push for legislation that the industry could act in a socially responsible way.

The public relations campaign conducted by the CMAA in its early years therefore was not aimed at lawmakers, but rather focused on civic and church organizations, the CMAA realizing that if the protests from these critics subsided, so would the call for additional legislation. The CMAA, in its first newsletter published in December 1955, reported that a number of these groups had passed resolutions commending the work of the CMAA, including the Protestant Episcopal Church, the American Legion, and the New York City Federation of Women's Clubs. Both CMAA President John Goldwater and the code administrator, Judge Charles Murphy, crisscrossed the country speaking to various organizations and explaining the work of the CMAA. In his first year, Murphy reported speaking to more than one hundred women's clubs, veterans organizations, and religious, civic, educational, and fraternal groups in addition to making television and radio appearances.

The CMAA was also careful to keep the members of the Senate Subcommittee on Juvenile Delinquency apprised of their activities and achievements. In August 1955, Sen. Estes Kefauver alarmed the CMAA with an announcement, reported in the *New York Times* on August 12, that his committee would reopen their investigation of comic books ("Comic Book Inquiry Set" 21). His comments came after the close of hearings conducted by the subcommittee in Nashville, Tennessee, designed to get input from religious and educational leaders about juvenile delinquency. During those hearings, members of the Committee on Subversive Literature of Knoxville called for national legislation against comic books. Judge Murphy immediately wrote to Kefauver, pointing out that the material Kefauver had criticized in his interim report was no longer being published and that the code authority was making progress in eliminating all objectionable material. In his August 12 letter, he added: "Therefore, I should greatly appreciate your calling to my attention any new trends that you feel might be open to criticism. It would also be most helpful if you could send me a copy of the testimony upon which your statement is based, together with any other material which you feel would guide us in our work" (Murphy to Kefauver). Kefauver was out of the country, and Murphy's letter was answered by General Counsel James Bobo, who told Murphy in his August 30 letter that it was Kefauver's feeling that the committee should do a follow-up study (Bobo to Murphy).

The promised investigation never materialized; Kefauver's' committee had moved on to other concerns. A photograph of Judge Murphy shaking hands with Senator Kefauver appeared in the CMAA newsletter in May 1956, and Murphy noted in his column that he had an opportunity to speak to Kefauver personally about the CMAA: "His gratifying comment on our program was: 'I think generally you are doing all right'" (Murphy, "Code Administrator's Column"). The CMAA continued to keep the Senate subcommittee informed about its work. When Murphy resigned as code administrator, CMAA President John Goldwater wrote to Kefauver on June 10, 1956, assuring him that the position would be filled immediately: "You will be kept advised of all developments in this matter. We assure you that whoever is selected will be the proper individual to carry on the same vigorous enforcement of the Code of Ethics as has been practiced heretofore" (Goldwater to Kefauver).

Other groups that monitored comics also responded favorably to the code. The National Office of Decent Literature noted that the comics code authority had cleaned up the comics magazine field, and NODL no longer listed any comics as "disapproved" ("NODL Head" 1). The Cincinnati Committee on the Evaluation of Comics, headed by Rev. Jesse L. Murrell, wrote to Code Administrator Mrs. Guy Percy Trulock that his organization had discontinued its regular evaluations for all comics and conducted only periodic spot checks of certain ones due to the improvement in quality ("Cincinnati Committee" 3).

The public relations campaign, while effective, proved costly. In 1955, the CMAA found itself several thousand dollars in debt. In addition to expenses related to bolstering the comic industry's public image, the CMAA found that the demise of several comic book publishing companies, along with a decline in sales, reduced its income substantially. The organization moved to cheaper office space, dispensed with the services of its public relations firm, and reduced its office staff. In his 1957 report to the association in November, CMAA President John Goldwater was able to report the trade group was back on solid financial ground.

By the CMAA's fifth year of operation, there were signs the industry was recovering. Goldwater reported to CMAA members that circulation of comics was approximately six hundred million annually, and while it was true that a number of companies had not survived, the overall circulation of the comic book industry had increased by almost 150 million annually. He urged members to experiment with new types of material and new approaches to material while maintaining high standards (CMAA Files [Address of the President, 14 Apr. 1959]). While funny animal, teen, and romance comics performed adequately on the newsstands, the publishers were in search of a genre that would appeal to the baby-boom youngsters who were now teenagers. Their "experiment" would be to resurrect the genre that started the industry, that of the superhero. National Comics led the way with the reintroduction of a 1940s character, the Flash. He made his debut in Showcase No. 4, cover-dated October 1956. His success was to launch a revival of the genre, and comic book historians use the reappearance of the Flash in 1956 as a marker to indicate the start of the Silver Age of comic books (Benton, *Comic Book* 177). Archie Comics hired

Jack Kirby and Joe Simon to revive their 1940s superhero, the Shield, but the revival lasted only two issues. Next, they tried an original character, the Fly, who had insect-like powers (Benton, *Comic Book* 59).

As DC revived more of its 1940s heroes, it decided to put them all together in the Justice League of America with an issue cover-dated October 1960. It was tremendously popular. Martin Goodman at Marvel, seeking to capitalize on the superhero team concept that had been successful at DC, gave writer Stan Lee the go-ahead to develop a team for Marvel. Lee's answer was the Fantastic Four (November 1961). The team consisted of a scientist who could stretch, a teenager who burst into flame, an invisible girl, and a monstrously ugly strongman. The team also represented a departure from the traditional superhero formula; instead of being perfect and god-like, these four behaved "more like human beings who happened to be superheroes than heroes who happened to be human" (Benton, *Comic Book* 63).

This new approach to superheroes would eventually pay off for Marvel. By 1965, every other comic book publisher was rushing to introduce its version of new-and-improved superhero characters. And the success of the campy Batman television series in 1966 created a new superhero craze. Sales of all comic books rose as a result, and the Batman comic book reached an all-time high of 900,000 copies, the best performance by a comic since the pre-code days. It was the revitalization of the superhero comic that lent impetus to making revisions in the comics code. The new breed of superheroes, with their human problems, were creatures of the 1960s, a decade very different from that of the Golden Age superheroes of the 1940s. The social upheaval of the 1960s, with its liberalization of attitudes toward sex and the rise of a drug culture, led publishers to push for a code that adhered to more contemporary standards.

But the first comic books to escape the constraints of the comics code came from outside the industry in the form of underground comics. These comics were the product of the counterculture that flourished in America in the late 1960s and early 1970s. At first, underground comic books were available only by mail order or directly from the artist, but eventually a network of retail outlets, including alternative record stores and bookstores, along with so-called head shops, was created for distribution. Historian Mark Estren identifies the first underground comic book as *God Nose*, produced by Jack Jackson under the name Jaxon, which appeared in

1963. It was not until 1967 that underground comics began to emerge as a unique medium. A whole new alternative comics culture was established, with its peak years coming between 1968 and 1974 (Estren 45, 50; Sabin 41).

Underground comics (sometimes spelled "comix" to distinguish them from their more mainstream counterparts) dealt with taboo subjects of interest to the counterculture, specifically sex and drugs. Most contained a liberal dose of graphic violence as well. Estren notes: "The comics of the forties and early fifties were very often cast in a cops-and-robbers format, while the violence in the underground comics is more likely to cut across all strata of society and to be completely pointless—an accurate reflection of present-day America" (146). The quality of drawing ranged from amateurish to polished and utilized a variety of artistic styles. Underground comics never completely died out, but they decreased in popularity after the decline of the counterculture. Also contributing to the decline of underground comics were increasing production costs in the 1970s, a wave of obscenity prosecutions, and the closing of head shops under new anti–drug paraphernalia laws (Sabin 174).

It was not the intention of the underground comics producers to compete with mainstream publishers for their audience. Rather, the underground artists, who grew up with comics books, found comic books to be the perfect medium to express their defiance of social norms. What better way to demonstrate their disdain of conservative taste than to pervert what the public perceived as children's entertainment? The underground comics represented no real challenge to the comic book industry, however. The limited circulation of underground comics posed no economic threat and also meant that there would be no public confusion about the mainstream product and the comics offered by the underground artists.

Despite their relatively short lifespan, underground comics were important to the mainstream comic book industry in three ways. First, they demonstrated that there was a market for adult comics. Second, the retail network developed for distribution was an important precursor to changes in the way more mainstream comics were distributed in the 1980s. And finally, some underground artists went on to make a name for themselves with the new mainstream adult comics that were to emerge in the 1980s. The most notable success was Art Spiegelman, who emerged from the underground with *Maus*, a tale of the holocaust in comic-book form.

While the "comix" added a new dimension to the medium, it was the rebirth of the superhero in the late 1950s and early 1960s that brought new life to the floundering industry. The number of teenage readers was growing, and the stories of superheroes whose human flaws (rather than their fantastic powers) were emphasized appealed to this older group. But just as it had in the 1940s, the interest in superhero comics waned; by the late 1960s the industry was desperately casting around for new material. One response was to introduce new "socially relevant" comics. The leader in this respect was a DC superhero team consisting of Green Lantern and Green Arrow. Comic book historians Will Jacobs and Gerald Jones note that the characters served as "a mouthpiece for [writer Denny O'Neil's] own 1960s radical orientation" (160). Despite its short run, lasting only fourteen issues, the *Green Lantern/Green Arrow* comic book opened the way for a challenge to the outdated rules of the code. O'Neil sought to introduce fantasy rooted in the issues of the day. Stories tackled problems such as overpopulation, racism, sexism, and judicial due process. One subject the comic could not deal with was drugs, a topic forbidden by the comics code (McCue and Bloom 52).

The code made crafting such socially relevant stories very difficult. Comic book characters lived in a perfect world where good and evil were supposed to be clearly defined and where figures of authority were never corrupt. This vision was not consistent with the social unrest that reverberated through the 1960s, when the Vietnam War, the civil rights movement, the feminist movement, and other issues led some to question the very structure of society. The 1954 code allowed no acknowledgement that the world had changed. To bring an element of realism to comics, the publishers had to go outside the code.

It was Marvel Comics, not DC, that broke new ground by producing a mainstream comic book dealing with drugs, publishing and distributing the comic without code approval. By doing so, Marvel Comics forced the Comics Magazine Association to reevaluate the comics code that had been in effect with no changes since 1954. The comic was *Spider-Man,* a top-selling Marvel title. Stan Lee, Marvel's editor-in-chief, received a letter from the Department of Health, Education and Welfare asking the company to do a *Spider-Man* story about the dangers of drugs. In a three-issue story, Spider-Man learns that his college roommate is a drug addict. Because the comics code forbade any mention of narcotics or their use, the story did not get code approval, but Marvel decided to publish the story anyway. Lee recalls that the story got favorable press nationwide, "and because of that, the Code was changed" (Daniels "Five Fabulous Decades" 152).

The publishers apparently considered Marvel's request that the company be allowed to publish their special Spider-Man stories at a meeting in June 1970. This request led to a discussion of whether the time had come to change the code, a discussion led by National's representative, Carmine Infantino. The minutes of the meeting stated: "It was decided each publisher, after discussions with his editorial staff, should prepare any suggested revisions he saw fit, and these should be submitted to the Board for its consideration at a subsequent meeting." However, the board rejected Marvel's request with this statement: "In the meantime, the Code Administration's ruling that no stories shall deal with narcotics addiction shall remain in effect" (CMAA Files [minutes, 9 June 1970]). Work on code revisions began immediately, and the association's board of directors reviewed specific provisions in a special meeting called December 7, 1970, for that purpose. The president of the association, John Goldwater, noted that he had always taken the position that if times and circumstances warranted it, changes in the code should be considered and made. He added: "However, such changes should be carefully considered, so that the self-regulation program, which has served the industry effectively for more than sixteen years, should not become ineffective" (CMAA Files [minutes, 7 Dec. 1970]).

Revisions were discussed and approved for most of the text of the code at that December meeting, and the publishers agreed that the new code would go into effect February 1, 1971 (see CMAA Code 1971). Many of the restrictions on the presentation of crime and horror were liberalized. Ghouls, vampires, and werewolves, which were prohibited under the original code, would now be allowed as long as they were "handled in the classic tradition such as Frankenstein, Dracula and other high calibre literary works... read in schools throughout the world." In addition, new provisions dealing specifically with narcotics were added. The revisions dealing with sex also reflected the relaxing of the strict morality imposed by the 1950s version of the code. Although illicit sex acts were not to be portrayed, they could now be hinted at. Although rape still could not be shown or suggested, seduction could be suggested (although not shown). The code provisions for advertising remained unchanged. Unlike other magazines, which relied heavily on advertising revenue, the revenue derived by comic book publishers for advertising was negligible. Nearly 95 percent of revenues came from newsstand sales.

A lengthy preamble was added to the 1971 code reaffirming the publishers' commitment to act responsibly in publishing comics. It praised comics as an "effective tool" for education and instruction and also noted the comics' emerging role as a contributor to "social commentary and criticism of contemporary life," recognizing the move in the industry to incorporate contemporary issues into story lines. The code changes were explained as necessary to making a positive contribution to "contemporary life." While the wording of some sections of the code was modified and a new section on how to handle drugs was added, the format of the code remained unchanged, with the emphasis remaining on the depiction of crime and authority figures. Comic book standards defined the reader as a child, and there was no acknowledgement on the part of the CMAA-member publishers that the medium should move beyond content suitable for an audience of all ages.

These changes were approved by the publishers at their meeting in December, but the publishers could not agree over the wording of Part C, which gave the code administrator broad powers to interpret the code for "all elements or techniques not specifically mentioned" in the code. That debate was carried over into the board's meeting January 28, 1971. National Periodical Publications had proposed amending that section of the code by adding a second paragraph that would read: "It is not the intent of the Code to prohibit the treatment of such realistic problems as drugs, generation gap, poverty, racial relations, abortions and political unrest handled in an instructive positive fashion. This provision shall not be unreasonably invoked" (CMAA Files [minutes, 28 Jan. 1971]). The debate centered around the provisions involving drugs and abortion. Although the amendment was supported by Charles Goodman, representing Marvel Comics, and Carmine Infantino, representing National, three other publishers opposed its adoption, including Goldwater (representing Archie Comics), Leon Harvey of Harvey Comics, and John Santangelo, representing Charlton Comics. The proposal failed, and Section C of the comics code remained unchanged.

At a meeting February 1, 1971, the association formally approved and implemented the new code. At that time, Charles Goodman, speaking on behalf of Marvel Comics, promised that after the publication of the three *Spider-Man* issues (cover-dated May–July 1971) the company would not publish any comics magazine without the seal of approval. The minutes specifically state that the February meeting was called "to receive assurances that the members would comply with the Code in the future" (CMAA Files [minutes, 1 Feb. 1971]).

Despite its softened stance, the 1971 code represents a lost opportunity for the industry. Its reaffirmation of comic books as a medium intended for children effectively shut the door on the possibility of attracting a broader audience for comic books. The underground comics had established that there was a new adult market for comic books, a generation of young adults who had grown up with comic books and were open to the possibilities of the comic book form. But the publishers were generally content with the status quo and unwilling to risk their economic health on experimentation that would challenge the public's perception of comic books. This conservative stance served to reinforce the idea that any significant changes in evolution of the medium would have to come from outside the major players in the industry.

The liberalization of the code had less impact on industry output in the 1970s than one might expect. Part of the reason was that the push for "relevance" in comics died not long after being introduced. Comics historians Greg McCue and Clive Bloom suggest that relevance failed to catch on because audiences wanted more allegorical and escapist entertainment from their superhero comics (53). The content of some comics did change under the 1971 code, however. For example, the relaxing of the restrictions on vampire and werewolf stories led to publication of a number of these types of stories, prompting some publishers to propose this amendment at an October 27, 1971, meeting: "No comics magazine shall use the word vampire or werewolf in its title, or bear illustrations of such characters on its cover" (CMAA Files [minutes, 27 Oct. 1971]). The motion was tabled at that meeting and defeated at the board's February 28, 1972 meeting. On June 19, 1973, the association clarified the use of the words *horror* and *terror*, specifying that while those words could be used in the body of a story, they could not be used in the title of the story. The prohibition of those words on the cover of comic books continued as well (CMAA Files [minutes, 29 June 1973]).

Comics also became somewhat more graphic in their depiction of violence and sex, and occasionally the code authority issued memos interpreting the code regulations. One such memo was issued April 13, 1974, and clarified the definitions of "excessive bloodshed and gore" as well as warning publishers about their treatment of sex. Code administrator Leonard Darvin wrote: "Running or dripping blood, or pools of blood, are not permitted. A very small stain around a wound may be acceptable, but must be kept to a minimum. There must be no impression of gore in any areas of objection by governmental and private agencies concerned with children" (CMAA Files [memorandum from Leonard Garvin, 13 Aug. 1974]). The memo also cautioned publishers that the topic of rape was forbidden, that the code prohibited any illustration or dialogue that indicates a sexual act is actually taking place, and that homosexuality or any suggestion of it by illustration, dialogue, or text was strictly forbidden.

Another memo, dealing with the topics of drug addiction, nudity, and alcohol, was issued in 1978. The memo, written by Darvin, noted that stories showing or describing any kind of drugs, including marijuana, had to definitely state or show it being a harmful substance. Publishers were also violating code standards of nudity by submitting artwork that showed nude buttocks or pictured them "so insufficiently covered as to amount to nudity" (CMAA Files [memorandum from Leonard Darvin, 13 Apr. 1974]). Darvin warned publishers that such representations were not allowed under state statutes that legally defined nudity. He also warned against showing the drinking of alcohol and instructed publishers to avoid gratuitous display of signs or scenes showing liquor, beer, or wine.

For the most part, however, the comic book industry of the 1970s resembled that of the 1950s. The superhero had fallen from favor, and it was a time of experimentation as readership declined. The devoted core audience of fans was too small to support the industry, and publishers introduced new genres in an effort to lure new readers. Some of the genres that were tried (with varying degrees of success) were sword-and-sorcery titles such as *Conan the Barbarian,* science fiction, and horror comics. Jacobs and Jones describe the 1970s as "a mad scramble for new ideas that would sell." Of all new comics introduced in the 1970s, half failed in the first ten issues, two-thirds failed by the first fifteen issues, and only seven survived into the 1980s (242).

Rising production costs drove the price of comic books up and out of the price range of many children. In addition, comic books, considered low-yield items, disappeared from drugstores, newsstands, and supermarkets. The two major publishers, Marvel and DC, made changes in corporate management. In 1976, outsider Jenette Kahn, with experience in children's publishing, was named publisher at DC. This appointment was followed by a cutback in the number of titles and a staff reduction. Marvel promoted Jim Shooter to editor-in-chief in 1978. He set out to train new talent in the basics of comic book storytelling and also trimmed titles (Jacobs and Jones 243–44).

The four publishers who remained active in the CMAA during the late 1970s and the 1980s—Archie, Marvel, Harvey, and DC—continued to challenge the need for a code. Marvel president James Galston, at a meeting of the board of directors in October 1976, questioned whether there was any need to continue the use of the seal. Others, however, felt that the seal remained "essential to the viability of the comics magazine industry" (CMAA Files [minutes, 19 Oct. 1976]). Galston's question was spurred in part by changes in the comic book publishing industry that would enable new publishers to bypass the CMAA and its code administrator entirely. Beginning in the late 1970s, an innovation was under way in comic book distribution that was to have tremendous impact on the way comic books were marketed and sold. That innovation was direct market distribution.

Changes in distribution during this period were linked to an earlier change in the industry, the rise of independent publishers. In the 1970s, there was a movement toward independent publishing, which initially served as an outlet for creator-owned properties. Until that time, all of the rights for characters were owned by companies, not by individual writers and artists. New publishing companies were started that allowed creators to retain the rights to their characters. At first, distribution was limited to mail order and a small number of specialty shops, and the profits were not high enough to lure top talent away from the major companies. But by the end of the decade, a proliferation of specialty shops and the emergence of direct market distribution created a market capable of sustaining these independent publishers (Jacobs and Jones 269).

Under the old system, which is still in place and accounts for about one-quarter of all comic book distribution, comic books are distributed by companies that also handle other periodicals and are sold in outlets that carry a variety of magazines. Retailers are able to return unsold copies to the publisher for credit. Under the direct market system, distributors who specialize in comic books and comics-related merchandise solicit orders for upcoming titles and sell comic books directly to retailers on a non-return basis. Their primary customers are comics specialty shops, which pay less for their comics through the direct market system but forfeit the right to return unsold copies. Store owners develop an inventory of back issues that then may be sold to fans and collectors at a later date. The number of specialty stores in the United States increased from an estimated twenty-five in the mid-1970s to between 3,500 and 5,000 by 1990 (Thompson 58).

The number of such stores is hard to estimate because many of these retail outlets were served by more than one distributor, and because distributors protected their customer lists.

As a result of this change in distribution, companies were able to eliminate some of the guesswork involved in production. Under the newsstand distribution system, as many of seven of every ten copies of a comic book were returned to the publisher. Because comic book orders for direct market sales are solicited before the comics are published, publishers know in advance how many copies of each title to print for distribution to specialty shops. Often, companies will print more copies of a particular title than were ordered so they can fill back orders. In addition, distributors may speculate on how well a particular issue of a comic book will sell and purchase more copies than retailers order. Particularly successful comic books may have additional press runs (Salicrup 38).

The new distribution system, which eliminated some of the risk in publishing comics, led to a boom in independent publishing in the 1980s. Independent companies who were early leaders in this trend included Aardvark-Vanaheim, created in 1977 to publish a *Conan* parody entitled *Cerebus;* and WaRP Graphics, started by Richard and Wendi Pini in 1978 to publish their comic, *Elfquest.* The first company to bring out regular-format comics among the independents was Pacific Comics, which published comics from 1981 to 1984. First Comics, started in 1983 in Chicago, was a strong performer in the 1980s before folding. The leading independent company in the early 1990s has been Image Comics, started by a group of creators who capitalized on their popularity with the fan community to produce titles that have outsold many comics marketed by the larger companies. While Marvel and DC still dominate the comic book industry in terms of number of titles, sales figures on their titles have dropped as independents cut into their market. Although some of these independent publishers, like Image, produce professional quality four-color comic books on a monthly schedule and compete successfully with the major publishers, many independent companies publish only one or two books, often on a highly erratic schedule, and the number of such companies fluctuates almost daily as smaller companies are started, merge, or fold.

These independent companies distribute comics only through the direct market system. Bypassing the newsstand distribution system, the enforcement arm of the comics code, these independent publishers do not submit their titles for code approval nor are they members of the Comics

Magazine Association of America. As a result, the CMAA and its code administrator have no say in the content of comic books which make up a significant part of the comic book industry today. It was inevitable that independent companies, freed from the constraints of the comics code, would produce adult-oriented material for the evolving market—which one study suggests has led the industry "once again—but this time not innocently—to confront the adult themes of violence, sexuality and obsession" (McCue and Bloom ix).

Unlike the underground comics, these new independently published comics did represent an economic challenge to the established publishers. And, more important, these comics demonstrated the possibilities of a distribution system that was more open to experimentation and to the expansion of the audience for comics. This paved the way for even the mainstream publishers to opt out of their own prepublication review system to take advantage of new marketing opportunities.

The pressure brought to bear by the change in distribution and the modest success of the independent publishers in the 1980s led to another code revision at the end of the decade. The possibility of revising the code a second time was first raised at a meeting December 17, 1982, when association members were told that the copies of the 1971 code booklet were almost gone. It was suggested that a request for changes, additions, and deletions be circulated before the booklet was sent to the printers. Apparently the publishers felt the current code was adequate, because no changes were incorporated at that time (CMAA Files [minutes, 17 Dec. 1982]). Five years later, the publishers began what would result in a major overhaul of the 1971 comics code.

The association contracted with Wally Green to draft a revised code for the association, to be submitted in April 1987. They provided him with a copy of the old code and the various rules of interpretation circulated to publishers and editors. He was instructed to meet with each publisher to determine what changes were desired. In addition, publishers agreed to provide Green with samples of comics being published (CMAA Files [letter to Wally Green, 9 Feb. 1987]). Green produced a lengthy, detailed revision of the code. The format of the revised code submitted by Green was somewhat different from the 1971 code, and the emphasis on what material would be prohibited reflected the changing nature of the content of comic books. The general preamble was replaced in Green's draft with a statement explaining the need and purpose of a comics code. In it, Green suggested that the comic book had a strong appeal to very young readers and with the advent of adult-oriented comic books, a code and seal was necessary to make sure objectionable material did not find its way into the hands of young children. It also noted that publishers recognized that the very young "do not yet have the protection of a fully-developed standard of ethical conduct or a well-formed set of moral values." The purpose of the comics code was to inspire trust in the industry and to assure parents that comics bearing the seal contained nothing but "wholesome reading pleasure" and that readers would be provided content that is "intellectually stimulating and morally sound."

Green then listed the grounds for finding material objectionable, including unacceptable moral and ethical standards; unacceptable treatment of social and political issues; unacceptable references to religious and racial matters; and general "repugnance." He noted that no categories of subject matter would be expressly forbidden, since such a move would be "dangerous as well as impractical." But, the introduction added, it was important that regulation of content be "clear and precise" so that editors and writers would find them "readily understandable and easy to follow."

The first set of regulations spelled out in Green's draft dealt with issues of sex, reflecting the maturing content of comic books. While total nudity was prohibited, implied nudity in a scene with members of the same sex would be permitted. Partial nudity was permissible under certain circumstances, but genitals, breasts, and buttocks still could not be exposed. The code continued to specify that anatomy should not be emphasized or needlessly displayed. Portrayal of the sex act would still be prohibited under the revised code, but it could be implied, as long as there was no gratuitous reference to the act and no provocative or tantalizing illustration. Promiscuity, homosexuality, and explicit depiction of child molestation were prohibited. In addition, sexual assaults or sadistic attacks with sexual undertones showing women being victimized were not allowed.

The reduced emphasis on crime and horror in Green's draft of the code demonstrates that this area was no longer the major concern of comic book publishers. Depictions of criminal acts would be allowed, so long as the wrongdoers were punished and a life of crime was not shown to be desirable. Public officials could be shown breaking the law as long as respect for the rule of law was upheld. The code still forbade the depiction of methods for committing crimes. Behavior that was reprehensible although not strictly criminal could not be shown to be acceptable. In addition, portraying drug use as pleasant was prohibited, and the code specified that the consequences of drug use must be clearly spelled out in the story. Under the section dealing with religion and prejudice, the code regulations suggested that no faith be shown as superior to another, that deformities and afflictions could not be treated frivolously and ridiculed, and that stories could not suggest such afflictions were "punishment imposed by a divine power."

The section dealing with depictions of violence was labeled "repugnance," and sixteen regulations dealing with violent acts were listed. The draft of the code noted that objections to depictions of violence, death, torture, pain, putrefaction, or extreme ugliness were often a matter of degree, and a key recommendation was restraint. In knife wounds, the point of entry could not be shown. Depicting dismemberment, blows to the skull, or kicks to the genitals was not permitted. Scenes of explicit torture were not permitted, and showing decomposed bodies or parts of bodies was prohibited. A locale that was "loathsome" should not be rendered so as to "revolt or terrorize the reader." Depictions of death were permitted, and blood could be shown; however, free-flowing blood and pools of blood were prohibited. In addition, characters could not be shown drinking blood. Cannibalism was prohibited, and it was not to be inferred that elderly persons, women, or children were fair game for robberies.

Under the language provisions, obscene or sacrilegious language was not permitted, and the Lord's name could not be used as an expletive. The words *hell* and *damn* were not permitted except when used in the literal sense. Language belittling ethnic speech patterns was prohibited, and publishers were warned to stay abreast of "street language" since "new dirty words are quickly added to the lexicon." Publishers were urged to show respect for the English language, using correct spelling and proper grammar when possible. A special section dealing with covers was added because Green believed that covers were a problem for the industry since they have high visibility and were often seen by readers for whom the comic book was not intended. Although covers should meet the code requirements, Green's code also stressed that it was important that the cover not mislead the reader about the contents. There were few changes made to the guidelines governing advertising, since that was an area with which publishers had little difficulty.

The most radical innovation Green introduced in his draft of the code were provisions that would impose standards of political and social "fairness" on writers. His draft called for stories that treated controversial social issues to do so "without bias and give a fair picture of the various sides" in order to demonstrate "respect for the diversity of opinion." In addition, stories were not allowed to "indulge in partisan politics." Green's draft also forbid treating criminal acts such as terrorist bombings or hostage-taking as social problems. Finally, this section forbade writers and artists to portray real people, even if disguised.

In the summary, the code stated that while it was impossible to apply the regulations uniformly due to the diversity of titles, the regulations did allow for the free expression of ideas and imagination. It also recommended that publishers print the following statement in each comic: "_____ Comics pledges to readers and to the parents that the Comics Magazine Association of America Seal of Approval on the cover is your guarantee that no offensive material appears in this book."

Green's new version of the code was much more detailed than what the publishers had in mind. Their response was varied, but none was happy with the changes Green proposed. Gladstone (publisher of the Disney comics) and Archie favored retaining the 1971 code. Although Marvel favored making a few minor changes in the 1971 code, they indicated a willingness to continue under that code. Harvey favored a new or revised code, but did not want to see a version liberalized "to the point of meaninglessness." It also advocated a separate designation for children's comics. DC indicated that it was considering eliminating the code seal from its books entirely and strongly advocated a revised code, calling the present code an embarrassment and a hindrance which restricted the creative talent of artists and writers. DC was pushing for a simple statement of key guidelines that were broad in scope.

Green's version of the code, with its specific guidelines, was rejected by the publishers, who then set out to rewrite the code by appointing an editorial task force of industry insiders to the task. The final version of the new code incorporated the suggestion made by DC to publish a general code as a "public document" and then issue a "working document" that would be circulated among editors, writers, and artists. In the two-part document, the first part was labeled "Principles of the Comics Code Authority" and was designed for dissemination to the general public. The second part, "Editorial Guidelines," was meant as an internal working document for publishers. It was adopted in 1989 (CMAA Files [memorandum from J. Dudley Waldner, executive director, 12 Apr. 1988]).

The format of the 1989 code was much different from the 1971 version (see CMAA Code 1989). There was still a preamble, which acknowledged that comic book publishers were committed to providing "decent and wholesome comic books as entertainment for children." It also promised that comics carrying the seal would be titles "that a parent can purchase with confidence that the contents uphold basic American moral and cultural values." Following the preamble were seven sections providing general statements on institutions, language, violence, characterization, substance abuse, crime, and attire and sexuality. The "principles" of the code also outlined the administrative procedure followed by the code office. Some of the provisions of the 1971 code and the revision drafted by Green were incorporated into these general statements, but the specific lists of what was and was not allowed were eliminated.

The second part of the 1989 code was the unpublished editorial guidelines given to all publishers, editors, and artists. The CMAA has forbidden its members to distribute the contents of these editorial guidelines to "nonmembers of the Comics Magazine Association of America or to members of the press or general public." For each of the seven sections listed in the "principles" section of the code, a corresponding "specific guidelines" section was issued. For example, the general statement concerning institutions and individuals specifies that "recognizable social, cultural, political, ethnic, racial and religious institutions, persuasions and authorities will be portrayed in a positive light." Under the specific guidelines issued to artists, writers, and editors, these are defined as including government, law enforcement agencies, the military, known religious organizations, ethnic agencies such as the NAACP, and foreign leaders. In dealing with sex, the general statement adopted by the CMAA specifies that relationships will be presented with "good taste, sensitivity, and in a manner which will be generally considered to be acceptable by a mass audience." The specific guidelines suggest: "Writers and editors should ask themselves, 'Is this story suitable for a seven-year-old whose parent is going to let the child select any comic with the Code Seal?' and 'Will the parent continue to let the child select any comic with the Code Seal?'"

This definition of audience is central to the ongoing debate over the content of comic books. In order to compete with the independent publishers, Marvel and DC had developed their own lines of adult-oriented, noncode comics intended for distribution to comics specialty stores through direct-market sales. Although the first draft of the code prepared in late

1988 made a distinction between the requirements for code-approved comic books intended for adult consumption and those comics intended for children, the final version of the code rejected that distinction and specified that all code-approved books would have to meet standards acceptable for a mass audience. The publishers decided the code seal of approval would be used to indicate to parents that the content of any comic book carrying the seal would be acceptable to parents, much like the "G" rating of the film code. Comic books targeted for the older audience would remain non-code approved (CMAA Files [memorandum from J. Dudley Waldner, 3 Feb. 1989]).

There was some concern over how to publicize the latest revision of the code. The association members agreed that the revision should be explained as a measure undertaken "to give the code a more contemporary wording and interpretation." Rather than seeking simply to implement the code without any announcement, the publishers decided to announce the code but to be careful not to imply that it was "a major, or earthshaking, change" (CMAA Files [memorandum from J. Dudley Waldner, 12 Apr. 1988]). Their strategy worked: the implementation of the code received no attention outside of the fan press.

In the mid-1990s, Archie, DC, and Marvel comics form the backbone of the CMAA. The companies voluntarily submit titles they wish to carry the code seal of approval to the CMAA's Comics Code Authority office. In addition, nonmembers are allowed to submit titles for prepublication review; the CMAA charges a $500 fee for each nonmember title reviewed. Each publisher pays a membership fee, based in part on the number of titles it releases per month. Since 1979, the CMAA has contracted with an organization that specializes in managing trade associations to oversee the programs of the CMAA, including the Comics Code Authority. Such an arrangements allows the CMAA to draw on the expertise provided by specialists in trade association management and also to share expenses with the other clients of the management company. The firm charges a yearly "management fee" and the CMAA splits the cost of renting office space with other clients.

One person serves as both the CMAA executive secretary and code administrator. In 1994, Holly Munter was serving in that capacity (Munter interview). She reviewed between 125 and 150 comic books a month for member publishers. While Munter did most of the reviewing herself, occasionally other staff members at the management company office were called upon to assist her. While neither Munter nor other staff members had a background in the comic book industry, she stressed that the most significant requirement for the job was to have a thorough understanding of the code guidelines and administrative procedures.

Major problems with code standards are rare, primarily because the editors are aware of the code provisions and screen the titles they edit at all stages of production to eliminate any problems. The review begins with the initial stage of production, the plotting and scripting of the comic book. When the script is sent to the penciller, editors make notes reminding the artist about restrictions on rendering certain scenes. Members of the creative team can also bring potential problems to the attention of the editor. In many cases, it is assumed that the creative team is familiar with the restrictions of the code and their own company's policies (Cavalieri and Morra interview).

Different companies submit their titles for review at different stages in the production process, but the office always works with black-and-white photocopies of the original art. The code administrator is expected to read the comic book and examine the artwork to determine if anything on the cover, in the book itself, or in the advertising violates code standards. It may take longer to review some titles than others due to the amount of dialogue or the complexity of the artwork, but in general it takes the code authority office about a week to complete the review. If a particular title is running behind schedule, however, the process can be completed in a day (Munter interview). Publishers are on the "honor system" concerning changes mandated by the Code Authority; artwork is not re-reviewed prior to publication. There is no formal penalty for comic book publishers who fail to make the changes recommended by the code office. The code office does monitor compliance by examining the completed comic books sent directly to the CMAA office by the members' printers.

Changes mandated by the code office are open to negotiation, and the formal appeal process is never invoked, simply because there is not time for such a process. Usually, if a panel or a page is "bounced" and the editor disagrees with the code administrator, the situation is resolved with a telephone call. In most cases, the changes asked for by the code office are made. Sometimes the publisher will decide not to make the changes and elect to publish the book without the seal, withdrawing it from newsstand distribution, but that does not happen often (Munter interview). If changes are required, they are usually made in-house because of deadline concerns, rather than being made by the creative team. Changes are generally done by putting a "patch" over the original artwork. That way, the artist can remove the change when the original artwork is returned to him or her (Cavalieri and Morra interview).

Perhaps one of the most significant changes in the industry is that not all comic books pass through this prepublication review process. In the 1989 code, the publishers acknowledged that even members of the CMAA have elected to publish non-code comics, including titles intended for adult readers. But the CMAA members agreed that such comics should not be distributed on the newsstand but only through direct distribution markets, since newsstand outlets "are serviced by individuals who are unaware of the content of specific publications before placing them on display." As noted above, this gave mainstream publishers the option of bypassing the strict code regulations in order to publish comics for a broader audience.

However, it is important to recognize that such a system allows publishers to abdicate their responsibility and shift the burden of monitoring content to the retailer. While some publishers have included warnings about content with labels such as "For mature readers," many adult comics carry no warning at all. This means the retailer ordering and displaying comics needs to be familiar with the content of all the comic books he or she carries and to make sure that inappropriate material does not fall into the wrong hands. It is a rather dangerous assumption to make that all retailers will be conscientious about reviewing and displaying the material they sell, and the strategy backfired on the industry when local officials began to investigate and arrest comic book retailers under obscenity statutes.

One case that generated a great deal of alarm was the arrest and conviction of a sales clerk at a comic book store in Lansing, Illinois. He was found guilty of intent to disseminate obscene material under Illinois law in January 1988, although that decision was overturned on appeal in 1989. While most such cases eventually are decided in favor of the retailer, the time and expense involved in legal battles have a chilling effect on retailers who might otherwise support alternative comics.

One response to this problem has been the creation of the Comic Book Legal Defense Fund, started by Denis Kitchen of Kitchen Sink Press. The CBLDF is a nonprofit group that aids retailers in fighting obscenity charges. The group is supported by donations and fundraising events often held in conjunction with comic book conventions. Many retailers, however, are not willing to go to the time and expense of a court battle. Much as retailers in the 1950s bowed to pressure from the Catholic National Organization for Decent Literature and from local law enforcement agencies, owners of comic book retail stores today, warned by police or challenged by irate parents, simply remove the offensive material from their shelves.

From this brief overview of the operation of the Comics Code Authority today, it is clear that the procedure put in place by the publishers in 1954 remains relatively intact. Revisions of the code in 1971 and again in 1989 reflected the changing nature of society, of the industry, and of the audience, and each new version of the code has loosened restrictions placed on the content of comic books. The process of prepublication review remains essentially the same. What has changed is the size of the staff, the number of titles reviewed, and the specific provisions of the code. The most important change, however, is not in the code itself, but in the industry's willingness to set aside the code. The underlying principle of the industry's program of self-regulation is the idea that the seal of approval carried on the cover of a comic book means that it contains nothing offensive and is appropriate for readers of all ages. By sidestepping the code, publishers have acknowledged for the first time that comic books are not just for children.

Conclusion

The Significance of the Code Today

From the beginning, the comic book controversy was constructed around children. For educators and librarians, the comic book was a threat to adult authority over children's reading and their leisure time; after the war, the comic book became a threat to adult authority in maintaining law and order. In both instances, the child audience was justification for taking action against comic books, as well as other mass media. Even with a lack of evidence proving that mass media sex and violence had harmful effects on children, common sense dictated that a steady diet of such material simply could not be good for young minds. Protection of children made a strong case for both community and political action. In cities across the United States, decency campaigns organized by church groups, civic organizations, and women's groups targeted local retailers. Threats of a boycott were usually enough to encourage shop owners to remove materials deemed offensive. Politicians, too, found the comic book crusade a worthy cause and launched investigations at the state and federal level, threatening to pass legislation censoring comic books. These investigations accomplished little in the way of legislation, but they quite effectively generated enough negative publicity to force the comic book publishers into action.

Psychiatrist Fredric Wertham played a pivotal role in focusing national attention on comic books and juvenile delinquency. Wertham brought to the crusade a lifelong interest in social influences on violent behavior, suggesting that intervention at the social, not the individual, level was the most effective way to deal with problems such as juvenile delinquency. Far from being a naive social scientist with a simplistic cause-and-effect model of media effects, Wertham fits more into the tradition of the Frankfurt School and its critique of mass culture. In fact, Wertham dismissed social science methodology, instead developing the "clinical method" of taking detailed case histories, which he believed was the only way of truly understanding the longitudinal impact of media effects. Because his medical colleagues rejected his call for the development of social psychiatry, he took his campaign for social reform to the public, capitalizing on the comic book controversy as a way of furthering his agenda for addressing issues of violence in society.

This revisionist history of Wertham should not be misinterpreted as an attempt to glorify his actions. Despite his efforts to frame the debate over comic books as a mental health issue, the legislation he pushed for was clearly censorship. In addition, he used comic books as a way to advance his social agenda, recognizing that a medium perceived by the public as catering to children—one that had little legitimacy as a literary or artistic form—would make an easy target. Most of the arguments he made about comic books and violence could have been applied to film or television, but those media were much less vulnerable to attack. By the time he wrote *Seduction of the Innocent,* Wertham made no attempt at neutrality. His loathing of the comic book medium and the industry that produced it was evident in his writing, and he skillfully manipulated public opinion with carefully selected anecdotal material and examples. But it is important to recognize that much of the condemnation of Wertham has been based on erroneous assumptions about his views and his methodology.

The adoption of a comics code and the appointment of a "czar" to oversee its implementation and enforcement was, in Wertham's eyes, a victory for the comic book industry. He was right. The code proved to be an effective public relations move, silencing most of the critics without substantially changing the structure of the industry. Modeled after the film code, the comics code targeted all material that could possibly be considered offensive, going beyond the regulation of crime and horror comics to mandate that comics should reflect dominant American values. The main impact of the code, beyond restricting the type of material that could be published, was that it forced the reorganization of the industry. Publishers of the crime and horror comics restricted or outlawed under the new code either had to adapt or to go out of business, and many did fold. The major problem faced by the survivors had less to do with the code and more to do with increasing competition for children's leisure time from television and with a crisis brought about by antitrust action against the industry's major distributor. Many scholars have argued that the code nearly destroyed the comic book industry. This simply is not true. The comics code, along with changing business conditions, resulted in a number of established companies, along with the more marginal publishers, closing their doors, but there was never any real danger that comic books would cease to exist.

Had the industry chosen to ride out the controversy over content, it is possible that much of the fervor over comics would have died down as the public turned its attention to other matters. But such defiance would have been difficult under the circumstances. William Gaines's proposal to hire researchers in an effort to prove scientifically that there were no ill effects from reading comic books seems logical, but unfortunately, such evidence most likely would have been dismissed by the public in much the same way that educators and parents rejected earlier academic research that demonstrated comic books had little effect on reading development in children. Further, comic book distribution depended on the goodwill of retailers. While publishers might have been able to insulate themselves from their critics and continue to publish what they wished, the retailers were on the front lines. They were the targets of boycotts and were subject to arrest under any laws that were passed making the sale of objectionable comics to minors illegal, even if such arrests were eventually thrown out on constitutional grounds. Publishers were justified in pursuing self-regulation as a solution to the comic book controversy.

However, the code could have acknowledged that not all comics should be suitable for children. Had the Motion Picture Association of America code been in place in the 1950s, rather than the earlier Film Production Code, the comics code might have been much different. The code was literally thrown together almost overnight, with little thought about the long-range impact such a document would have. A more thoughtful, less hurried approach to the problem might have resulted in a more visionary structure for the code based on the idea there should be different rating categories depending on the intended audience. Such a code would have paved the way for the comic book industry to cater to its child audience while at the same time considering ways it could expand its market to encompass older adolescents and young adults to help stem the loss of its audience to television.

Instead, the code represented a tacit agreement with the critics. The lasting legacy of the comics code has been the comic book industry's acquiescence to defining the comic book as a form of entertainment solely for children and the reinforcement of that perception in the minds of the public. Such limitations, many have argued, were a major setback in the development of the comic book. This argument that the comics code had a negative effect on the creative growth of the medium is more difficult to assess than the code's influence on the industry. While the focus of this study has been the code's impact on publishing, no discussion of the code would be complete without an attempt to address the issue of the comics code's effect on the comic book itself. Even without a systematic study of pre-code and post-code comic books, it is obvious that adoption of a self-regulatory code changed comic book content. Gone were the gruesome horror comics. In their place, historians note, were stories featuring the supernatural, emphasizing suspense over terror (Benton *Horror Comics* 53–55; Sabin 165). With vampires and werewolves banned under the code, writers and artists began to borrow the giant monsters of the movies, such as Godzilla and The Blob (Benton, *Horror Comics* 57). While the code did not forbid crime comics, the urban crime story became a thing of the past under the new code regulations (Williams 66). Instead, the genre shifted to detective mysteries or focused on police stories patterned after popular television series (Sabin 166).

It is difficult to say what would have happened to crime and horror comics if there had never been a comics code. By the time the code went into effect, sales of crime comics had already begun to decline. It is possible that horror comics, then at their peak, would have decreased in popularity as well, to be replaced by other genres—a pattern typical in popular culture in general, as evidenced by the rise and fall of the western in film and on television, for example. In fact, horror comics enjoyed a brief resurgence during the 1970s after the first revision of the code, but this resurgence was short lived. While the Silver Age heroes stepped into the vacuum left by the departure of the horror comics, their rebirth was due as much to the rise of a new generation of artists raised on the Golden Age superheroes and their desire to recreate the characters of their youth as it was to the demise of the horror genre. It is likely that the coming of the new superhero titles would have displaced many of the surviving horror and crime comics.

The biggest impact that the code has had on the content of comic books was the maintenance of the superhero comic as the dominant genre in the years following the code's adoption. The code discourages experimentation with its strict prohibitions on subject matter; as a result, the super-hero comic, the staple of the industry, is reworked in endless variations that seldom pose a challenge to the code or to public perception of the medium (Williams 66). Another factor, of course, is that the superhero has been a successful (and profitable) formula, and established companies prefer to remain with the tried-and-true rather than take risks with more innovative material. This fact is typical of media producers in general, not just comic book publishers.

Much more damaging to the creative development of the comic book than the restrictions on crime and horror comics was the code's insistence that all comics published adhere to a rigid value structure that forbid any challenge to authority. Under the 1954 comics code, there was a unified view in the world of comic books, one in which social institutions and authority figures were always benign in their concern with upholding traditional values and in which rebellion against the "establishment" was nearly impossible. Without the freedom to question the status quo, comic book content remained for the most part quite innocuous. This innocuousness was not an issue with most critics, who rejected the notion that comic books could contribute to any meaningful exchange of ideas. One of the few groups to speak out for the potential of comic books was the American Civil Liberties Union. They actually favored legislation over industry regulation (ACLU 6–8). The group argued in a pamphlet published in 1955 that postpublication punishment based on laws at least allowed for the due process of law and a jury that reflected a community's taste. Prior censorship, in the form of a prepublication review process, concentrated power in the hands of the few with no legal recourse. Industry codes, the ACLU argued, inevitably have the effect of inhibiting the free expression of ideas: "Collective adherence to a single set of principles in a code has the effect of limiting different points of view, because individual publishers—as well as writers—are fearful of departing from the accepted norm lest they be held up to scorn or attack and suffer economic loss" (7).

But publishers in the 1950s had little interest in protecting comic books as a medium of self-expression. Their motivations were primarily economic. Since the beginning, comic book publishing had focused on production, not creation. In the early days of comic books, companies did not hire their own writers and artists. Instead, they contracted with a number of shops set up to provide creative services to the publishers. Writers and artists churned out pages of material in a factory system in which each task, from drawing the figures and the backgrounds to inking to lettering the word balloons, was carried out by someone different. There was no creator controlling the product. The goal was quantity, not quality (McAllister 59). Even after comic book companies dispensed with the services of such "shops" and began to assemble in-house staffs and later to contract the work out to free-lance artists, the collaborative nature of production precluded any recognition of the individual roles in the creative process. The publishers owned the rights to the characters and kept the finished artwork. Much as the film industry had resisted the star system, the comic book industry wanted its creative talent to be largely interchangeable. As a result, there was no creative "voice" to speak up against the adoption of a comics code in the mid-1950s.

This situation began to change with the advent of the direct distribution system, supported by an increasingly influential fan market. In fact, the rise of the direct market has had far more impact on both the creative development of comic books and on industry practices than the code has ever had. As Roger Sabin notes, the institution of direct sales changed relationships between the industry and the creators and between the industry and the fans (66–68). Independent publishers, in order to lure popular artists and writers away from the larger companies, began to offer royalties and copyright control. This, in turn, allowed top-selling creators to break free of the work-for-hire system, using their new bargaining power to push for greater flexibility in their choice and presentation of subject matter and to experiment with new techniques, such as painting rather than drawing both the cover and interior artwork. The fans, who had been able to build collections of comics through the purchase of the unsold "back copies" that became part of the inventory of the specialty shops, began to parlay their hobby into an investment. They searched for old comics in top condition to complete their collections and began to speculate on which newer comics would increase in value, buying multiple copies of comic books. The industry responded to what Sabin terms this new "fan capitalism" by producing limited editions of comics with special covers and other gimmicks to encourage multiple-copy buying. These fan-collectors became the driving force behind comic book publishing, creating a boom in the 1980s.

As noted in the last chapter, these changes led the major publishers to revamp the comics code in 1989 and for the first time to acknowledge that there was a place in the market for the non-code comic. The major publishers still supported the code and submitted most of their titles for pre-publication review, so much of the output of the industry was still governed by the code. Shifting sales of comics from newsstand distribution to specialty shops significantly weakened the enforcement mechanism of the code, however, since distribution and sales were no longer tied to compliance with the code standards. The result is that today, the industry's output is divided into two distinct categories: on the one hand, code-approved comics that adhere to strict regulations concerning the use of language, nudity, sexual situations, and excessive violence, designed for an audience that fits with the public perception of what a comic book is; and on the other, non-code comic books, many produced by small, independent publishers, that seek to challenge the way in which the medium has been defined.

While the direct market may have been good for the aesthetic development of comic books, allowing them to escape the constraints of the code, encouraging experimentation with new techniques and subject matter, and giving the creators more control over content and form, the benefits for the industry are less clear, for two reasons. First, in 1995 the distribution system that had served the market so well in the 1970s and 1980s went through a major reorganization that sent shock waves through the industry; and second, there was a backlash by fans against what were increasing perceived as manipulative marketing techniques.

The direct market was served by a number of distributors, including the two major companies, Diamond Distributors, based in Maryland, and Capital City Comics, located in Wisconsin. In December 1994, Marvel announced it was acquiring the third largest distributor, Heroes World Distribution Company, and shortly after that, decided that Heroes World would distribute Marvel products exclusively. Since the distribution of Marvel comics made up a significant portion of the business for distributors, there was an immediate scramble among the remaining distributors to sign other publishers to exclusive contracts. Diamond Distributors announced in April 1995 that it had reached such an agreement with DC Comics. Capital City Distribution sued both Marvel and DC under the Wisconsin Fair Dealership law, settling out of court for an undisclosed amount, but eventually bowed to the inevitable and closed its doors. In 1997, Marvel shut down Heroes World, leaving Diamond Distribution with a near-monopoly in direct-market distribution. There are both economic and creative ramifications from this arrangement. The discounts offered by Diamond are not nearly as large now that there is less competition for business, and many have predicted that a number of specialty stores operating on an already slim profit margin will eventually be driven out of business. Perhaps less obvious is the impact on the creative growth of the medium. There are, operating in the margins of the industry, individuals who self-publish. Until now, these individuals could sometimes persuade a distributor to offer their titles through the direct market, even though sales would be insignificant compared to the titles published by the larger companies. One example is Kevin Eastman and Peter Laird, creators of the *Teenage Mutant Ninja Turtles,* a title that began as a small self-published comic but went on to become one of the industry's best known success stories. While one could argue that Eastman and Laird's success had little impact on the creative growth of the medium, it does demonstrate the possibilities when non-mainstream material is allowed access to an audience. But Diamond has little incentive to offer such marginal titles to its retail outlets, effectively shutting out the smaller creator from the distribution system. While comic book conventions and mail-order distribution are alternatives for these publishers, wider dissemination of their work is nearly impossible without support from the distributors.

The second factor, the fan backlash, has resulted in a decease in sales on titles whose circulation numbers were artificially inflated by the marketing gimmicks employed by publishers. This downturn has renewed the industry's interest in opening up new markets for comic books. One attempt to market outside fandom was the "creation" of the graphic novel (Sabin 86). In the late 1980s, the publication of three titles—*Maus, Batman Returns,* and *Watchmen*—caught the fancy of the mainstream press, and journalists unfamiliar with the industry heralded them "as constituting a new and historically unique trend" (93). Publishers capitalized on this notion of a "new breed" of comics to cultivate a new outlet for comics: bookstores (94). But as comics attempted to make the transition from "comics culture" to "book culture," the "graphic" element of the graphic novel was left behind. As Sabin notes, graphic novels were reviewed in book sections, writers were profiled rather than artists, and the quality of writing was held in higher esteem than the quality of artwork. In short, the co-option of comic books by literary interests was doomed to failure because, as Sabin writes, "it served to remake comics in prose literature's image" (247). The bookstores' interest waned and graphic novels began to disappear from shelves.

If the graphic novel is not the solution, what is? And what does all this have to do with the comics code? The answer to these two questions is related. Many of the outlets for comics in the 1950s, such the corner drug store or grocery store, are gone, replaced by chain stores that have little interest in handling a large volume of comic book business. Many involved in comic book publishing and sales agree, however, that the comic book industry must expand beyond its core fan audience. There has been a lot of debate about the best way to achieve this goal, but whatever method is used, the industry must find a way to make the comic book more "mainstream." The comic book will never again be a "mass" medium in the truest sense of the word, but enhancing its visibility outside of the limited audience that now exists is necessary if new readers are to be introduced to the medium. There are risks involved, however, in moving beyond the specialized audience and reaching out to new readers. For example, in 1989, Joe Queenan wrote an article for the *New York Times Magazine* titled "Drawing on the Dark Side." In his article, Queenan noted that while journalists have written reams about the new "avant-garde" maturity of comic books, "what seems to have escaped attention is that over the last decade, comics have forsaken campy repartee and outlandishly byzantine plots for a steady diet of remorseless violence" (32). He wrote that a host of superhero titles that are generally unknown to the public but "are far more popular within the comic book-subculture" offer heavy doses of sex and violence (34). He suggested: "In many ways, the comics industry seems to be playing with the same fire that nearly destroyed it in the early 1950s" (79).

If the comic book becomes more visible, it also will be more vulnerable to such outside criticism. The adoption of a new television rating system by that industry in 1997 after government pressure, stemming from protests about violence and sex on television, demonstrates that the issue of media content is an enduring one. The comics code, while it has helped perpetuate the idea that comics are a children's medium, also protects the industry from a public that perceives comics as strictly juvenile fare by continuing to designate certain titles as appropriate for readers of all ages. Retaining the comics code, in some form, is a defensive mechanism that publishers cannot yet afford to abandon; until the comic book is able to recreate itself as a legitimate art form and change the public perception of it as juvenile entertainment, the seal of approval will remain a necessity.

Association of Comics Magazine Publishers
Comics Code
1948

The Association of Comics Magazine Publishers, realizing its responsibility to the millions of readers of comics magazines and to the public generally, urges its members and others to publish comics magazines containing only good, wholesome entertainment or education, and in no event include in any magazine comics that may in any way lower the moral standards of those who read them. In particular:

1. Sexy, wanton comics should not be published. No drawing should show a female indecently or unduly exposed, and in no event more nude than in a bathing suit commonly worn in the United States of America.

2. Crime should not be presented in such a way as to throw sympathy against law and justice or to inspire others with the desire for imitation. No comics shall show the details and methods of a crime committed by a youth. Policemen, judges, Government officials, and respected institutions should not be portrayed as stupid or ineffective, or represented in such a way as to weaken respect for established authority.

3. No scenes of sadistic torture should be shown.

4. Vulgar and obscene language should never be used. Slang should be kept to a minimum and used only when essential to the story.

5. Divorce should not be treated humorously nor represented as glamorous or alluring.

6. Ridicule or attack on any religious or racial group is never permissible.

Comics Magazine Association of America
Comics Code
1954

CODE FOR EDITORIAL MATTER

General Standards Part A

1. Crimes shall never be presented in such a way as to create sympathy for the criminal, to promote distrust of the forces of law and justice, or to inspire others with a desire to imitate criminals.

2. No comics shall explicitly present the unique details and methods of a crime.

3. Policemen, judges, government officials and respected institutions shall never be presented in such a way as to create disrespect for established authority.

4. If crime is depicted it shall be as a sordid and unpleasant activity.

5. Criminals shall not be presented so as to be rendered glamorous or to occupy a position which creates a desire for emulation.

6. In every instance good shall triumph over evil and the criminal punished for his misdeeds.

7. Scenes of excessive violence shall be prohibited. Scenes of brutal torture, excessive and unnecessary knife and gun play, physical agony, gory and gruesome crime shall be eliminated.

8. No unique or unusual methods of concealing weapons shall be shown.

9. Instances of law enforcement officers dying as a result of a criminal's activities should be discouraged.

10. The crime of kidnapping shall never be portrayed in any detail, nor shall any profit accrue to the abductor or kidnapper. The criminal or the kidnapper must be punished in every case.

11. The letters of the word "Crime" on a comics magazine cover shall never be appreciably greater in dimension than the other words contained in the title. The word "crime" shall never appear alone on a cover.

12. Restraint in the use of the world "crime" in titles or sub-titles should be exercised.

General Standards Part B

1. No comic magazine shall use the word horror or terror in its title.

2. All scenes of horror, excessive bloodshed, gory or gruesome crimes, depravity, lust, sadism, masochism shall not be permitted.

3. All lurid, unsavory, gruesome illustrations shall be eliminated.

4. Inclusion of stories dealing with evil shall be used or shall be published only where the intent is to illustrate a moral issue and in no case shall evil be presented alluringly nor so as to injure the sensibilities of the reader.

5. Scenes dealing with, or instruments associated with walking dead, torture, vampires and vampirism, ghouls, cannibalism and werewolfism are prohibited.

General Standards Part C

All elements or techniques not specifically mentioned herein, but which are contrary to the spirit and intent of the Code, and are considered violations of good taste or decency, shall be prohibited.

DIALOGUE

1. Profanity, obscenity, smut, vulgarity, or words or symbols which have acquired undesirable meanings are forbidden.

2. Special precautions to avoid references to physical afflictions or deformities shall be taken.

3. Although slang and colloquialisms are acceptable, excessive use should be discouraged and wherever possible good grammar shall be employed.

RELIGION

Ridicule or attack on any religious or racial group is never permissible.

COSTUME

1. Nudity in any form is prohibited, as is indecent or undue exposure.

2. Suggestive and salacious illustration or suggestive posture is unacceptable.

3. All characters shall be depicted in dress reasonably acceptable to society.

4. Females shall be drawn realistically without exaggeration of any physical qualities.

NOTE: It should be recognized that all prohibitions dealing with costume, dialogue or artwork applies as specifically to the cover of a comic magazine as they do to the contents.

Marriage and Sex

1. Divorce shall not be treated humorously nor represented as desirable.

2. Illicit sex relations are neither to be hinted at nor portrayed. Violent love scenes as well as sexual abnormalities are unacceptable.

3. Respect for parents, the moral code, and for honorable behavior shall be fostered. A sympathetic understanding of the problems of love is not a license for morbid distortion.

4. The treatment of love-romance stories shall emphasize the value of the home and the sanctity of marriage.

5. Passion or romantic interest shall never be treated in such a way as to stimulate the lower and baser emotions.

7. Sex perversion or any inference [*sic*] to same is strictly forbidden.

Code for Advertising Matter

These regulations are applicable to all magazines published by the members of the Comics Magazine Association of America, Inc. Good taste shall be the guiding principle in the acceptance of advertising.

1. Liquor and tobacco advertising is not acceptable.

2. Advertisement of sex or sex instruction books are unacceptable.

3. The sale of picture postcards, "pin-ups" "art studies," or any other reproduction of nude or semi-nude figures is prohibited.

4. Advertising for the sale of knives, concealable weapons or realistic gun facsimiles is prohibited.

5. Advertising for the sale of fireworks is prohibited.

6. Advertising dealing with the sale of gambling equipment or printed matter dealing with gambling shall not be accepted.

7. Nudity with meretricious purpose and salacious posture shall not be permitted in the advertising of any product; clothed figures shall never be presented in such a way as to be offensive or contrary to good taste or morals.

8. To the best of his ability, each publisher shall ascertain that all statements made in advertisements conform to fact and avoid misinterpretation.

9. Advertisement of medical, health, or toiletry products of questionable nature are to be rejected. Advertisements for medical, health or toiletry products endorsed by the American Medical Association, or the American Dental Association, shall be deemed acceptable if they conform with all other conditions of the Advertising Code.

Comics Magazine Association of America
Comics Code
1971

Originally adopted in 1954, and revised in 1971 to meet contemporary standards of conduct and morality, the enforcement of this code is the basis for the comic magazine industry's program of self-regulation.

PREAMBLE

The comics magazine, or as it is more popularly known, the comic book medium, having come of age on the American cultural scene, must measure up to its responsibilities.

Constantly improving techniques and higher standards go hand in hand with these responsibilities.

To make a positive contribution to contemporary life, the industry must seek new areas for developing sound, wholesome entertainment. The people responsible for writing, drawing, printing, publishing and selling comic books have done a commendable job in the past, and have been striving toward this goal.

Their record of progress and continuing improvement compares favorably with other media. An outstanding example is the development of comic books as a unique and effective tool for instruction and education. Comic books have also made their contribution in the field of social commentary and criticism of contemporary life.

Members of the industry must see to it that gains made in this medium are not lost and that violations of standards of good taste, which might tend toward corruption of the comic book as an instructive and wholesome form of entertainment, will not be permitted.

Therefore, the Comics Magazine Association of America, Inc., has adopted this Code, and placed its enforcement in the hands of an independent Code Authority.

Further, members of the Association have endorsed the purpose and spirit of this code as a vital instrument to the growth of the industry.

To this end, they have pledged themselves to conscientiously adhere to its principles and to abide by all decisions based on the Code made by the Administrator.

CODE FOR EDITORIAL MATTER

General Standards — Part A

1. Crimes shall never be presented in such a way as to promote distrust of the forces of law and justice, or to inspire others with a desire to imitate criminals.

2. No comics shall explicitly present the unique details and methods of a crime, with the exception of those crimes that are so far-fetched or pseudo-scientific that no would-be lawbreaker could reasonably duplicate.

3. Policemen, judges, government officials and respected institutions shall not be presented in such a way as to create disrespect for established authority. If any of these is depicted committing an illegal act, it must be declared as an exceptional case and that the culprit pay the legal price.

4. If crime is depicted it shall be as a sordid and unpleasant activity.

5. Criminals shall not be presented in glamorous circumstances, unless an unhappy end results from their ill-gotten gains, and creates no desire for emulation.

6. In every instance good shall triumph over evil and the criminal punished for his misdeeds.

7. Scenes of excessive violence shall be prohibited. Scenes of brutal torture, excessive and unnecessary knife and gun play, physical agony, gory and gruesome crime shall be eliminated.

8. No unique or unusual methods of concealing weapons shall be shown, except where such concealment could not reasonably be duplicated.

9. Instances of law enforcement officers dying as a result of a criminal's activities should be discouraged, except when the guilty, because of their crime, live a sordid existence and are brought to justice because of the particular crime.

10. The crime of kidnapping shall never be portrayed in any detail, nor shall any profit accrue to the abductor or kidnapper. The criminal or the kidnapper must be punished in every case.

11. The letters of the word "crime" on a comics magazine cover shall never be appreciably greater in dimension than the other words contained in the title. The word "crime" shall never appear alone on a cover.

12. Restraint in the use of the word "crime" in titles or subtitles shall be exercised.

General Standards — Part B

1. No comic magazine shall use the word horror or terror in its title. These words may be used judiciously in the body of the magazine. (The Board of Directors has ruled that a judicious use does not include the words "horror" or "terror" in story titles within the magazine.)

2. All scenes of horror, excessive bloodshed, gory or gruesome crimes, depravity, lust, sadism, masochism shall not be permitted.

3. All lurid, unsavory, gruesome illustrations shall be eliminated.

4. Inclusion of stories dealing with evil shall be used or shall be published only where the intent is to illustrate a moral issue and in no case shall evil be presented alluringly nor so as to injure the sensibilities of the reader.

5. Scenes dealing with, or instruments associated with walking dead or torture shall not be used. Vampires, ghouls and werewolves shall be permitted to be used when handled in the classic tradition such as Frankenstein, Dracula and other high calibre literary works written by Edgar Allen Poe, Saki (H.H. Munro), Conan Doyle and other respected authors whose works are read in schools throughout the world.

6. Narcotics or Drug addiction shall not be presented except as a vicious habit.

Narcotics or Drug addiction or the illicit traffic in addiction-producing narcotics or drugs shall not be shown or described if the presentation:

a. tends in any manner to encourage, stimulate or justify the use of such narcotics or drugs; or

b. stresses, visually, by text or dialogue, their temporarily attractive effects; or

c. suggests that the narcotics or drug habit may be quickly or easily broken; or

d. shows or describes details of narcotics or drug procurement, or the implements or devices used in taking narcotics or drugs, or of the taking of narcotics or drugs in any manner; or

e. emphasizes the profits of the narcotics or drug traffic; or

f. involves children who are shown knowingly to use or traffic in narcotics or drugs; or

g. shows or implies a casual attitude towards the taking of narcotics or drugs; or

h. emphasizes the taking of narcotics or drugs throughout, or in a major part, of the story, and leaves the denouement to the final panels.

General Standards—Part C

All elements or techniques not specifically mentioned herein, but which are contrary to the spirit and intent of the Code, and are considered violations of good taste or decency, shall be prohibited.

DIALOGUE

1. Profanity, obscenity, smut, vulgarity, or words or symbols which have acquired undesirable meanings—judged and interpreted in terms of contemporary standards—are prohibited.

2. Special precautions to avoid disparaging references to physical afflictions or deformities shall be taken.

3. Although slang and colloquialisms are acceptable, excessive use should be discouraged and wherever possible good grammar shall be employed.

RELIGION

1. Ridicule or attack on any religious or racial group is never permissible.

COSTUME

1. Nudity in any form is prohibited. Suggestive and salacious illustration is unacceptable.

2. Females shall be drawn realistically without undue emphasis on any physical quality.

MARRIAGE AND SEX

1. Divorce shall not be treated humorously nor represented as desirable.

2. Illicit sex relations are not to be portrayed and sexual abnormalities are unacceptable.

3. All situations dealing with the family unit should have as their ultimate goal the protection of the children and family life. In no way shall the breaking of the moral code be depicted as rewarding.

4. Rape shall never be shown or suggested. Seduction may not be shown.
5. Sex perversion or any inference to same is strictly forbidden.

CODE FOR ADVERTISING MATTER

(Remains unchanged from the 1954 version)

Comics Magazine Association of America
Comics Code
1989

PREAMBLE

The Comics Magazine Association of America was formed in 1954 by a group of publishers committed to the principle that the public deserved decent and wholesome comic books as entertainment for children. To that end, those publishers set content guidelines, created a reviewing authority and established the Comics Code Seal. This seal was to appear on covers of the CMAA member comics as a way of communicating to the public their shared commitment to uphold these standards.

While the comic book industry has changed over the intervening three decades, as has almost every other facet of American life, the publisher members of the CMAA remain committed to providing decent and wholesome comic books for children. This new updated version of the Comics Code is a reaffirmation of that commitment.

The member publishers of the Comics Magazine Association of America hereby reaffirm our joint commitment to our shared principle: that comics carrying the Comics Code Seal be ones that a parent can purchase with confidence that the contents uphold basic American moral and cultural values.

INSTITUTIONS

In general recognizable national, social, political, cultural, ethnic and racial groups, religious institutions, and law enforcement authorities will be portrayed in a positive light. These include the government on the national, state, and municipal levels, including all of its numerous departments, agencies and services; law enforcement agencies such as the state and municipal police, and other actual law enforcement agencies such as the FBI, the Secret Service, the CIA, etc.; the military, both United States and foreign; known religious organizations; ethnic advancement agencies; foreign leaders and representatives of other governments and national groups; and social groups identifiable by lifestyle, such as homosexuals, the economically disadvantaged, the economically privileged, the homeless, senior citizens, minors, etc.

Socially responsible attitudes will be favorably depicted and reinforced. Socially inappropriate, irresponsible, or illegal behavior will be shown to be specific actions of a specific individual or group of individuals, and not meant to reflect the routine activity of any general group of real persons.

If, for dramatic purposes, it is necessary to portray such group of individuals in a negative manner, the name of the group and its individual members will be fictitious, and its activities will not be clearly identifiable with the routine activities of any real group.

Stereotyped images and activities will be not used to degrade specific national, ethnic, cultural, or socioeconomic groups.

LANGUAGE

The language in a comic book will be appropriate for a mass audience that includes children. Good grammar and spelling will be encouraged. Publishers will exercise good taste and a responsible attitude as to the use of language in their comics. Obscene and profane words, symbols, and gestures are prohibited.

References to physical handicaps, illnesses, ethnic backgrounds, sexual preferences, religious beliefs, and race, when presented in a derogatory manner for dramatic purposes, will be shown to be unacceptable.

VIOLENCE

Violent actions or scenes are acceptable within the context of a comic book story when dramatically appropriate. Violent behavior will not be shown as acceptable. If it is presented in a realistic manner, care should be taken to present the natural repercussions of such actions. Publishers should avoid excessive levels of violence, excessively graphic depictions of violence, and excessive bloodshed or gore. Publishers will not present detailed information instructing readers how to engage in imitable violent actions.

CHARACTERIZATIONS

Character portrayals will be carefully crafted and show sensitivity to national, ethnic, religious, sexual, political and socioeconomic orientations.

If it is dramatically appropriate for one character to demean another because of his or her sex, ethnicity, religion, sexual preference, political orientation, socioeconomic status, or disabilities, the demeaning words or actions will be clearly shown to be wrong or ignorant in the course of the story. Stories depicting characters subject to physical, mental, or emotional problems or with economic disadvantages should never assign ultimate responsibility for these conditions to the character themselves. Heroes should be role models and should reflect the prevailing social attitudes.

SUBSTANCE ABUSE

Healthy, wholesome lifestyles will be presented as desirable. However, the use and abuse of controlled substances, legal and illicit, are facts of modern existence, and may be portrayed when dramatically appropriate.

The consumption of alcohol, narcotics, pharmaceuticals, and tobacco will not be depicted in a glamorous way. When the line between the normal, responsible consumption of legal substances and the abuse of these substances is crossed, the distinction will be made clear and the adverse consequences of such abuse will be noted.

Substance abuse is defined as the use of illicit drugs and the self-destructive use of such products as tobacco (including chewing tobacco), alcohol, prescription drugs, over-the-counter drugs, etc.

Use of dangerous substances both legal and illegal should be shown with restraint as necessary to the context of the story. However, storylines should not be detailed to the point of serving as instruction manuals for substance abuse. In each story, the abuser will be shown to pay the physical, mental, and/or social penalty for his or her abuse.

CRIME

While crimes and criminals may be portrayed for dramatic purposes, crimes will never be presented in such a way as to inspire readers with a desire to imitate them nor will criminals be portrayed in such a manner as to inspire readers to emulate them. Stories will not present unique imitable techniques or methods of committing crimes.

ATTIRE AND SEXUALITY

Costumes in a comic book will be considered to be acceptable if they fall within the scope of contemporary styles and fashions.

Scenes and dialogue involving adult relationships will be presented with good taste, sensitivity, and in a manner which will be considered acceptable by a mass audience. Primary human sexual characteristics will never be shown. Graphic sexual activity will never be depicted.

ADMINISTRATIVE PROCEDURE

I

All comics which member publishers wish to bear the Comics Code Seal will be submitted to the Code administrator for review prior to publication. The administrator will review them according to the guidance he has received from the permanent committee and will either approve them to bear the seal, or return them to the publisher with comments. The responsible editor from the publisher will either revise the comic in accordance with those comments, or discuss with the administrator the concerns raised with him and reach agreement on how the comic can properly bear the Code Seal either without being revised or with a mutually-agreeable set of alternative revisions. In the event no agreement can be reached between the editor and the administrator, the matter can be referred to the permanent committee, which will act promptly to determine if, or under what conditions, the comic in question can bear the Code Seal. Decisions of the permanent committee will be binding on the publishers, who agree not to place the Code Seal on any comic on which it is not authorized.

II

The members of the Comics Magazine Association of America include publishers who elect to publish comics that are not intended to bear the Code Seal, and that therefore need not go through the approval process described above. Among the comics in this category may be titles intended for adult readers. Member publishers hereby affirm that we will distribute these publications only through distribution channels in which it is possible to notify retailers and distributors of their content, and thus help the publications reach their intended audiences. The member publishers agree to refrain from distributing these publications through those distribution channels that, like the traditional newsstand, are serviced by individuals who are unaware of the content of specific publications before placing them on display.

III

Recognizing that no document can address all of the complex issues and concerns that face our changing society, the member publishers have established a permanent committee composed of the senior editor of each member's staff. The committee will meet regularly to review those issues and concerns as they affect our publications, and to meet with and guide the administrator of the Comics Code, and will replace the previous written guidelines of the Comics Code.

Notes

1. See, for example, Nathan Abelson, "Comics Are a Serious Business," *Advertising and Selling,* July 1946, 41; Nathan Abelson, "Comics Are a Serious Business; Part II of a Study of Comics Magazines," *Advertising and Selling,* August 1946, 80–92; Paul Witty, Ethel Smith, and Anne Coomer, "Reading the Comics in Grades VII and VIII," *Journal of Educational Psychology* 33 (1942): 173–82; Paul Witty, "Children's Interest in Reading the Comics," *Journal of Experimental Education* 10 (1941): 100–109; Paul Witty and Anne Coomer, "Reading the Comics in Grades IV–VII," *Educational Administration and Supervision* 28 (1942): 344–53; Paul Witty, "Reading the Comics—A Comparative Study," *Journal of Experimental Education* 10 (1941): 105–9; Harvey Zorbaugh, "The Comics—There They Stand," *Journal of Educational Sociology* 18 (1944): 196–203.

2. This account of the work of the New York legislature is constructed from many sources. Two unpublished master's theses dealt with the work of the committee: John E. Twomey, "The Anti–Comic Book Crusade," M.A. thesis, University of Chicago, 1955; and Steven E. Mitchell, "Evil Harvest: Investigating the Comic Book, 1948–1954," M.A. thesis, Arkansas State University, 1982 (also serialized in the trade publication *Comics Buyer's Guide*).

    Newspapers and magazines provided detailed accounts: "Comic Book Curb Vetoed by Dewey," *New York Times,* 20 April 1949, 20; "State Bill to Curb Comic Books Filed," *New York Times,* 14 January 1949, 18; "Comics Censorship Bill Passes New York Senate," *Publishers' Weekly,* 5 March 1949, 1160; "Comic Book Bill Assailed," *New York Times,* 11 March 1949, 23; "State Laws to Censor Comics Protested by Publishers," *Publishers' Weekly,* 12 March 1949, 1244; "New York Censors" (editorial), *Editor and Publisher,* 12 March 1949, 38; Editorial, *New York Times,* 25 February 1949, 22; "State Senate Acts to Control Comics," *New York Times,* 24 February 1949, 17; "Delayed Comic-Book Curb," *New York Times,* 18 January 1950, 23; "Witnesses Favor Comic Book Curbs," *New York Times,* 14 June 1950, 29; "Hold Hearings on New State Curb on Comics," *Advertising Age,* 19 June 1950, 65; "Comics

Publishers Speak Up against State Regulation," *Advertising Age,* 14 August 1950, 38; "Oppose State Regulation," *New York Times,* 9 August 1950, 24; "Psychiatrist Asks Crime Comics Ban," *New York Times,* 14 December 1950, 50; "New York Legislature Gives Warning to Comics Publishers," *Advertising Age,* 26 March 1951, 16; Comics Producers Get Censor Warning," *New York Times,* 27 April 1951, 15; "Comics Publishers Warned of Possible Legislative Action," *Advertising Age,* 7 May 1951, 74; "Health Law Urged to Combat Comics," *New York Times,* 4 December 1951, 35; "Comics Trade Solid to Balk State Rule," *New York Times,* 5 December 1951, 37; "New Move Likely on Car Inspection," *New York Times,* 7 March 1952, 21; "Comic Book Curbs Vetoed in Assembly," *New York Times,* 13 March 1952, 42; "Auto Inspections Backed in Albany," *New York Times,* 14 March 1952, 17; "Comic Book Curb Vetoed by Dewey," *New York Times,* 15 April 1952, 29.

The committee itself issued three reports: Joint Legislative Committee to Study the Publication of Comics, *Interim Report* (Albany: Williams Press Inc., 1950); idem, *Report,* Legislative Document No. 15 (Albany: Williams Press Inc., 1951); idem, *Report,* Legislative Document No. 64 (Albany: Williams Press Inc., 1952). Additional information was found in recorded testimony, *Hearings before the New York Joint Legislative Committee to Study the Publication of Comics,* 4 February 1955.

Governor Thomas Dewey's opinions and correspondence were contained in Governor's Bill Jacket, Veto no. 117, New York State Archives, Albany, New York.

3. Information on the Senate hearings was drawn from a number of sources. In addition to secondary sources as indicated, I used the following: U.S. Congress, *Juvenile Delinquency (Comic Books): Hearings before the Senate Subcommittee on Juvenile Delinquency,* 83d Cong., 2d sess., 21–22 April 1954 and 24 June 1954 (designated "Senate Hearings" in the text and followed by a page number); archival records, U.S. Congress, Senate, Records of the Subcommittee to Investigate Juvenile Delinquency, Committee on the Judiciary, 1953–1961, National Archives (designated "Senate Records" in the text); the report on comics compiled by the committee on organized crime, U.S. Congress, Special Committee to Investigate Organized Crime in Interstate Commerce, *A Compilation of Information and Suggestions Submitted to the Special Senate Committee to Investigate Organized Crime in Interstate Commerce Relative to the Incidence of Possible Influence Thereon of So-Called Crime Comic Books During the Five-Year Period 1945 to 1950,* 81st Cong., 2d sess., 1950, Committee Print (designated "Organized Crime Committee, Committee Print" in the text and followed by a page number); Estes Kefauver, Papers, Hoskins Library, University of Tennessee, Knoxville, TN; and the report issued by the Senate subcommittee, U.S. Congress, Senate, Subcommittee to Investigate Juvenile Delinquency, *Interim Report: Comic Books and Juvenile Delinquency,* 84th Cong., 1st sess., 1955, (designated "Senate Report" in the text).

4. Much of the information in this chapter comes from archival sources and interviews. The files of the Comics Magazine Association of America contained some

documents about the origins of the code, correspondence, reports, and the minutes of the various meetings of the CMAA. Those files are located at the Comics Magazine Association of America, New York, New York, and are designated in the text as "CMAA Files" followed by a description of the source and the date in brackets. The newsletters of the CMAA also were a valuable resource. I was able to locate a collection of them at the State Historical Society, Madison, Wisconsin. They are cited in the text as "CMAA Newsletter," followed by the date.

In addition, material was taken from unpublished interviews with the following: Leonard Darvin, former executive director of the CMAA, telephone interview with author, 7 June 1993; John Goldwater, former president of the CMAA, personal interview with author, 29 July 1992; William Gaines, interview with John Tebbel, 4 August 1986; Lyle Stuart, remarks at a memorial service for William Gaines, transcribed by John Tebbel, 5 June 1992; Elliott Caplin, member of the organizing committee of the CMAA, telephone interview with author, 11 July 1994.

References

Abelson, Nathan. "Comics Are a Serious Business." *Advertising and Selling*, July 1946, 41.

———. "Comics Are a Serious Business; Part II of a Study of Comic Magazines." *Advertising and Selling*, Aug. 1946, 80–92.

Adams v. Hinkle, 332 P.2d 844 (1958).

Aldrich, Julian C. "Comics Are a Serious Business." *Scholastic*, 10–15 Nov. 1941, T-1.

American Civil Liberties Union. "Censorship of Comic Books: A Statement." New York, NY, 1955.

Andrae, Thomas. "From Menace to Messiah: The Prehistory of the Superman in Science Fiction Literature." *Discourse* 2 (1980): 84–111.

Anttonen, Eva J. "On Behalf of Dragons." *Wilson Library Bulletin* 10 (1941): 567.

"Association of Comics Publishers." *Advertising and Selling*, July 1947, 102.

Baisden, Greg. "Friendly Frank's Wins on Appeal." *Comics Journal*, Dec. 1989, 13–15.

"Ban on Comics Held Unconstitutional." *Editor and Publisher*, 31 Dec. 1949, 10.

Barcus, Francis E. "A Content Analysis of Trends in Sunday Comics, 1900–1959." *Journalism Quarterly* 38 (1961): 171–80.

Barker, Martin. *A Haunt of Fears: The Strange History of the British Horror Comics Campaign*. London: Pluto, 1984.

Barnouw, Erik. *The Golden Web: A History of Broadcasting in the United States, Vol. II 1933–1953*. New York: Oxford UP, 1968.

Baughman, James L. *The Republic of Mass Culture: Journalism, Filmmaking, and Broadcasting in America since 1941*. Baltimore: Johns Hopkins UP, 1992.

Beard, James. Letter to Senate Subcommittee. 26 Sept. 1954. Records of the Senate Subcommittee on Juvenile Delinquency. National Archives, Washington, DC.

Bechtel, Louise Seaman. "The Comics and Children's Books." *The Horn Book*, July 1941, 296–303.

Bender, Lauretta, and Reginald S. Lourie. "The Effect of Comic Books on the Ideology of Children." *American Journal of Orthopsychiatry* 11 (1941): 540–50.

Benton, Mike. *The Comic Book in America: An Illustrated History*. Dallas: Taylor, 1989.

———. *Horror Comics: The Illustrated History*. Dallas: Taylor, 1991.

———. *Superheroes of the Golden Age: An Illustrated History*. Dallas: Taylor, 1992.

Berger, Arthur. "Comics and Culture." *Journal of Popular Culture* 5 (1971): 164–77.

"Better than Censorship." *Christian Century*, 28 July 1948, 750.

"Biblical Comic Books." *Newsweek*, 3 Aug. 1942, 55–56.

Blanchard, Paul. *The Right to Read: The Battle Against Censorship*. Boston: Beacon, 1955.

Bobo, James. Letter to Charles Murphy. 30 Aug. 1955. Records of the Senate Subcommittee on Juvenile Delinquency. National Archives, Washington, DC.

"Book Week Audience Hears About Comics." *Publishers' Weekly*, 22 Nov. 1941, 1953.

Boyer, Paul S. *Purity in Print: The Vice-Society Movement and Book Censorship in America*. New York: Scribner's, 1968.

———. *Urban Masses and Moral Order in America, 1820–1920*. Cambridge: Harvard UP, 1978.

Brady, Margaret E. "Comics — To Read or Not to Read." *Wilson Library Bulletin*, May 1950, 662–68.

Branley, Franklyn M. "The Plague of the Comics." *Elementary English Review* 19 (1942): 181–82.

Brim, Orville G., Jr. *Education for Child Rearing*. New York: Russell Sage, 1959.

Broun, Heywood, and Margaret Leech. *Anthony Comstock: Roundsman of the Lord*. New York: Literary Guild of America, 1927.

Brown, John Mason. "The Case against the Comics." *Saturday Review of Literature*, 20 Mar. 1948, 32–33.

Brumbaugh, Florence. "The Comics and Children's Vocabularies." *Elementary English Review* 16 (1939): 63–64.

Butts, R. Freeman, and Lawrence A. Cremin. *A History of Education in American Culture*. New York: Holt, 1953.

Cable, Mary. *The Little Darlings: A History of Child Rearing in America*. New York: Scribner's, 1975.

Campbell, C. Mactie. "Adolph Meyer." *Archives of Neurology and Psychiatry* 37 (1937): 715–25.

"Canadian Senate Bans Crime Comics." *Advertising Age*, 19 Dec. 1949, 18.

Caplin, Elliott. Telephone interview with author. 11 July 1994.

Capp, Al. "The Case for the Comics." *Saturday Review of Literature*, 20 Mar. 1948, 32–33.

"Cartoon Magazines for Children Big Success." *Publishers' Weekly*, 8 Mar. 1941, 1127.

"Cause of Delinquency." *Science News Letter*, 1 May 1954, 275.

Cavalieri, Joey, and Matthew Morra. Interview with author. New York, NY, 26 May 1994.

"Censorship of Comics." *Editor and Publisher*, 18 Dec. 1948, 36.

"Censorship Proposals Deluge Lawmakers." *Editor and Publisher,* 12 Feb. 1949, 9.

"Cincinnati Committee Lauds Continued Favorable Trend in Quality of Comics." *CMAA Newsletter,* Oct. 1959, 3.

"Circulation Bust." *Business Week,* 11 May 1946, 71–75.

"Classic Comics Sell a Hundred Million." *Publishers' Weekly,* 23 Mar. 1946, 1736.

Cleverly, John, and D. C. Phillips. *Visions of Childhood: Influential Models from Locke to Spock.* New York: Teachers College, 1986.

Clifford, Katherine. "Comic Sense about Comics." *Parents' Magazine,* Oct. 1948, 30.

CMAA Files. Records of the Comics Magazine Association of America, New York, NY.

"The Code Administrator's Column." *CMAA Newsletter,* Dec. 1955, 3.

"Code for the Comics." *Time,* 12 July 1948, 62.

Coleman, James S. *The Adolescent Society: The Social Life of the Teenager and Its Impact on Education.* New York: Free Press of Glencoe, 1961.

"Comfort for Comics." *Newsweek,* 9 Jan. 1950, 46.

"Comic Book Curb Vetoed by Dewey." *New York Times,* 20 Apr. 1949, 20.

"Comic Book Inquiry Set." *New York Times,* 12 Aug. 1955, 21.

Comic Book Legal Defense Fund. Papers. Comic Book Legal Defense Fund, Lathrup Village, MI.

"Comic Menace." *Wilson Library Bulletin* 15 (1941): 846–47.

"Comics: The Exception of Press Censorship." *Violence in the Print Media.* Vol. 4 of *Report of the Royal Commission on Violence in the Communications Industry.* Ontario: Royal Commission on Violence in the Communications Industry, 1976.

"Comics Censorship Bill Passes New York Senate." *Publishers' Weekly,* 12 Mar. 1949, 1244.

"Comics Code Authority Completes First Year." *CMAA Newsletter,* Dec. 1955, 1.

"Comics 'Czar' Invites Newspaper Compliance." *Editor and Publisher,* 1 Jan. 1955, 47.

"Comics Group Plans to Test Los Angeles Ban." *Editor and Publisher,* 23 Oct. 1948, 32.

Comics Magazine Association of America. "Fact Kit." New York: Comics Magazine Association of America, 1955.

———. *Facts about Code-Approved Comics.* New York: Comics Magazine Association of America, 1959.

———. Papers. Comics Magazine Association of America, New York, NY.

"Comics Publishers Organize for Self Regulation." *Advertising Age,* 6 Sept. 1954, 3.

"Comics Publishers Speak Up against State Regulation." *Advertising Age,* 14 Aug. 1950, 38.

"Comics Publishers Warned of Possible Legislative Action." *Advertising Age,* 7 May 1951, 74.

"Comics Trade Solid to Balk State Rule." *New York Times,* 5 Dec. 1951, 37.

Comstock, Anthony. *Traps for the Young.* New York: Funk, 1884.

Coontz, Stephanie. *The Way We Never Were: American Families and the Nostalgia Trap.* New York: Basic, 1992.

Coren, Robert W., et al. *Guide to the Records of the United States Senate at the National Archives.* Washington, DC: National Archives and Records Administration, 1989.

Cowan, Geoffrey. *See No Evil: The Backstage Battle over Sex and Violence on Television.* New York: Simon, 1979.

Crider, Allen Billy. *Mass Market Publishing in America.* Boston: C. K. Hall, 1982.

Crist, Judith. "Horror in the Nursery." *Collier's,* 29 Mar. 1948, 22–23.

Curti, Merle. *Probing Our Past.* New York: Harper, 1955.

"Daily is Leader of Comic Book Cleanup Drive," *Editor and Publisher,* 26 June 1954, 38.

Daniels, Les. *Comix: A History of Comic Books in America.* New York: Bonanza, 1971.

———. *Marvel: Five Fabulous Decades of the World's Greatest Comics.* New York: Abrams, 1991.

Darvin, Leonard. Telephone interview with author. 7 June 1993.

Davis, Kenneth C. *Two-Bit Culture: The Paperbacking of America.* Boston: Houghton, 1984.

deGrazia, Edward, and Roger K. Newman. *Banned Films: Movies, Censors and the First Amendment.* New York: Bowker, 1982.

"Delays Comic-Book Curb." *New York Times,* 18 Jan. 1950, 23.

Dias, Earl J. "Comic Books—A Challenge to the English Teacher." *English Journal* 35 (1946): 142–45.

"The Dirt and Trash that Kids Are Reading." *Changing Times,* Nov. 1954, 25–29.

Dooley, Dennis. "The Man of Tomorrow and the Boys of Yesterday." *Superman at Fifty: Persistence of a Legend.* Ed. Dennis Dooley and Gary Engle. Cleveland: Octavia, 1987. 19–36.

Dooley, Dennis, and Gary Engle. "The Man Who Changed Comics." *Superman at Fifty: Persistence of a Legend.* Ed. Dennis Dooley and Gary Engle. Cleveland: Octavia, 1987. 59–61.

Doyle, Thomas F. "What's Wrong with the 'Comics'?" *Catholic World,* Feb. 1943, 548–57.

Duke, Judith. *Children's Books and Magazines: A Market Study.* White Plains, NY: Knowledge Industry, 1979.

Editorial. *New York Times,* 25 Feb. 1949, 38.

Ellison, Ralph. "Harlem is Nowhere." *Shadow and Act.* New York: Random, 1953. 294–302.

Elson, Ruth Miller. *Guardians of Tradition: American Schoolbooks of the Nineteenth Century.* Lincoln: U of Nebraska P, 1964.

Ernst, Morris, and Alexander Lindey. *The Censor Marches On: Recent Milestones in the Administration of the Obscenity Law in the United States.* New York: Doubleday, 1940.

Ernst, Morris L., and William Seagle. *To the Pure: A Study of Obscenity and the Censor.* New York: Viking, 1928.

Estren, Mark J. *A History of Underground Comics*. 3d ed. Berkeley, CA: Ronin, 1993.

Exton, Elaine. "Countering Crime-Laden Comics." *School Board Journal* 117 (1948): 47–50.

Facey, Paul W. *The Legion of Decency: A Sociological Analysis of the Emergence and Development of a Social Pressure Group*. New York: Arno, 1974.

Fackler, Mark. "Moral Guardians of the Movies and Social Responsibility of the Press: Two Movements toward a Moral Center." *Mass Media Between the Wars: Perceptions of Cultural Tension, 1918–1941*. Ed. Catherine L. Covert and John D. Stevens. Syracuse, NY: Syracuse UP, 1984.

The Fan-Addict Club Bulletin. No. 3, June 1954. Records of the Senate Subcommittee on Juvenile Delinquency. National Archives, Washington, DC.

"The Fawcett Formula." *Time*, 19 Mar. 1945, 63–66.

Feder, Edward L. *Comic Book Regulation*. Berkeley: University of California, Bureau of Public Administration, 1955.

Feiffer, Jules. *The Great Comic Book Heroes*. New York: Bonanza, 1965.

Finn, David. *The Corporate Oligarch*. New York: Simon, 1969.

Fontenay, Charles L. *Estes Kefauver: A Biography*. Knoxville: U of Tennessee P, 1980.

Frakes, Margaret. "Comics Are No Longer Comic." *Christian Century*, 4 Nov. 1942, 1349–51.

Frank, Josette. "Let's Look at the Comics." *Child Study* 19 (1942): 76.

———. "People in the Comics." *Progressive Education* 19 (1942): 28–31.

Frank, Josette, and Mrs. Hugh Grant Straus. "Looking at the Comics." *Child Study* 20 (1943): 112–18.

Fulton, E. D. "How Canada Has Dealt with the Comic Book Situation through Legislation." *Religious Education* 49 (1954): 415–18.

Gaines, William. Interview by John Tebbel. 4 Aug. 1986.

———. Letter to Robert Hendrickson. 21 May 1954. Records of the Senate Subcommittee on Juvenile Delinquency. National Archives, Washington, DC.

Gardiner, Harold C., S.J. *Catholic Viewpoint on Censorship*. Garden City, NY: Hanover House, 1958.

Gay, Roger C. "A Teachers Reads the Comics." *Harvard Educational Review* 7 (1937): 198–209.

Gibbs, W. "Keep Those Paws to Yourself, Space Rat." *New Yorker*, 8 May 1954, 134–41.

Gilbert, James. *Cycle of Outrage: America's Reaction to the Juvenile Delinquent in the 1950s*. New York: Oxford UP, 1986.

Gleason, Mona. "The Crime Comic Debate: Children, Family and Popular Culture in Postwar Canada." Paper presented at the annual meeting of the Popular Culture Association, New Orleans, Apr. 1993.

Goldwater, John. *Americana in Four Colors: A Decade of Self-Regulation by the Comics Magazine Industry*. New York: Comics Magazine Association of America, 1964.

———. "Editorial." *CMAA Newsletter*, July 1957, 1.

————. Interview with author. New York, NY, 29 July 1992.

————. Letter to Estes Kefauver. 10 June 1956. Records of the Senate Subcommittee on Juvenile Delinquency. National Archives, Washington, DC.

Gorman, Joseph Bruce. *Kefauver: A Political Biography.* New York: Oxford UP, 1971.

Goulart, Ron. *Cheap Thrills: An Informal History of the Pulp Magazines.* New Rochelle, NY: Arlington House, 1972.

————. *Over Fifty Years of American Comic Books.* Lincolnwood, IL: Publications International, 1991.

————. *Ron Goulart's Great History of Comic Books.* Chicago: Contemporary Books, 1986.

Gourley, Myrtle. "A Mother's Report on Comic Books." *National Parent-Teacher,* Dec. 1954, 27–29.

Haney, Robert W. *Comstockery in America: Patterns of Censorship and Control.* Boston: Beacon, 1960.

Harker, Jean Gray. "Youth's Librarians Can Defeat Comics." *Library Journal,* 1 Dec. 1948, 1705–7.

Harrison, Emma. "Magistrate Is Made Comics 'Czar.'" *New York Times,* 17 Sept. 1954, 1.

Hart, James D. *The Popular Book: A History of America's Literary Taste.* Berkeley: U of California P, 1963.

Hawes, Joseph M. *Children in Urban Society: Juvenile Delinquency in Nineteenth Century America.* New York: Oxford UP, 1971.

"Health Law Urged to Combat Comics." New York Times, 4 Dec. 1951, 35.

Heisler, Florence. "A Comparison between Those Elementary School Children Who Attend Moving Pictures, Read Comic Books, and Listen to Serial Radio Programs to an Excess, with Those Who Indulge in These Activities Seldom or Not at All." *Journal of Educational Research* 42 (1948): 182–90.

————. "A Comparison of Comic Book and Non-Comic Book Readers of the Elementary School." *Journal of Educational Research* 40 (1947): 458–64.

Hendrickson, Robert. Letter to Mrs. Mario Levy. 24 Sept. 1954. Records of the Senate Subcommittee on Juvenile Delinquency. Box 169, National Archives, Washington, DC.

————. Letter to William Gaines (draft). Robert Hendrickson Papers, Syracuse University Library, Syracuse, NY.

————. Papers. Syracuse University Library, Syracuse, NY.

Hill, George. "Taking the Comics Seriously." *Childhood Education* 17 (1941): 413–14.

Hill, George, and M. Estelle Trent. "Children's Interests in Comic Strips." *Journal of Educational Research* 34 (1940): 30–36.

Hitzig, William M. "Murder Every Forty-Five Minutes." *Saturday Review of Literature,* 7 May 1949, 9–10.

"Hold Hearings on New State Curb on Comics." *Advertising Age,* 19 June 1950, 65.

Hoult, Thomas Ford. "Comic Books and Juvenile Delinquency." *Sociology and Social Research* 33 (1949): 279–84.

Hoult, Thomas, and Lois Hoult. "Are Comic Books a Menace?" *Today's Health,* June 1950, 20–21.

"How About the Comics?" *Newsweek,* 15 Mar. 1948, 56.

"How Much of a Menace Are the Comics?" *School and Society,* 15 Nov. 1941, 436.

Hughes, Mabel W. "Newsstand Nightmares." *National Parent-Teacher,* Nov. 1948, 3.

Hutchinson, Earl R. "Obscenity, the Censors, and Their Foes," *Mass Media and the Law: Freedom and Restraint.* Ed. David G. Clark and Earl R. Hutchinson. New York: Wiley-Interscience, 1970. 281–83.

Inge, M. Thomas. *Comics as Culture.* Jackson: UP of Mississippi, 1990.

———. Roundtable Discussion on Comics Scholarship. Twenty-second Annual Convention, Popular Culture Association, Mar. 1992, Louisville, KY.

Inglis, Ruth A. *Freedom of the Movies: A Report on Self-Regulation from the Commission on Freedom of the Press.* Chicago: U of Chicago P, 1947.

Jacobs, Frank. *The Mad World of William M. Gaines.* Secaucus, NJ: Lyle Stuart, 1972.

Jacobs, Will, and Gerard Jones. *The Comic Book Heroes from the Silver Age to the Present.* New York: Crown, 1985.

Kahn, E. J., Jr. "Why I Don't Believe in Superman." *New Yorker,* 29 June 1940, 56–58.

Karp, Etta. "Crime Comic Book Role Preferences." Ph.D. diss., New York University, 1954.

Karpman, Benjamin, ed. *Symposia on Child and Juvenile Delinquency.* Washington, DC: Psychodynamics Monograph Series, 1959.

Katzev v. County of Los Angeles, 341 P.2d 310 (1959).

Kefauver, Estes. Letter to William Jenner. 31 Jan. 1955. Kefauver Papers, Hoskins Library, University of Tennessee, Knoxville, TN.

———. Papers. Hoskins Library, University of Tennessee, Knoxville, TN.

Kihss, Peter. "Senator Charges 'Deceit' on Comics." *New York Times,* 23 Apr. 1954, 29.

Kinneman, Fleda Cooper. "The Comics and Their Appeal to the Youth of Today." *English Journal* 32 (1943): 331–35.

Kurtzman, Harvey. *From Aargh to Zap: Harvey Kurtzman's Visual History of the Comics.* New York: Prentice, 1991.

Landsdowne, James D. "The Viciousness of the Comic Book." *Journal of Education* 127 (1944): 14–15.

Lee, Harriet E. "Discrimination in Reading." *English Journal* 21 (1942): 677–79.

Leff, Leonard, and Jerold Simmons. *The Dame in the Kimono: Hollywood, Censorship and the Production Code from the 1920s to the 1960s.* New York: Grove Weidenfield, 1990.

Legman, Gerson. "The Comic Books and the Public." *American Journal of Psychotherapy* 11 (1948): 473–77.

"Less Paper." *Time,* 11 Jan. 1943, 71.

"Let Children Read the Comics; Science Gives Its Approval." *Science News Letter,* 23 Aug. 1941, 124–25.

Levine, Murray, and Adeline Levine. *Helping Children: A Social History*. New York: Oxford UP, 1992.

"Librarian Named on Comics Advisory Committee." *Library Journal*, 1 Jan. 1949, 37.

"Libraries, to Arms!" *Wilson Library Bulletin* 15 (1941): 670–71.

Littledale, Clara Savage. "What to Do about the Comics." *Parents' Magazine*, Mar. 1941, 26.

Lomax, Elizabeth M. R., Jerome Kagan, and Barbara Rosenkrantz. *Science and Patterns of Child Care*. San Francisco: W. H. Freeman, 1978.

"Los Angeles Ordinance Bans All Crime Comics." *Editor and Publisher*, 2 Oct. 1948, 18.

Lowery, Shearon, and Melvin DeFleur, eds. "Seduction of the Innocent: The Great Comic Book Scare." *Milestones in Mass Communication Research*. New York: Longman, 1983. 233–66.

Luckiesh, Matthew, and Frank K. Moss. "Legibility in Comic Books." *Sight-Saving Review* 12 (1942): 19–24.

Luke, Carmen. *Constructing the Child Viewer: A History of the American Discourse on Television and Children, 1950–1980*. New York: Praeger, 1990.

———. *Pedagogy, Printing and Protestantism: The Discourse on Childhood*. Albany: State U of New York P, 1989.

Lupoff, Dick, and Don Thompson, eds. *All in Color for a Dime*. New Rochelle, NY: Arlington House, 1970.

MacDonald, Andrew, and Virginia MacDonald. "Sold American: The Metamorphosis of Captain America." *Journal of Popular Culture* 10 (1976): 249–58.

Mackey, David R. "The Development of the National Association of Broadcasters." *Journal of Broadcasting* 1 (1957): 305–25.

MacLeod, Anne Scott. *A Moral Tale: Children's Fiction and American Culture, 1820–1860*. Hamden, CT: Archon Books, 1975.

Mannes, Marya. "Junior Has a Craving." *New Republic*, 17 Feb. 1947, 20–23.

Marston, William Moulton. "Why 100,000,000 Americans Read Comics." *American Scholar* 13 (1943–1944): 35–44.

Martin, Olga J. *Hollywood's Movie Commandments: A Handbook for Motion Picture Writers and Reviewers*. New York: H. H. Wilson, 1937.

Martin, Ralph G. "Doctor's Dream in Harlem." *New Republic*, 3 June 1946, 798–800.

McAllister, Matthew P. "Cultural Argument and Organizational Constraint in the Comic Book Industry." *Journal of Communication* 40 (1990): 55–71.

McChesney, Robert W. "Franklin Roosevelt, His Administration, and the Communications Act of 1934." *American Journalism* 5 (1988): 204–29.

McCord, David Frederick. "The Social Rise of the Comics." *The American Mercury*, July 1935, 360–64.

McCue, Greg, and Clive Bloom. *Dark Knights: The New Comics in Context*. Boulder, CO: Pluto, 1993.

McGraw, Curtis. Letter to Governor Thomas Dewey. 4 Apr. 1949. Governor's Bill Jacket, Veto #117, New York State Archives, Albany, NY.

McMahon, Robert Sears. *Federal Regulation of the Radio and Television Broadcast Industry in the United States 1927–1959.* New York: Arno, 1979.

McMaster, Jane. "Comics Ratings Bring Comment about Taboos." *Editor and Publisher,* 11 Feb. 1950, 46.

Medhurst, Andy. "Batman, Deviance and Camp." *The Many Lives of the Batman: Critical Approaches to a Superhero and His Media.* Ed. Roberta E. Pearson and William Uricchio. New York: Routledge, 1991. 149–63.

Meigs, Cornelia, et al. *A Critical History of Children's Literature.* New York: Macmillan, 1969.

Memorandum filed with Senate Bill Introductory Number 1862, Printed Number 2939, n.d. Governor's Bill Jacket, Veto #117, New York State Archives, Albany, NY.

Mennel, Robert M. *Thorns and Thistles: Juvenile Delinquency in the United States, 1825–1940.* Hanover, NH: UP of New England, 1973.

Mitchell, Steve. "The Best Is the Worst: Love, 'Classics,' and the ACMP." *Comics Buyer's Guide,* 19 July 1985.

———. "Evil Harvest: Investigating the Comic Book, 1948–1954." M.A. thesis, Arkansas State University, 1982.

———. "The Red-Hot Thrill: The Comic Book Crisis of 1948, Part I." *Comics Buyer's Guide,* 21 June 1985.

———. "The Red-Hot Thrill: The Comic-Book Crisis of 1948, Part II." *Comics Buyer's Guide,* 28 June 1985.

———. "Slaughter of the Innocents." *Comics Buyer's Guide,* 17 May 1985.

———. "Superman in Disguise: The New York State Investigations." *Comics Buyer's Guide,* 9 May 1986.

Moley, Raymond. *The Hays Office.* New York: Bobbs, 1945.

Moore, William Howard. *The Kefauver Committee and the Politics of Crime, 1950–1952.* Columbia: U of Missouri P, 1974.

Morgan, Joy Elmer. "The Ubiquitous Comics." *NEA Journal,* Dec. 1948, 570.

Munter Holly. Telephone interview with author. 23 June 1994.

Murphy, Charles F. "The Code Administrator's Column." *CMAA Newsletter,* May 1956.

———. Letter to Estes Kefauver. 12 Aug. 1955. Records of Senate Subcommittee on Juvenile Delinquency. National Archives, Washington, DC.

———. "The Role of the Code Administrator." *Violence and the Mass Media.* Ed. Otto N. Larson. New York: Harper, 1968. 244–49.

Murrell, Jesse. "Cincinnati Rates the Comics." *Parents' Magazine,* Feb. 1950, 44–45.

———. "Annual Rating of Comics Magazines." *Parents' Magazine,* Aug. 1954, 48.

Mussey, "Books—5 Cents, 10 Cents and Up." *Publishers' Weekly,* 1 Oct. 1938, 1280–83.

Nation, 19 Mar. 1949, 319.

"New Canadian Law Declares Crime Comics Illegal." *Publishers' Weekly,* 7 Jan. 1950, 45.

Newson, John and Elizabeth Newson. "Cultural Aspects of Childrearing in the English Speaking World." *Rethinking Childhood: Perspectives on Development and Society.* Ed. Arlene Skolnick. Boston: Little, 1976. 325–46.

"New York Censors." *Editor and Publisher,* 12 Mar. 1949, 38.

"New York Gives Warning to Comics Publishers." *Advertising Age,* 26 Mar. 1951, 16.

"New York Officials Recommend Code for Comics Publishers." *Publishers' Weekly,* 19 Feb. 1949, 978.

New York State Legislature. Joint Legislative Committee to Study the Publication of Comics. *Interim Report.* Albany: Williams, 1950.

———. *Report.* Legislative Document No. 15. Albany: Williams, 1951.

———. *Report.* Legislative Document No. 64. Albany: Williams, 1952.

———. *Hearings before the New York Joint Legislative Committee to Study the Publication of Comics,* 4 Feb. 1955.

Nisbet, Peter. "Collecting, Connecting: Fredric Wertham and His Art." *The Fredric Wertham Collection.* Cambridge: Busch-Reisinger Museum, Harvard University, 1990.

Noble, William. *Bookbanning in America: Who Bans Books—And Why?* Middlebury, VT: Erikssen, 1990.

"NODL Head Says Comics Code Authority Definitely Cleaned Up Comics." *CMAA Newsletter,* July 1957, 1.

North, Sterling. "The Antidote for Comics." *National Parent-Teacher,* Mar. 1941, 16–17.

———. "A National Disgrace." Rpt. in *Childhood Education* 17 (1940): 56.

"Not So Funny." *Time,* 4 Oct. 1948, 46.

"N.Y. Legislature Gives Warning to Comics Publishers." *Advertising Age,* 26 Mar. 1951, 16.

Nystrom, Elsa. "A Rejection of Order: The Development of the Newspaper Comic Strip in America, 1830–1920." Ph.D. diss., Loyola University of Chicago, 1989.

"The Old Folks Take It Harder Than Junior." *Collier's,* 9 July 1949, 74.

"Oppose State Regulation." *New York Times,* 9 Aug. 1950, 24.

"Our Comic Culture." *Educational Forum* 6 (1941): 84–85.

"Outlawed." *Time,* 19 Dec. 1949, 33.

Overstreet, Robert M. *The Official Overstreet Price Guide, 1989–1990.* 19th ed. New York: The House of Collectibles, 1989.

Parsons, Patrick. "Batman and His Audience: The Dialectic of Culture." *The Many Lives of the Batman: Critical Approaches to a Superhero and His Media.* Ed. Roberta E. Pearson and William Uricchio. New York: Routledge, 1991. 66–89.

Paul, James C. N., and Murry L. Schwartz. *Federal Censorship: Obscenity in the Mail.* New York: Free Press of Glencoe, 1961.

Pearson, Edmund. *Books in Black and Red.* New York: Macmillan, 1923.

————. *Dime Novels: Following an Old Trail in Popular Literature.* Port Washington, NY: Kennikat, 1968.

"Personal and Otherwise." *Harper's,* July 1951, 8.

Peterson, Theodore. *Magazines in the Twentieth Century.* Urbana: U of Illinois P, 1964.

Pivar, David J. *Purity Crusade: Sexual Morality and Social Control 1868–1900.* Westport, CT: Greenwood, 1973.

"Plan of Action Against Unwholesome Comics, Motion Pictures, and Radio Programs." *National Parent-Teacher,* Nov. 1948, 12.

Postman, Neil. *The Disappearance of Childhood.* New York: Dell, 1982.

Powers, Thom. "Friendly Frank's Manager Found Guilty." *Comics Journal,* Mar. 1988, 5.

"President's Column." *CMAA Newsletter,* Feb. 1957, 1.

"Psychiatrist Asks Crime Comics Ban." *New York Times,* 14 Dec. 1950, 50.

"Psychiatrist Charges Stalling Tactics on Legislation to Control Comic Books." *New York Times,* 24 Jan. 1950, 9.

"Psychiatry in Harlem." *Time,* 1 Dec. 1947, 50–52.

Pulliam, John D. *The History of Education in America.* 5th ed. New York: Macmillan, 1991.

"Purified Comics." *Newsweek,* 12 July 1948, 56.

Queenan, Joe. "Drawing on the Dark Side." *New York Times Magazine,* 30 Apr. 1989, 32–34.

Reibman, James E. "The Life of Dr. Fredric Wertham." *The Fredric Wertham Collection.* Cambridge: Busch-Reisinger Museum, Harvard University, 1990.

Reidelbach, Maria. *Completely MAD: A History of the Comic Book and Magazine.* Boston: Little, 1991.

Reitberg, Reinhold, and Wulfgang Fuchs. *Comics: Anatomy of a Mass Medium.* Boston: Little, 1971.

"Religious Editor Hits Comic Books." *Editor and Publisher,* 10 July 1954, 50.

Reynolds, George R. "The Child's Slant on the Comics." *School Executive* 62 (1942): 17.

Rhyne, Charles S. *Comic Books—Municipal Control of Sale and Distribution—A Preliminary Study.* National Institute of Municipal Law Officers Report No. 4. Washington, DC, 1948.

Richardson, Theresa R. *The Century of the Child: The Mental Hygiene Movement and Social Policy in the United States and Canada.* Albany: State U of New York P, 1989.

Rothe, Anna, ed. *Current Biography: Who's News and Why.* New York: H. W. Wilson, 1949.

Rowland, Willard D., Jr. *The Politics of TV Violence: Policy Uses of Communication Research.* Beverly Hills: Sage, 1983.

Rudy, Willis. *Schools in an Age of Mass Culture: An Exploration of Selected Themes in the History of Twentieth-Century American Education.* Englewood Cliffs, NJ: Prentice, 1965.

Sabin, Roger. *Adult Comics: An Introduction.* London: Routledge, 1993.

Salicrup, Jim. "Editor: Dick Giordano." *Comics Interview,* June 1983, 38.

Sarno, Edward F., Jr. "The National Radio Conferences." *Journal of Broadcasting* 13 (1969): 189–202.

Savage, William. *Comic Books and America, 1945–1954.* Norman: U of Oklahoma P, 1990.

Scheffer, Ruth. Letter to Senate Subcommittee. 8 Sept. 1954. Records of the Senate Subcommittee on Juvenile Delinquency. Box 169, National Archives, Washington, DC.

Schick, Frank. *The Paperbound Book in America: The History of Paperbacks and Their European Background.* New York: Bowker, 1958.

Schreuders, Piet. *Paperbacks, U.S.A.: A Graphic History.* San Diego: Blue Dolphin, 1981.

Schultz, Henry E. "Censorship or Self Regulation?" *Journal of Educational Sociology* 23 (1949): 215–24.

———. Letter to Governor Thomas Dewey. 1 Apr. 1949. Governor's Bill Jacket, Veto #117, New York State Archives, Albany, NY.

"Senate Committee Will Take Comics Under Consideration." *Advertising Age,* 23 Nov. 1953, 1.

Senn, Milton J.E. "Insights on the Child Development Movement in the United States." *Monographs of the Society for Research in Child Development* 40 (1975), No. 161.

Skolnick, Arlene. *Rethinking Childhood: Perspectives of Development and Society.* Boston: Little, 1976.

Smith, Ruth Emily. "Publishers Improve Comic Books." *Library Journal,* 15 Nov. 1948, 1649–53.

"Some Milestone Comics Drop Comics Code." *Comics Journal,* June 1993, 12.

Sones, W. W. D. "Comic Books as Teaching Aids." *The Instructor* 51 (1942): 14.

Sperzel, Edith Z. "The Effect of Comic Books on Vocabulary Growth and Reading Comprehension." *Elementary English* 25 (1948): 109–13.

"State Bill to Curb Comic Books Filed." *New York Times,* 14 Jan. 1949, 18.

"State Laws to Censor Comics Protested by Publishers." *Publishers' Weekly,* 12 Mar. 1949, 243–44.

"State Senate Acts to Control Comics." *New York Times,* 24 Feb. 1949, 17.

Steranko, James. *The Steranko History of Comics.* 2 vols. Reading, PA: Supergraphics, 1972.

Strang, Ruth. "Why Children Read the Comics." *Elementary School Journal* 43 (1943): 336–42.

Stuart, Lyle. Letter to James Bobo. 11 Aug. 1955. Records of the Senate Subcommittee on Juvenile Delinquency. National Archives, Washington, DC.

———. Remarks at a memorial service for William Gaines. Transcribed by John Tebbel (unpublished), 5 June 1992.

"Study Course Outlines: What Are Comic Books?" *National Parent-Teacher,* Mar. 1949, 34–35.

"Superman Scores." *Business Week,* 18 Apr. 1942, 54–56.

"Supersuit." *Newsweek,* 14 Apr. 1947, 65–66.

Suransky, Valeria Polakov. *The Erosion of Childhood.* Chicago: U of Chicago P, 1982.

"Survey of E.C. Fan-Addict Club Letters." Records of the Senate Subcommittee on Juvenile Delinquency. National Archives, Washington, DC.

"Survey Reveals High Readership." *Advertising Age,* 27 Sept. 1943, 54.

"Survey Shows Ninety-Five Percent of Youngsters Read, Like Comic Books." *Advertising Age,* 9 Jan. 1950, 46.

Swados, Harvey. *Standing Up for the People: The Life and Times of Estes Kefauver.* New York: Dutton, 1972.

Thomas, Mrs. Letter to Senate Subcommittee. 23 Sept. 1954. Records of the Senate Subcommittee on Juvenile Delinquency. Box 169, National Archives, Washington, DC.

Thompson, Maggie. "The Comics Industry: 1989." *Comics Buyers Guide,* 31 Mar. 1989, 58.

Thorndike, Robert L. "Words and the Comics." *Journal of Experimental Education* 10 (1941): 110–13.

Thrasher, Frederic M. "The Comics and Delinquency: Cause or Scapegoat?" *Journal of Educational Sociology* 23 (1949): 195–205.

Tielman, Adrian. "Comic Books and Democracy." *Educational Administration and Supervision* 35 (1949): 299–301.

"'Tis True, 'Tis Comic, and Comic 'Tis 'Tis True." *School and Society,* 10 May 1941, 598.

"To Burn or Not to Burn?" *Senior Scholastic,* 2 Feb. 1949, 5.

"Too Many Magazines?" *Time,* 17 June 1946, 48–49.

Towne, Charles L. "Hartford Is Aroused by Comic Book Expose." *Editor and Publisher,* 10 Apr. 1954, 11.

Twomey, John E. "The Anti-Comic Book Crusade." M.A. thesis, University of Chicago, 1955.

———. "The Citizen's Committee and Comic Book Control: A Study of Extragovernmental Restraint." *Law and Contemporary Problems* 20 (1955): 623–29.

"Unfunny Comic Books Banned in Los Angeles." *New York Times,* 23 Sept. 1948, 38.

United States of America v. The American News Company and the Union News Company, U.S. District Court, Southern District of New York, Civil Action No. 77-193. Filed 17 July 1952. Records of the Senate Subcommittee on Juvenile Delinquency. National Archives, Washington, DC.

U.S. Congress. House. *Investigation of Literature Allegedly Containing Objectionable Material: Hearings before the Select Committee on Current Pornographic Materials,* 82d Cong., 2d sess., 1–5 Dec. 1952.

U.S. Congress. Senate. Special Committee to Investigate Organized Crime in Interstate Commerce. *A Compilation of Information and Suggestions Submitted to the Special Senate Committee to Investigate Organized Crime in Interstate Commerce Relative to the Incidence of Possible Influence Thereon of So-Called Crime Comic Books During the Five-Year Period 1945 to 1950.* 81st Cong., 2d sess., 1950. Committee Print.

———. Records of the Subcommittee to Investigate Juvenile Delinquency, Committee on the Judiciary, 1953–1961. National Archives, Washington, DC.

———. *Juvenile Delinquency (Comic Books): Hearings before the Senate Subcommittee on Juvenile Delinquency,* 83d Cong., 2d sess, 21–22 Apr. 1954 and 24 June 1954.

———. *Television Programs: Hearings before the Senate Subcommittee on Juvenile Delinquency,* 83d Cong., 2d sess., 5 June 1954 and 19–20 Oct. 1954.

———. Subcommittee to Investigate Juvenile Delinquency. *Interim Report: Comic Books and Juvenile Delinquency,* 84th Cong., 1st sess., 1955.

———. *Motion Pictures: Hearings before the Senate Subcommittee on Juvenile Delinquency,* 84th Cong., 1st sess., 15–18 June 1955.

Vaughn, Stephen. "Morality and Entertainment: The Origins of the Motion Picture Production Code." *Journal of American History,* June 1990, 39–65.

Vlamos, James Frank. "The Sad Case of the Funnies." *American Mercury,* Apr. 1941, 411–16.

Vosburgh, John R. "How the Comic Book Started." *Commonweal,* 20 May 1942, 146–48.

Warshow, Robert. "Paul, the Horror Comics, and Dr. Wertham." *Commentary,* June 1954, 596–604.

Wartella, Ellen, and Sharon Mazzarella. "A Historical Comparison of Children's Use of Leisure Time." *For Fun and Profit: The Transformation of Leisure into Consumption.* Ed. Richard Butsch. Philadelphia: Temple UP, 1990, 173–94.

Wartella, Ellen, and Byron Reeves. "Historical Trends in Research on Children and the Media: 1900–1960." *Journal of Communication* 35 (1985): 118–33.

Waugh, Colton. *The Comics.* New York: Macmillan, 1947; Rpt. Jackson: UP of Mississippi, 1991.

Wertham, Fredric. "The Air-Conditioned Conscience." *Saturday Review of Literature,* 1 Oct. 1949, 6–8.

———. "The Betrayal of Childhood: Comic Books." *Proceedings of the 78th Annual Congress of Correction, American Prison Association,* 1948, 57–59.

———. *The Circle of Guilt.* New York: Rinehart, 1956.

———. "The Comics . . . Very Funny!" *Saturday Review of Literature,* 29 May 1948, 6–7.

———. "Critique of the Report to the Surgeon General from the Committee on Television and Social Behavior." *American Journal of Psychotherapy* 26 (1972): 216–19.

———. "The Curse of the Comic Book: The Value Patterns and Effects of Comic Books." *Religious Education* 49 (1954): 394–406.

———. "Is TV Hardening Us to the War in Vietnam?" *Violence and the Mass Media.* Ed. Otto N. Larson. New York: Harper, 1968. 50–54.

———. "It's Still Murder: What Parents Don't Know About Comic Books." *Saturday Review of Literature,* 9 Apr. 1955, 11–121.

———. "Nine Men Speak to You: Jim Crow in the North." *The Nation,* 12 June 1954, 497–99.

———. "Psychiatry and the Prevention of Sex Crimes." *Journal of Criminal Law and Criminology* 28 (1938): 847–53.

———. "The Psychopathology of Comic Books." Proceedings of the Association for the Advancement of Psychotherapy. *American Journal of Psychotherapy* 11 (July 1948): 472–90.

———. "Reading for the Innocent." *Wilson Library Bulletin* 29 (1955): 610–13.

———. "The Scientific Study of Media Effects." *American Journal of Psychiatry* 119 (1962): 306–11.

———. *Seduction of the Innocent.* New York: Rinehart, 1954.

———. *The Show of Violence.* Garden City, NY: Doubleday, 1949.

———. *A Sign for Cain: An Exploration of Human Violence.* New York: Macmillan, 1966.

———. "Wham! Socko! Pow!: *Harper's,* Sept. 1951, 16.

———. "What to Do Till the Doctor Goes." *The Nation,* 2 Sept. 1950, 67–69.

———. "Who Will Guard the Guardians." *New Republic,* 29 Oct. 1945, 578–80.

———. *The World of Fanzines: A Special Form of Communication.* Carbondale: Southern Illinois UP, 1973.

"Wertham on Murder." *Newsweek,* 9 May 1949, 51–52.

West, Mark I. *Children, Culture and Controversy.* Hamden, CT: Archon Books, 1988.

West, Mrs. Max. *Infant Care.* Washington, DC: U.S. Children's Bureau Publication No. 8, 1914. Rpt. in *Children and Youth in America: A Documentary History, Vol. II.* Ed. Robert H. Bremner. Cambridge: Harvard UP, 1971. 1866–1922.

Westerhoff, John H., III. *McGuffy and His Readers: Piety, Morality and Education in Nineteenth Century America.* Nashville: Parthenon, 1978.

White, Kenneth. Letter to Senate Subcommittee. 7 July 1954. Records of the Senate Subcommittee on Juvenile Delinquency. Box 169, National Archives, Washington, DC.

White, Llewellyn. *The American Radio: A Report on the Broadcasting Industry in the United States from the Commission on Freedom of the Press.* New York: Arno, 1974.

Williams, Gweneira, and Jane Wilson. "They Like It Rough." *Library Journal,* 1 Mar. 1942, 204–6.

Williams, J. P. "Why Superheroes Never Bleed: The Effects of Self-Censorship on the Comic Book Industry." *Free Speech Yearbook, Vol. 26.* Ed. Stephen A. Smith. Carbondale: Southern Illinois UP, 1987. 60–69.

Winters v. New York, 68 S.Ct. 665 (1948).

"Wisconsin District Attorney Finds Comics O.K." *CMAA Newsletter,* Dec. 1957, 4.

Wisconsin Session Laws. Adjourned session of the Legislature, Vol. 2, Madison, WI, 1957.

"Witnesses Favor Comic Book Curbs." *New York Times,* 14 June 1950, 29.

Witty, Paul. "Children's Interest in Reading the Comics." *Journal of Experimental Education* 10 (1941): 100–104.

———. "Comics and Television: Opportunity or Threat?" *Today's Health,* Oct. 1952, 18.

———. "Reading the Comics—A Comparative Study." *Journal of Experimental Education* 10 (1941): 105–9.

———. "Those Troublesome Comics." *National Parent-Teacher,* Jan. 1942, 29–30.

Witty, Paul, and Anne Coomer. "Reading the Comics in Grades IV–VII." *Educational Administration and Supervision* 28 (1942): 344–53.

Witty, Paul, Ethel Smith, and Anne Coomer. "Reading the Comics in Grades VII and VIII." *Journal of Educational Psychology* 33 (1942): 173–82.

Wolf, Katherine M., and Marjorie Fiske. "Children Talk about Comics." *Communications Research 1948–1949.* Ed. Paul Lazarsfeld and Frank Stanton. New York: Harper, 1949. 3–50.

Wright, Ethel C. "A Public Library Experiments with the Comics." *Library Journal,* 15 Oct. 1943, 832–35.

Zimmerman, Thomas L. "What to Do about Comics." *Library Journal,* 15 Sept. 1954, 1605–7.

Zorbaugh, Harvey. "Editorial." *Journal of Educational Sociology* 18 (1944): 193–94.

———. "The Comics—There They Stand." *Journal of Educational Sociology* (1940): 196–203.

———. "What Adults Think of Comics as Reading for Children." *Journal of Educational Sociology* 23 (1949): 225–35.

Index

E.C. Comics, 59–60, 63–64, 66, 74, 104, 108, 118, 120, 122–24; Fan-Addict Club, 121; "New Direction" comics, 117, 122; "New Trend" comics, 60

Educational comics, 8. See also *Classics Illustrated;* Comic books, educational tools

Educational Comics Company, 118

Eliot, Martha, 55

Entertaining Comics company. *See* E.C. Comics

Estrow, Stanley, 110

Extra, 117

Famous Funnies, 105, 110

Fan-Addict Club Bulletin, 120–21

Fantastic Four, The, 137

Fanzines, 103

Fawcett Publications, 104, 127; advisory board, 15; in-house code, 107

Feinberg, Benjamin, 42–43

Feldstein, Al, 118

Fiction House, 124

Film: censorship, 3; and children, 3; effects, 3; self-regulation, 3, 23, 98, 113, 151, 156

Film Production Code, 157

Finn, David, 111–12, 116. *See also* Ruder and Finn

First Amendment, 27, 39–40, 48, 50

First Comics, 145

Fitzpatrick, James, 43, 56, 78–79

Flash, The, 136

Fourteenth Amendment, 39

Frank, Josette, 14–15, 75–77, 107

Frankfurt school, 86, 94, 155

Freund, Arthur, 130

Friedman, William, 59, 80

Froehlich, Monroe, 59, 80, 110

Fulton, E. D., 56, 78

Gaines, Max, 8, 117–18

Gaines, William: and E.C. Comics, 118, 124; and formation of CMAA, 108–09, 157; relationship with CMAA, 104, 117–18, 122–24; testimony before Senate, 56, 59–66, 73–75, 80, 119–20

Gallup, George, 7

Galston, James, 144

Gilbertson Publications, 117

Gladstone comics, 149

Gleason, Lev, 45

Glueck, Sheldon and Eleanor, 108–09, 130

God Nose, 137

Golden Age of comics, 5, 137, 158

Golden Willow press, 105

Goldwater, John, 109–10, 112, 126, 130–31, 134–36, 140–41

Goodman, Martin, 126, 137, 141

Gosnell, Charles, 105

Graphic novels, 162–63

Green Lantern/Green Arrow, 139

Green, Wally, 146–49

Gruenberg, Sidonie M., 15, 107

Hannoch, Herbert, 61

Hardy, Allen, 110

Harvey Comics, 126–27, 141, 144, 149

Harvey, Leon, 141

Haunt of Fear, 118

Hay's Office, 98, 112

Hecht, George, 7, 31. See also *Parents' Magazine*

Hendrickson, Robert, 51, 53, 77, 79, 83, 119–20

Hennings, Thomas, 63

Heroes World Distribution Company, 161

Hesketh, Florence, 87

Hillman Periodicals, 105

Munter, Holly, 151–52. *See also* Comics code, administrator

Murphy, Charles: appointment by CMAA, 110–11; as code administrator, 99, 114–16, 123, 129, 131, 134–35; resignation from CMAA, 130; testimony by, 114–16

Murrell, Jesse, 29, 136. *See also* Committee for the Evaluation of Comics

Muzzey, David, 7

NAACP, 93

National Advisory Committee on Comic Books, 131

National Comics, 8, 75–76, 106, 110, 127, 136, 140–41. *See also* DC Comics

National Congress of Parents and Teachers, 37

National Education Association, 37

National Office of Decent Literature: and comic book legislation, 27; formation of, 23; impact, 27–28, 136; procedure for decency crusade, 25–26; procedure for reviewing, 24–25; Publications Disapproved for Youth, 23; standards for comics, 24, 27, 29, 31. *See also* Catholic Church; Decency crusades

National Organization for Decent Literature, 23, 154. *See also* National Office of Decent Literature

National Periodical Publications. *See* DC Comics; National Comics

New York City Federation of Women's Clubs, 130, 134

New York Department of Education, and comic books, 43, 48, 49

New York Joint Legislative Committee to Study the Publication of Comics: formation, 44; hearings, 44–45, 47–48,

93, 114–15, 117; and legislation, 50; and Senate Subcommittee, 55–56, 78

New York Legislature. *See* New York Joint Legislative Committee to Study the Publication of Comics

New York Penal Code, 38, 42, 48

New York Society for the Suppression of Vice, 2, 22. *See also* Decency crusades

NODL. *See* National Office of Decent Literature

North, Sterling, 3–6, 15

Obscenity and pornography, 22, 26, 28–29, 39, 50, 113, 138, 148, 153

O'Neil, Denny, 139

Orbit Publications, 105

Osborne, Ernest, 15, 107

Pacific Comics, 145

Panic magazine, 74

Panken, Harold, 44

Parents' Institute, 105

Parents' Magazine: and comic books, 6–8, 31; and comic book ratings, 23, 29. See also *True Comics*

Peck, Harris, 59

Pepard, S. Harcourt, 107

Phipps Psychiatric Clinic, 87–88

Picture Stories from the Bible, 8

Pini, Richard and Wendy, 145

Piracy, 117

Popular culture, and elites, 4

Premium Service Company, 105

Production Code Administration, 3

Protestant Motion Picture Council, 131

Psychoanalysis, 117

Publishers' Weekly, 7

Pulp fiction, 17

Quality Comics Group, 125